ACCOUNTING
The Language of Business

SEVENTH EDITION

Sidney Davidson, Ph.D., CPA
University of Chicago

Clyde P. Stickney, D.B.A., CPA
Dartmouth College

Roman L. Weil, Ph.D., CPA, CMA
University of Chicago

THOMAS HORTON AND DAUGHTERS
26662 S. New Town Drive ● Sun Lakes, Arizona 85248

For Our Children

ISBN 0-913878-38-3

Library of Congress Cataloging in Publication Data

Davidson, Sidney 1919-
    Accounting: the language of business, seventh edition

I. Accounting—Terminology.   2. Accounting.

I . Stickney, Clyde P., 1944-   joint author.
II . Weil, Roman Lee, 1940-   joint author.
III. Title.
HF5621.D28   657.03   87-5974

Preface

Business increases in importance. Accounting is the language of business. Understanding accounting, therefore, increases in importance. We hope this book will assist the student in becoming familiar with the language required to understand business communications. The first edition appeared in 1974. Since that time feedback from readers about the contents of the book has enabled us to refine the presentation—adding here, deleting there—to suit the wishes of teacher and students as well as those earning a living in business, generally. Although some of the material here will seem too advanced for the beginner, we think the book has something cost-effective for all interested in business.

WE ARE PROFIT-ORIENTED and are eager to learn from you how we can make the book more successful. We will pay the first person who makes a given suggestion incorporated in subsequent editions. Such suggestions might include typographical errors ($1), additional cross references ($1), errors of fact or substance ($2), and additional terms with their explanation ($2).

This edition contains the following sections.

Glossary. Accounting's vocabulary comprises many words that have other meanings in ordinary usage. Understanding the concepts and using accounting reports require that the reader know how to interpret the words used and their special meaning. Students of accounting and readers of accounting reports will find the tasks easier the sooner they learn, for example, the difference between the meanings of *revenue* and *receipt*, between *fund* and *reserve*. The Glossary defines these and some 1,400 other terms. A glossary is not a dictionary, so that we have given definitions of terms only as they are, or should be, used in accounting.

Students and readers of financial reports will not encounter all the terms in the Glossary. We have tried to include, however, all the terms that are used in a wide range of textbooks, problems, financial reports, financial periodicals, and newspapers.

Many words and phrases in the Glossary are defined in terms of other entries in the Glossary. Terms in a given definition that are themselves explained elsewhere are *italicized*. Many of the entries in the Glossary are multiple-word phrases because much of the specialized terminology of accounting depends upon such phrases. We have tried to anticipate the most likely phrase that will occur to the reader and have used that phrase in the Glossary. Nevertheless, we probably have failed in some cases to put the explanation by the word or phrase that occurs to you. As Jim Schindler (our co-author before his death) used to say, "If you can't find what you're looking for under one listing, keep looking under others."

Words and phrases are alphabetized using the word-by-word principle. Thus, the following terms are defined in the order shown: *account, account form, account payable, accountancy, accounting, accounting standards, accounts receivable turnover.*

There are a few words in accounting, for example *cost* and *expense*, that mean different things to different people. We believe that the more precise the meaning of the words used, the easier is the understanding of accounting. Consequently, we give the restricted definition, for example, of *cost* that we think enhances the user's ability to understand but we also give the variants in meaning often used in practice. Further, certain terms used widely in the accounting profession, for example, *prepaid expenses* seem to us to be self-contradictory given our preference for restricted and unambiguous definitions. We point out these contradictions knowing that many people, nevertheless, use these terms.

General Electric Company's Annual Report. GE's annual report is consistently among the best published. We reproduce GE's annual report issued in 1987 along with our own comments and notes which should help in understanding it, and, we hope, other financial statements as well.

Penn Central Transportation Company's Balance Sheet Just Before Its Bankruptcy. One of the most widely known bankruptcies, and one of the largest, was that of Penn Central. We reproduce the balance sheet so that the reader can see the limitations of analyzing the stockholders' equity section of the balance sheet in forecasting bankruptcy. The annual report shows retained earnings of almost half a billion dollars and stockholders' equity of almost $2 billion. Yet soon after the report was issued, the company petitioned for bankruptcy because it could not meet its obligations.

Accounting Magic. This example shows how generally accepted accounting principles allow a range of accounting treatments so that two firms, exactly alike in all respects except for their accounting methods, can report drastically different incomes.

Pronouncements Governing Generally Accepted Accounting Principles. We include a list of pronouncements governing generally accepted accounting principles and their dates of issuance.

We gratefully acknowledge the permission of the Dryden Press to reproduce material from our *Financial Accounting, Intermediate Accounting*, and *Managerial Accounting* texts published by them. Special thanks to Peter M. Hinzelman for his comments on a draft of our notes for the GE financial statements. Ruth Dabrowski, Cheryl Greenland and Eli Worman designed the book and planned the layout. We thank them for their help.

Table of Contents

Glossary[1]

A

AAA. *American Accounting Association.*

Abacus. A scholarly journal containing articles on theoretical aspects of accounting. Published twice a year by the Sydney University Press, Sydney, Australia.

abatement. A complete or partial cancellation of a levy imposed by a government unit.

abnormal spoilage. Actual spoilage exceeding that expected when operations are normally efficient. Usual practice treats this cost as an *expense* of the period rather than as a *product cost*. Contrast with *normal spoilage*.

aboriginal cost. In public utility accounting, the *acquisition cost* of an *asset* incurred by the first *entity* devoting that asset to public use. Most public utility regulation is based on aboriginal cost. If it were not, then public utilities could exchange assets among themselves at ever-increasing prices in order to raise the rate base and, then, prices based thereon.

absorbed overhead. *Overhead* costs allocated to individual products at some *overhead rate*. Also called *applied overhead*.

absorption costing. See *full absorption costing*.

---

[1]Many words and phrases in the Glossary are defined in terms of other words and phrases. Terms in a given definition that are themselves (or variants thereof) explained elsewhere under their own listings are *italicized*.

Accelerated Cost Recovery System. A form of *accelerated depreciation* enacted by the Congress in 1981 and amended in 1986. The system provides percentages of the asset's cost to be depreciated each year for tax purposes. *Salvage value* is ignored. These amounts are generally not used for *financial accounting*.

accelerated depreciation. Any method of calculating *depreciation* charges where the charges become progressively smaller each period. Examples are *double-declining-balance* and *sum-of-the-years'-digits* methods.

acceptance. A written promise to pay that is equivalent to a *promissory note*.

account. Any device for accumulating additions and subtractions relating to a single *asset, liability, owners' equity* item, including *revenues* and *expenses*.

account analysis method. A method of separating *fixed* from *variable costs* involving the classification of the various *product cost accounts*. For example, *direct labor* and *direct material* are classified as variable and *depreciation* on the factory building as fixed.

account form. The form of *balance sheet* where *assets* are shown on the left and *equities* are shown on the right. Contrast with *report form*. See also *T-account*.

account payable. A *liability* representing an amount owed to a *creditor*, usually arising from purchase of *merchandise* or materials and supplies; not necessarily due or past due. Normally, a *current* liability.

account receivable. A claim against a *debtor* usually arising from sales or services rendered; not necessarily due or past due. Normally, a *current* asset.

accountability center. *Responsibility center.*

accountancy. The British word for *accounting*. In the United States, it means the theory and practice of accounting.

Accountants' Index. A publication of the *AICPA* that indexes, in detail, the accounting literature of the period.

accountant's opinion. *Auditor's report.*

accountant's report. *Auditor's report.*

accounting. An *information system* conveying information about a specific *entity*. The information is in financial terms and is restricted to information that can be made reasonably precise. The *AICPA* defines accounting as a service activity whose "function is to provide quantitative information, primarily financial in nature, about economic entities that is intended to be useful in making economic decisions."

accounting changes. As defined by *APB Opinion No. 20*, a change in (a) an *accounting principle* (such as a switch from *FIFO* to *LIFO* or from *sum-of-the-years'-digits* to *straight-line depreciation*), (b) an accounting estimate (such as estimated useful lives or salvage value of depreciable assets and estimates of *warranty* costs or *uncollectible accounts*), and (c) the reporting *entity*. Changes of type (a) should be disclosed. The cumulative effect of the change on *retained earnings* at the start of the period during which the change was made should be included in reported earnings for the period of change. Changes of type (b) should be treated as affecting only the period of change and, if necessary, future periods. The reasons for changes of type (c) should be disclosed and, in statements reporting on operations of the period of the change, the effect of the change on all other periods reported for comparative purposes should also be shown. In some cases (such as a change from *LIFO* to other inventory *flow assumptions* or in the method of accounting for long-term construction contracts), changes of type (a) are treated like changes of type (c). That is, for these changes all statements shown for prior periods must be restated to show the effect of adopting the change for those periods as well. See *all-inclusive concept* and *accounting errors*.

accounting conventions. Methods or procedures used in accounting. This term tends to be used when the method or procedure has not been given official authoritative sanction by a pronouncement of a group such as the *APB, EITF, FASB,* or *SEC*. Contrast with *accounting principles*.

accounting cycle. The sequence of accounting procedures starting with *journal entries* for various transactions and events and ending with the *financial statements* or, perhaps, the *post-closing trial balance*.

accounting entity. See *entity.*

accounting equation. *Assets = Equities. Assets = Liabilities + Owners' Equity.*

accounting errors. Arithmetic errors and misapplications of *accounting principles* in previously published financial statements that are corrected in the current period with direct *debits* or *credits* to *retained earnings*. In this regard, they are treated like *prior-period adjustments*, but, technically, they are not classified by *APB Opinion No. 9* as prior-period adjustments. See *accounting changes* and contrast with changes in accounting estimates as described there.

accounting event. Any occurrence that is recorded in the accounting records.

accounting methods. *Accounting principles.* Procedures for carrying out accounting principles.

accounting period. The time period for which *financial statements* that measure *flows*, such as the *income statement* and the *statement of cash flows*, are prepared. Should be clearly identified on the financial statements. See *interim statements.*

accounting policies. *Accounting principles* adopted by a specific *entity.*

accounting principles. The methods or procedures used in accounting for events reported in the *financial statements*. This term tends to be used when the method or procedure has been given official authoritative sanction by a pronouncement of a group such as the *APB, EITF, FASB,* or *SEC*. Contrast with *accounting conventions* and *conceptual framework.*

Accounting Principles Board. See *APB.*

accounting procedures. See *accounting principles*, but usually this term refers to the methods for implementing accounting principles.

accounting rate of return. Income for a period divided by average investment during the period. Based on income, rather than discounted cash flows and, hence, is a poor decision making aid or tool. See *ratio.*

Accounting Research Bulletin. ARB. The name of the official pronouncements of the former *Committee on Accounting Procedure* of the *AICPA*. Fifty-one bulletins were issued between 1939 and 1959. *ARB No. 43* summarizes the first forty-two bulletins.

Accounting Research Study. ARS. One of a series of studies published by the Director of Accounting Research of the *AICPA* "designed to provide professional accountants and others interested in the development of accounting with a discussion and documentation of accounting problems." Fifteen such studies were published between 1961 and 1974.

The Accounting Review. Scholarly publication of the *American Accounting Association.*

Accounting Series Release. ASR. See *SEC.*

accounting standards. *Accounting principles.*

Accounting Standards Executive Committee. AcSEC. The senior technical committee of the *AICPA* authorized to speak for the AICPA in the areas of *financial accounting* and reporting as well as *cost accounting.*

accounting system. The procedures for collecting and summarizing financial data in a firm.

Accounting Terminology Bulletin. ATB. One of four releases of the Committee on Terminology of the *AICPA* issued in the period 1953-1957.

Accounting Trends and Techniques. An annual publication of the *AICPA* that surveys the reporting practices of 600 large corporations. It presents tabulations of specific practices, terminology, and disclosures along with illustrations taken from individual annual reports.

accounts receivable turnover. Net *sales on account* divided by average *accounts receivable.* See *ratio.*

accretion. See *amortization.* When a *book value* grows over time, such as a *bond* originally issued at a *discount,* the correct technical term is "accretion," not "amortization." Also, increase in economic worth through physical change, usually sid of a natural resource such as an orchard, caused by natural growth. Contrast with *appreciation.*

accrual. Recognition of an *expense (or revenue)* and the related *liability (or asset)* that is caused by an *accounting event,* frequently by the passage of time, and that is not signaled by an explicit cash transaction. For example, the recognition of interest expense or revenue (or wages, salaries, or rent) at the end of a period even though no explicit cash transaction is made at that time. Cash flow follows accounting recognition; contrast with *deferral.*

accrual basis of accounting. The method of recognizing *revenues* as *goods* are sold (or delivered) and as *services* are rendered, independent of the time when cash is received. *Expenses* are recognized in the period when the related revenue is recognized independent of the time when cash is paid out. *SFAC No. 1* says "accrual accounting attempts to record the financial effects on an enterprise of transactions and other events and circumstances that have cash consequences for the enterprise in the periods in which those transactions, events, and circumstances occur rather than only in the periods in which cash is received or paid by the enterprise." Contrast with the *cash basis of accounting.* See *accrual* and *deferral.* The basis would more correctly be called "accrual/deferral" accounting.

accrued. Said of a *revenue (expense)* that has been earned (recognized) even though the related *receivable (payable)* is not yet due. This adjective should not be used as part of an account title. Thus, we prefer to use Interest Receivable (Payable) as the account title, rather than Accrued Interest Receivable (Payable). See *matching convention.* See *accrual.*

accrued depreciation. An incorrect term for *accumulated depreciation.* Acquiring an asset with cash, capitalizing it, and then amortizing its cost over periods of use is a process of *deferral* and allocation, not of *accrual.*

accrued payable. A *payable* usually resulting from the passage of time. For example, *salaries* and *interest* accrue as time passes. See *accrued.*

accrued receivable. A *receivable* usually resulting from the passage of time. See *accrued.*

accumulated benefit obligation. See *projected benefit obligation* for definition and contrast.

accumulated depreciation. A preferred title for the *contra-asset* account that shows the sum of *depreciation* charges on an asset since it was acquired. Other titles used are *allowance* for *depreciation* (acceptable term) and *reserve* for *depreciation* (unacceptable term).

accurate presentation. The qualitative accounting objective suggesting that information reported in financial statements should correspond as precisely as possible with the economic effects underlying transactions and events. See *fair presentation* and *full disclosure.*

acid test ratio. *Quick ratio.*

acquisition cost. Of an *asset,* the net *invoice* price plus all *expenditures* to place and ready the asset for its intended use. The other expenditures might include legal fees, transportation charges, and installation costs.

ACRS. *Accelerated Cost Recovery System.*

AcSEC. *Accounting Standards Executive Committee* of the *AICPA.*

activity accounting. *Responsibility accounting.*

activity-based depreciation. *Production method of depreciation.*

activity basis. *Costs* are *variable* or *fixed* (*incremental* or *unavoidable*) with respect to some activity, such as production of units (or the undertaking of some new project). This activity is referred to as the "activity basis."

actual cost (basis). *Acquisition* or *historical cost.* Also contrast with *standard cost.*

actual costing (system). Method of allocating costs to products using actual *direct materials,* actual *direct labor,* and actual *factory overhead.* Contrast with *normal costing* and *standard cost system.*

actuarial. Usually said of computations or analyses that involve both *compound interest* and probabilities, such as the computation of the *present value* of a life-contingent *annuity.* Sometimes the term is used if only one of the two is involved.

actuarial accrued liability. A 1981 report of the Joint Committee on Pension Terminology (of various actuarial societies) stated that this term is the preferred one for *prior service cost.*

additional paid-in capital. An alternative acceptable title for the *capital contributed in excess of par (or stated) value* account.

additional processing cost. *Costs* incurred in processing *joint products* after the *splitoff point*.

adequate disclosure. *Fair presentation* of *financial statements* requires *disclosure* of *material* items. This *auditing standard* does not, however, require publicizing all information detrimental to a company. For example, the company may be threatened with a lawsuit and disclosure might seem to require a *debit* to a *loss* account and a *credit* to an *estimated liability*. But the mere making of this entry might adversely affect the actual outcome of the suit. Such entries need not be made although impending suits should be disclosed.

adjunct account. An *account* that accumulates additions to another account. For example, Premium on Bonds Payable is adjunct to the liability Bonds Payable; the effective liability is the sum of the two account balances at a given date. Contrast with *contra account*.

adjusted acquisition (historical) cost. Sometimes said of the *book value* of a *plant asset*. Also, cost adjusted to a *constant dollar* amount to reflect *general price level changes*.

adjusted bank balance of cash. The *balance* shown on the statement from the bank plus or minus amounts, such as for unrecorded deposits or outstanding checks, to reconcile the bank's balance with the correct cash balance. See *adjusted book balance of cash*.

adjusted basis. The *basis* used to compute gain or loss on disposition of an *asset* for tax purposes. Also, see *book value*.

adjusted book balance of cash. The *balance* shown in the firm's account for cash in bank plus or minus amounts, such as for *notes* collected by the bank or bank service charges, to reconcile the account balance with the correct cash balance. See *adjusted bank balance of cash*.

adjusted trial balance. *Trial balance* taken after *adjusting entries* but before *closing entries*. Contrast with *pre* and *post-closing trial balances*. See *unadjusted trial balance* and *post-closing trial balance*. See also *work sheet*.

adjusting entry. An entry made at the end of an *accounting period* to record a *transaction* or other *accounting event*, which for some reason has not been recorded or has been improperly recorded during the accounting period. An entry to update the accounts. See *work sheet*.

adjustment. A change in an *account* produced by an *adjusting entry*. Sometimes the term is used to refer to the process of restating *financial statement* amounts to *constant dollars*.

administrative expense. An *expense* related to the enterprise as a whole as contrasted to expenses related to more specific functions such as manufacturing or selling.

admission of partner. Legally, when a new partner joins a *partnership*, the old partnership is dissolved and a new one comes into being. In practice, however, the old accounting records may be kept in use and the accounting entries reflect the manner in which the new partner joined the firm. If the new partner merely purchases the interest of another partner, the only accounting is to change the name for one capital account. If the new partner contributes *assets* and *liabilities* to the partnership, then the new assets must be recognized with debits and the liabilities and other source of capital, with credits. See *bonus method*.

ADR. See *asset depreciation range*.

advances from (by) customers. A preferred title for the *liability* account representing *receipts* of *cash* in advance of delivering the *goods* or rendering the *service* (that will cause *revenue* to be recognized). Sometimes called "deferred revenue" or "deferred income."

advances to affiliates. *Loans* by a parent company to a *subsidiary*. Frequently combined with "investment in subsidiary" as "investments and advances to subsidiary" and shown as a *noncurrent asset* on the parent's *balance sheet*. These advances are eliminated in *consolidated financial statements*.

advances to suppliers. A preferred term for the *asset account* representing *disbursements* of cash in advance of receiving *assets* or *services*.

adverse opinion. An *auditor's report* stating that the financial statements are not fair or are not in accord with *GAAP*.

affiliated company. Said of a company controlling or controlled by another company.

after closing. *Post-closing*; said of a *trial balance* at the end of the period.

after cost. Said of *expenditures* to be made subsequent to *revenue* recognition. For example, *expenditures* for *repairs* under warranty are after costs. Proper recognition of after costs involves a debit to expense at the time of the sale and a credit to an *estimated liability*. When the liability is discharged, the debit is to the estimated liability and the credit is to the assets consumed.

agency fund. An account for *assets* received by governmental units in the capacity of trustee or agent.

agency theory. A branch of economics relating the behavior of principals (such as owner non managers or bosses) and their *agents* (such as nonowner managers or subordinates). The principal assigns responsibility and authority to the agent but the agent has his or her own risks and preferences different from those of the principal. The principal is unable to observe all activities of the agent. Thus the principal must be careful about the kinds of observations of or reports sought from the agent, perhaps through an independent *auditor*, and the sorts of incentive contracts that the principal makes with the agent.

agent. One authorized to transact business, including executing contracts, for another.

aging accounts receivable. The process of classifying *accounts receivable* by the time elapsed since the claim came into existence for the purpose of estimating the amount of uncollectible accounts receivable as of a given date. See *sales contra, estimated uncollectibles* and *allowance for uncollectibles.*

aging schedule. A listing of *accounts receivable*, classified by age, used in *aging accounts receivable.*

AICPA. American Institute of Certified Public Accountants. The national organization that represents *CPAs., See AcSEC.* It oversees the writing and grading of the Uniform CPA Examination. Each state, however, sets its own requirements for becoming a CPA in that state. See *certified public accountant.*

all-capital earnings rate. *Rate of return on assets.*

all-inclusive (income) concept. Under this concept, no distinction is drawn between *operating* and *nonoperating revenues* and *expenses;* thus the only entries to retained earnings are for *net income* and *dividends.* Under this concept all *income, gains,* and *losses* are reported in the *income statement;* thus, events usually reported as *prior-period adjustments* and as *corrections of errors* are included in net income. This concept in its pure form is not the basis of *GAAP,* but *APB Opinions Nos. 9 and 30* move far in this direction. They do permit retained earnings entries for prior-period adjustments and correction of errors.

allocate. To spread a *cost* from one *account* to several accounts, to several products, or activities, or to several periods.

allocation base. *Joint costs* are assigned to *cost objectives* in some systematic fashion. The allocation base specifies the fashion. For example, the cost of a truck might be assigned to periods based on miles driven during the period; the allocation base is miles. Or, the cost of a factory supervisor might be assigned to product based on *direct labor* hours; the allocation base is direct labor hours.

allocation of income taxes. See *deferred income tax.*

allowance. A balance sheet *contra account* generally used for *receivables* and depreciable assets. See *sales* (or *purchase) allowance* for another use of this term.

allowance for funds used during construction. One principle of public utility regulation and rate setting is that customers should pay the full costs of producing the services (e.g., electricity) that they use nothing more and nothing less. Thus an electric utility is even more careful than other businesses to capitalize into an *asset account* the full costs, but no more, of producing a new electric power generating plant. One of the costs of building a new plant is the *interest* cost on money tied up during construction. If *funds* are explicitly borrowed by an ordinary business, the journal entry for interest of $1,000 is typically:

Interest Expense	1,000	
Interest Payable		1,000
Interest expense for the period.		

If the firm is constructing a new plant, then another entry would be made capitalizing interest into the plant-under-construction account:

Construction Work in Progress	750	
Interest Expense		750
Capitalize relevant portion of interest relating to construction work in progress into the asset account.		

The cost of the *plant asset* is increased; when the plant is used, *depreciation* is charged; the interest will become an expense through the depreciation process in the later periods of use, not currently as the interest is paid. Thus the full cost of the electricity generated during a given period is reported as expense in that period. But suppose, as is common, that the electric utility does not explicitly borrow the funds, but uses some of its own funds, including funds raised from equity issues as well as from debt. Even though there is no explicit interest expense, there is the *opportunity cost* of the funds. Put another way, the cost of the plant under construction is not less in an economic sense just because the firm used its own cash, rather than borrowing. The public utility using its own funds, on which $750 of interest would be payable if the funds had been explicitly borrowed, will make the following entry:

Construction Work in Progress	750	
Allowance for Funds Used During Construction		750
Recognition of interest, an opportunity cost, on own funds used.		

The allowance account is a form of *revenue*, to appear on the income statement, and will be closed to Retained Earnings, increasing it. On the *funds statement, it is an income or revenue item not producing funds and so must be subtracted from net income in deriving funds provided by operations. SFAS No. 34* specifically prohibits non-utility companies from capitalizing the opportunity cost (interest) on own funds used into plant under construction.

allowance for uncollectibles (accounts receivable). A *contra* to Accounts Receivable that shows the estimated amount of *accounts receivable* that will not be collected. When such an allowance is used, the actual *write-off* of specific accounts receivable (*debit* allowance, *credit* specific account) does not affect *revenue* or *expense* at the time of the write off. The revenue reduction is recognized when *bad debt expense* is *debited* and the allowance is credited; the amount of the credit to the allowance may be based on a percentage of sales on account for a period of time or computed from *aging accounts receivable.* This contra account enables an estimate to be shown of the amount of receivables that will be collected without identifying specific uncollectible accounts. See *allowance method.*

allowance method. A method of attempting to *match* all *expenses* of a transaction with its associated *revenues.*

Usually involves a debit to expense and a credit to an *estimated liability*, such as for estimated warranty expenditures, or a debit to a revenue (*contra*) account and a credit to an asset (*contra*) account, such as in some firms' accounting for uncollectible accounts. See *allowance for uncollectibles* for further explanation. When the allowance method is used for *sales discounts*, sales are recorded at *gross invoice* prices (not reduced by the amounts of discounts made available). An estimate of the amount of discounts to be taken is debited to a *revenue contra account* and *credited* to an allowance account, shown contra to *accounts receivable*.

American Accounting Association. AAA. An organization primarily for academic accountants, but open to all interested in accounting. It publishes *The Accounting Review*.

American Institute of Certified Public Accountants. See *AICPA*.

American Stock Exchange. AMEX. ASE. A public market where various corporate *securities* are traded.

AMEX. *American Stock Exchange.*

amortization. Strictly speaking, the process of liquidating or extinguishing ("bringing to death") a *debt* with a series of payments to the *creditor* (or to a *sinking fund*). From that usage has evolved a related use involving the accounting for the payments themselves: "amortization schedule" for a mortgage which is a table showing the allocation between *interest* and *principle*. The term has come to mean writing off ("liquidating") the cost of an asset. In this context it means the general process of *allocating acquisition cost* of an asset to either the periods of benefit as *expenses* or to *inventory* accounts as *product costs*. Called *depreciation* for *plant assets*, *depletion* for *wasting assets* (natural resources), and "amortization" for *intangibles*. *SFAC No. 6* refers to amortization as "the accounting process of reducing an amount by periodic payments or write-downs." The expressions "unamortized debt discount or premium" and "to amortize debt discount or premium" relate to *accruals*, not to *deferrals*. The expressions "amortization of long-term assets" and "to amortize long-term assets" refer to deferrals, not accruals. Contrast with *accretion*.

analysis of variances. See *variance analysis*.

annual report. A report for shareholders and other interested parties prepared once a year, includes a *balance sheet*, an *income statement*, a *statement of cash flows*, a reconciliation of changes in *owners' equity* accounts, a *summary of significant accounting principles*, other explanatory *notes*, the *auditor's report*, and, comments from management about the year's events. See *10-K* and *financial statements*.

annuitant. One who receives an *annuity*.

annuity. A series of payments, usually made at equally spaced time intervals.

annuity certain. An *annuity* payable for a definite number of periods. Contrast with *contingent annuity*.

annuity due. An *annuity* whose first payment is made at the start of period 1 (or at the end of period 0). Contrast with *annuity in arrears*.

annuity in advance. An *annuity due*.

annuity in arrears. An *ordinary annuity* whose first payment occurs at the end of the first period.

annuity method of depreciation. See *compound interest depreciation*.

antidilutive. Said of a *potentially dilutive security* that will increase *earnings per share* if it is *exercised* or *converted* into common stock. In computing *primary* and *fully diluted earnings per share*, antidilutive securities may not be assumed to be exercised or converted and hence do not increase reported earnings per share in a given period.

APB. Accounting Principles Board of the *AICPA*. It set *accounting principles* from 1959 through 1973, issuing 31 *APB Opinions*. It was superseded by the *FASB*.

APB Opinion. The name given to pronouncements of the *APB* that make up much of *generally accepted accounting principles*; there are 31 *APB Opinions*, issued from 1962 through 1973.

APB Statement. The *APB* issued four *Statements* between 1962 and 1970. The *Statements* were approved by at least two thirds of the Board, but they are recommendations, not requirements. For example, *Statement No. 3* (1969) suggested the publication of *constant dollar financial statements* but did not require them.

APBs. An abbreviation used for *APB Opinions*.

applied cost. A *cost* that has been *allocated* to a department, product, or activity; need not be based on actual costs incurred.

applied overhead. *Overhead costs* charged to departments, products or activities. Also called *absorbed overhead*.

appraisal. The process of obtaining a valuation for an *asset* or *liability* that involves expert opinion rather than evaluation of explicit market transactions.

appraisal method of depreciation. The periodic *depreciation* charge is the difference between the beginning and end-of-period appraised value of the *asset* if that difference is positive. If negative, there is no charge. Not based on *historical cost* nor, hence, generally accepted.

appreciation. An increase in economic worth caused by rising market prices for an *asset*. Contrast with *accretion*.

appropriated retained earnings. See *retained earnings, appropriated*.

appropriation. In governmental accounting, an *expenditure* authorized for a specified amount, purpose, and time.

appropriation account. In governmental accounting, an account set up to record specific authorizations to spend; it is credited with appropriation amounts. *Expenditures* during the period and *encumbrances* outstanding at the end of the period are closed (debited) to this account at the end of the period.

approximate net realizable value method. A method of assigning joint costs to *joint products* based on revenues minus *additional processing costs* of the end products.

ARB. Accounting Research Bulletin.

arbitrage. Strictly speaking, the simultaneous purchase in one market and sale in another of a *security* or commodity in hope of making a *profit* on price differences in the different markets. Often this term is loosely used when the item sold is somewhat different from the item purchased; for example, the sale of shares of *common stock* and the simultaneous purchase of a *convertible bond* that is convertible into identical common shares.

arm's length. Said of a transaction negotiated by unrelated parties, each acting in his or her own self-interest; the basis for a *fair market value* determination.

arrears. Said of *cumulative preferred stock dividends* that have not been declared up to the current date. See *annuity in arrears* for another context.

ARS. Accounting Research Study.

articles of incorporation. Document filed with state authorities by persons forming a corporation. When the document is returned with a certificate of incorporation, it becomes the corporation's *charter.*

articulate. Said of the relationship between any operating statement (for example, *income statement* or *statement of cash flows*) and *comparative balance sheets*, where the operating statement explains (or reconciles) the change in some major balance sheet category (for example, *retained earnings* or *working capital*).

ASE. American Stock Exchange.

ASR. Accounting Series Release.

assess. To value property for the purpose of property taxation; the assessment is computed by the taxing authority. To levy a charge on the owner of property for improvements thereto, such as for sewers or sidewalks.

assessed valuation. A dollar amount for real estate or other property used by a government as a basis for levying taxes. The amount may or may not bear some relation to *market value.*

asset. *SFAC No. 6* defines assets as "probable future economic benefits obtained or controlled by a particular entity as a result of past transactions. An asset has three essential characteristics: (a) it embodies a probable future benefit that involves a capacity, singly or in combination with other assets, to contribute directly or indirectly to future net cash inflows, (b) a particular enterprise can obtain the benefit and control others' access to it, and (c) the transaction or other event giving rise to the enterprise's right to or control of the benefit has already occurred." A footnote points out that "probable" means that which can be reasonably expected or believed but is neither certain nor proved. May be *tangible* or *intangible*, *short-term* (current) or *long-term* (noncurrent).

asset depreciation range. ADR. The range of *depreciable lives* allowed by the *Internal Revenue Service* for a specific depreciable *asset.*

asset turnover. Net sales divided by average assets. See *ratio.*

assignment of accounts receivable. Transfer of the legal ownership of an *account receivable* through its sale. Contrast with *pledging* accounts receivable where the receivables serve as *collateral* for a *loan.*

ATB. Accounting Terminology Bulletin.

at par. Said of a *bond* or *preferred stock* issued or selling at its *face amount.*

attachment. The laying claim to the *assets* of a borrower or debtor by a lender or creditor when the borrower has failed to pay debts on time.

attest. Rendering of an *opinion* by an auditor that the *financial statements* are fair. This procedure is called the "attest function" of the CPA. See *fair presentation.*

attribute measured. When making physical measurements, such as of a person, one needs to decide the units with which to measure, such as inches or centimeters or pounds or grams. One chooses the attribute height or weight independently of the measuring unit English or metric. In conventional accounting the attribute measured in *historical cost* and the measuring unit is *nominal dollars.* Some theorists argue that accounting is more useful when the attribute measured is *current cost.* Others argue that accounting is more useful when the measuring unit is *constant dollars.* Some, including us, think both changes from conventional accounting should be made. The attribute historical cost can be measured in nominal dollars or in constant dollars. The attribute current cost can also be measured in nominal dollars or constant dollars. Choosing between two attributes and two measuring units implies four different accounting systems. Each of these four has its uses.

audit. Systematic inspection of accounting records involving analyses, tests, and *confirmations.* See *internal audit.*

audit committee. A committee of the board of directors of a *corporation* usually consisting of outside directors who nominate the independent auditors and discuss the auditors' work with them. If the auditors believe certain matters should be brought to the attention of shareholders, the auditors first bring these matters to the attention of the audit committee.

Audit Guides. See Industry Audit Guides.

audit program. The procedures followed by the *auditor* in carrying out the *audit.*

audit trail. A reference accompanying an *entry*, or *posting*, to an underlying source record or document. A good audit trail is essential for efficiently checking the accuracy of accounting entries. See *cross-reference*.

Auditing Research Monograph. Publication series of the *AICPA*.

auditing standards. A set of ten standards promulgated by the *AICPA*, including three general standards, three standards of field work, and four standards of reporting. According to the AICPA, these standards "deal with the measures of the quality of the performance and the objectives to be attained," rather than with specific auditing procedures.

Auditing Standards Advisory Council. An *AICPA* committee.

Auditing Standards Board. Operating committee of the *AICPA* promulgating auditing rules.

auditor. One who checks the accuracy, fairness, and general acceptability of accounting records and statements and then *attests* to them.

auditor's opinion. *Auditor's report.*

auditor's report. The auditor's statement of the work done and an opinion of the *financial statements*. Opinions are usually unqualified ("clean"), but may be *qualified*, or the auditor may disclaim an opinion in the report. Often called the "accountant's report." See *adverse opinion*.

AudSEC. The former Auditing Standards Executive Committee of the *AICPA*, now functioning as the *Auditing Standards Board*.

authorized capital stock. The number of *shares* of stock that can be issued by a corporation; specified by the *articles of incorporation*.

average. The arithmetic mean of a set of numbers; obtained by summing the items and dividing by the number of items.

average collection period of receivables. See *ratio*.

average-cost flow assumption. An *inventory flow assumption* where the cost of units is the *weighted average* cost of the *beginning inventory* and purchases. See *inventory equation*.

average tax rate. The rate found by dividing *income tax expense* by *net income* before taxes. Contrast with *marginal tax rate, statutory tax rate*.

avoidable cost. A *cost* that will cease if an activity is discontinued. An *incremental* or *variable cost*. See *programmed cost*.

B

backlog. Orders for which insufficient *inventory* is on hand for current delivery and which will be filled in a later period.

backlog depreciation. In *current cost accounting*, a problem arising for the *accumulated depreciation* on *plant assets*. Consider an *asset* costing $10,000 with a 10-year life depreciated with the *straight-line method*. Assume that a similar asset has a current cost of $10,000 at the end of the first year but $12,000 at the end of the second year. Assume that the depreciation charge is based on the average current cost during the year, $10,000 for the first year and $11,000 for the second. The depreciation charge for the first year is $1,000 and for the second is $1,100 (= .10 x $11,000), so the *accumulated depreciation account* is $2,100 after 2 years. Note that at the end of the second year, 20 percent of the asset's future benefits have been used, so the accounting records based on current costs must show a *net book value* of $9,600 (= .80 x $12,000), which would result if accumulated depreciation of $2,400 were subtracted from a current cost of $12,000. But the sum of the depreciation charges has been only $2,100. The *journal entry* to increase the accumulated depreciation account requires a *credit* to that account of $300. The question arises, what account is to debited? That is the problem of backlog depreciation. Some theorists would *debit* an *income* account and others would *debit* a *balance sheet owners' equity* account without reducing current-period earnings. The answer to the question of what to do with the debit is closely tied to the problem of how *holding gains* are recorded. When the asset account is debited for $2,000 to increase the recorded amount from $10,000 to $12,000, a holding gain or $2,000 must be recorded with a credit. Many theorists believe that whatever account is credited for the holding gains is the same account that should be debited for backlog depreciation. Sometimes called "catch-up depreciation."

bad debt. An *uncollectible account receivable*; see *bad debt expense* and *sales contra, estimated uncollectibles*.

bad debt expense. The name for the *account debited* in both the *allowance method* for *uncollectibles* and the *direct write-off method*.

bad debt recovery. Collection, perhaps partial, of a specific account receivable previously written off as uncollectible. If the *allowance method* is used, the *credit* is usually to the *allowance* account. If the *direct write-off method* is used, the credit is to a *revenue account*.

bailout period. In a *capital budgeting* context, the total time that must elapse before net accumulated cash inflows from a project including potential *salvage value* of assets at various times equal or exceed the accumulated cash outflows. Contrast with *payback period*, which assumes completion of the project and uses terminal salvage value. Bailout is superior to payback because bailout takes into account, at least to some degree, the *present value* of the cash flows after termination date being considered. The potential salvage value at any time includes some estimate of the flows that can occur after that time.

balance. As a noun, the sum of *debit* entries minus the sum of *credit* entries in an *account*. If positive, the difference is called a debit balance; if negative, a credit balance. As a verb, to find the difference described above.

balance sheet. Statement of financial position that shows *Total Assets* = Total Liabilities + Owners' Equity.

balance sheet account. An account that can appear on a balance sheet. A *permanent account*; contrast with *temporary account*.

balloon. Most *mortgage* and *installment loans* require relative equal periodic payments. Sometimes, the loan requires relatively equal periodic payments with a large final payment. The large final payment is called a "balloon" payment. Such loans are called "balloon" loans. Although a *coupon bond* meets this definition, the term is seldom, if ever, applied to bond loans.

bank balance. The amount of the balance in a checking account shown on the *bank statement*. Compare with *adjusted bank balance* and see *bank reconciliation schedule*.

bank prime rate. See *prime rate*.

bank reconciliation schedule. A schedule that shows how the difference between the book balance of the cash in bank account and the bank's statement can be explained. Takes into account the amount of such items as checks issued that have not cleared or deposits that have not been recorded by the bank as well as errors made by the bank or the firm.

bank statement. A statement sent by the bank to a checking account customer showing deposits, checks cleared, and service charges for a period, usually one month.

bankrupt. Said of a company whose *liabilities* exceed its *assets* where a legal petition has been filed and accepted under the bankruptcy law. A bankrupt firm is usually, but need not be, *insolvent*.

base stock method. A method of inventory valuation that assumes that there is a minimum normal or base stock of goods that must be kept on hand at all times for effective continuity of operations. This base quantity is valued at *acquisition cost* of the inventory on hand in the earliest period when inventory was on hand. The method is not allowable for income tax purposes and is no longer used, but is generally considered to be the forerunner of the *LIFO* method.

basic accounting equation. *Accounting equation*.

basis. *Acquisition cost*, or some substitute therefore, of an *asset* or *liability* used in computing gain or loss on disposition or retirement. *Attribute measured*. This term is used in both *financial* and *tax reporting*, but the basis of a given item need not be the same for both purposes.

basket purchase. Purchase of a group of *assets* (and *liabilities*) for a single price; *costs* must be assigned to each of the items so that the individual items can be recorded in the *accounts*.

bear. One who believes that security prices will fall. A "bear market" refers to a time when stock prices are generally declining. Contrast with *bull*.

bearer bond. See *registered bond* for contrast and definition.

beginning inventory. Valuation of *inventory* on hand at the beginning of the *accounting period*.

behavioral congruence. *Goal congruence*.

betterment. An *improvement*, usually *capitalized*.

bid. An offer to purchase, or the amount of the offer.

big bath. A *write off* of a substantial amount of costs previously treated as *assets*. Usually caused when a corporation drops a line of business that required a large investment but that proved to be unprofitable. Sometimes used to describe a situation where a corporation takes a large write off in one period in order to free later periods of gradual write offs of those amounts. In this sense it frequently occurs when there is a change in top management.

Big Eight. The eight largest U.S. *public accounting (CPA)* partnerships; in alphabetical order: Arthur Andersen & Co.; Coopers & Lybrand; Deloitte Haskins & Sells; Ernst & Whinney; Peat Marwick Main & Co.; Price Waterhouse & Co.; Touche Ross & Co.; and Arthur Young & Company.

bill. An *invoice* of charges and *terms of sale* for *goods* and *services*. Also, a piece of currency.

bill of materials. A specification of the quantities of *direct materials* expected to be used to produce a given job or quantity of output.

board of directors. The governing body of a corporation elected by the shareholders.

bond. A certificate to show evidence of debt. The *par value* is the *principal* or face amount of the bond payable at maturity. The *coupon rate* is the amount of interest payable in one year divided by the principal amount. Coupon bonds have attached to them coupons that can be redeemed at stated dates for interest payments. Normally, bonds carry semiannual coupons.

bond conversion. The act of exchanging *convertible bonds* for *preferred* or *common stock*.

bond discount. From the standpoint of the issuer of a *bond* at the issue date, the excess of the *par value* of a bond over its initial sales price; at later dates the excess of par over the sum of (initial issue price plus the portion of discount already *amortized*). From the standpoint of a bondholder, the difference between par value and selling price when the bond sells below par.

bond indenture. The contract between an issuer of *bonds* and the bondholders.

bond premium. Exactly parallel to *bond discount* except that the issue price (or current selling price) is higher than *par value*.

bond ratings. Ratings of corporate and *municipal bond* issues by Moody's Investors Service and by Standard & Poor's Corporation, based on the issuer's existing *debt* level, its previous record of payment, the *coupon rate* on the bonds, and the safety of the *assets* or *revenues* that are committed to paying off *principal* and *interest*. Moody's top rating is Aaa; Standard & Poor's is AAA.

bond redemption. Retirement of *bonds*.

bond refunding. To incur *debt*, usually through the issue of new *bonds*, intending to use the proceeds to retire an *outstanding* bond issue.

bond sinking fund. See *sinking fund*.

bond table. A table showing the current price of a *bond* as a function of the *coupon rate*, years to *maturity*, and effective *yield to maturity* (or *effective rate*).

bonus. Premium over normal *wage* or *salary*, paid usually for meritorious performance.

bonus method. When a new partner is admitted to a *partnership* and the new partner is to be credited with *capital* in excess proportion to the amount of *tangible* assets he or she contributes, two methods may be used to recognize this excess, say $10,000. First, $10,000 may be transferred from the old partners to the new one. This is the bonus method. Second, goodwill in the amount of $10,000 may be recognized as an asset with the credit to the new partner's capital account. This is the *goodwill method*. (Notice that the new partner's percentage of total ownership is not the same under the two methods.) If the new partner is to be credited with capital in smaller proportion than the amount of contribution, then there will be bonus or goodwill for the old partners.

book. As a verb, to record a transaction. As a noun, usually plural, the *journals* and *ledgers*. As an adjective, see *book value*.

book cost. *Book value*.

book inventory. An *inventory* amount that results, not from physical count, but from the amount of beginning inventory plus *invoice* amounts of net purchases less invoice amounts of *requisitions* or withdrawals; implies a *perpetual* method.

book of original entry. A *journal*.

book value. The amount shown in the books or in the *accounts* for an *asset, liability,* or *owners' equity* item. Generally used to refer to the *net* amount of an *asset* or group of assets shown in the account which records the asset and reductions, such as for *amortization*, in its cost. Of a firm, the excess of total assets over total liabilities. *Net assets*.

book value per share of common stock. Common *shareholders' equity* divided by the number of shares of *common stock outstanding*. See *ratio*.

bookkeeping. The process of analyzing and recording transactions in the accounting records.

boot. The additional money paid (or received) along with a used item in a trade-in or exchange transaction for another item. See *trade-in transaction*.

borrower. See *loan*.

branch. A sales office or other unit of an enterprise physically separated from the home office of the enterprise but not organized as a legally separate *subsidiary*. The term is rarely used to refer to manufacturing units.

branch accounting. An accounting procedure that enables the financial position and operations of each *branch* to be reported separately but later combined for published statements.

breakeven analysis. See *breakeven chart*.

breakeven chart. Two kinds of breakeven charts are shown here. The charts are based on the information for a month shown below. Revenue is $30 per unit.

Cost Classification	Variable Cost, Per Unit	Fixed Cost, Per Month
Manufacturing costs:		
Direct material	$ 4	—
Direct labor	9	—
Overhead.	4	$3,060
Total manufacturing costs.	$17	$3,060
Selling, general and administrative costs	5	1,740
Total costs.	$22	$4,800

The cost-volume-profit graph presents the relationship of changes in volume to the amount of *profit*, or *income*. On such a graph, total *revenue* and total *costs* for each volume level are indicated and profit or loss at any volume can be read directly from the chart. The profit-volume graph does not show revenues and costs but more readily indicates profit (or loss) at various output levels. Two caveats should be kept in mind about these graphs. Although the curve depicting *variable cost* and total cost is shown as being a straight line for its entire length, it is likely that at low or high levels of output, variable cost would probably differ from $22 per unit. The variable cost figure was probably established by studies of operations at some broad central area of production, called the *relevant range*. For low (or high) levels of activity, the chart may not be applicable. For this reason, the total cost and profit-loss curves are sometimes shown as dotted lines at lower (or higher) volume levels. Second, this chart is simplified because it assumes a single product firm. For a multiproduct firm, the horizontal axis would have to be stated in dollars rather than in physical units of output. Breakeven charts for multiproduct firms necessarily assume that constant proportions of the several products are sold and changes in this mixture as well as in costs or selling prices would invalidate such a chart.

breakeven point. The volume of sales required so that total *revenues* and total *costs* are equal. May be expressed in units (*fixed costs/contribution per unit*) or in sales dollars selling price per unit x (*fixed costs/contribution per unit*).

budget. A financial plan that is used to estimate the results of future operations. Frequently used to help control future operations. In governmental operations, budgets often become the law.

A. Cost-Volume-Profit Graph

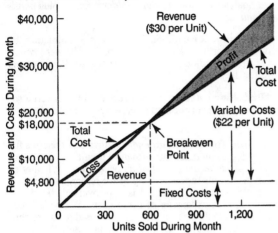

B. Profit-Volume Graph

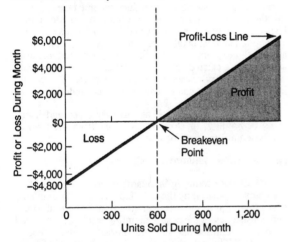

budgetary accounts. In governmental accounting, the accounts that reflect estimated operations and financial condition, as affected by estimated *revenues, appropriations,* and *encumbrances.* In contrast to *proprietary accounts* that record the transactions.

budgetary control. Management of governmental (nongovernmental) unit in accordance with an official (approved) *budget* in order to keep total expenditures within authorized (planned) limits.

budgeted cost. See *standard cost* for definition and contrast.

budgeted statements. *Pro forma statements* prepared before the event or period occurs.

bull. One who believes that security prices will rise. A "bull market" refers to a time when stock prices are generally rising. Contrast with *bear.*

burden. See *overhead costs.*

burn rate. A new business usually begins life with cash-absorbing operating losses, but with a limited amount of cash. The "burn rate" measures how long the new business can survive before operating losses must stop or a new infusion of cash will be necessary. The measurement is ordinarily stated in terms of months.

business combination. As defined in *APB Opinion No. 16,* the bringing together into a single accounting *entity* of two or more incorporated or unincorporated businesses. The *merger* will be accounted for either with the *purchase method* or the *pooling-of-interests method.* See *conglomerate.*

business entity. *Entity. Accounting entity.*

bylaws. The rules adopted by the shareholders of a corporation that specify the general methods for carrying out the functions of the corporation.

by-product. A *joint product* whose sales value is so small relative to the sales value of the other joint product(s) that it does not receive normal accounting treatment. The costs assigned to by-products reduce the costs of the main product(s). By-products are allocated a share of joint costs such that the expected gain or loss upon their sale is zero. Thus, by-products are shown in the *accounts* at *net realizable value.*

C

CA. *Chartered accountant.*

call. An option to buy *shares* of a publicly-traded corporation at a fixed price during a fixed time span. Contrast with *put.*

call premium. See *callable bond.*

call price. See *callable bond.*

callable bond. A *bond* for which the issuer reserves the right to pay a specific amount, the call price, to retire the obligation before *maturity* date. If the issuer agrees to pay more than the *face amount* of the bond when called the excess of the payment over the face amount is the "call premium."

Canadian Institute of Chartered Accountants. The national organization that represents *chartered accountants* in Canada.

cancelable lease. See *lease.*

capacity. Stated in units of product, the amount that can be produced per unit of time. Stated in units of input, such as *direct labor* hours, the amount of input that can be used in production per unit of time. This measure of output or input is used in allocating *fixed costs* if the amounts producible are normal, rather than maximum, amounts.

capacity cost. A *fixed cost* incurred to provide a firm with the capacity to produce or to sell. Consists of *standby costs* and *enabling costs.* Contrast with *programmed costs.*

capacity variance. *Production volume variance.*

capital. *Owners' equity* in a business. Often used, equally correctly, to mean the total assets of a business. Sometimes used to mean *capital assets.*

capital asset. Properly used, a designation for income tax purposes that describes property held by a taxpayer, except *cash*, inventoriable *assets*, goods held primarily for sale, most depreciable property, *real estate, receivables*, certain *intangibles*, and a few other items. Sometimes this term is imprecisely used to describe *plant* and *equipment*, which are clearly not capital assets under the income tax definition. Often the term is used to refer to an *investment* in *securities*.

capital budget. Plan of proposed outlays for acquiring long-term *assets* and the means of *financing* the acquisition.

capital budgeting. The process of choosing *investment* projects for an enterprise by considering the *present value* of cash flows and deciding how to raise the funds required by the investment.

capital consumption allowance. The term used for *depreciation expense* in national income accounting and the reporting of funds in the economy.

capital contributed in excess of par (or stated) value. A preferred title for the account that shows the amount received by the issuer for *capital stock* in excess of *par (or stated) value.*

capital expenditure (outlay). An *expenditure* to acquire long-term *assets.*

capital gain. The excess of proceeds over *cost*, or other *basis*, from the sale of a *capital asset* as defined by the Internal Revenue Code. If the capital asset has been held for a sufficiently long time before sale, then the tax on the gain is computed at a rate lower than is used for other gains and ordinary income.

capital lease. A *lease* treated by the *lessee* as both the borrowing of funds and the acquisition of an *asset* to be *amortized*. Both the *liability* and the asset are recognized on the balance sheet. Expenses consist of *interest* on the *debt* and *amortization* of the asset. The *lessor* treats the lease as the sale of the asset in return for a series of future cash receipts. Contrast with *operating lease.*

capital loss. A negative capital gain; see *capital gain.*

capital rationing. In a *capital budgeting* context, the imposing of constraints on the amounts of total capital expenditures in each period.

capital stock. The ownership shares of a corporation. Consists of all classes of *common* and *preferred stock.*

capital structure. The composition of a corporation's equities; the relative proportions of *short-term debt, long-term debt*, and *owners' equity.*

capital surplus. An inferior term for *capital contributed in excess of par (or stated) value.*

capitalization of a corporation. A term used by investment analysts to indicate *shareholders' equity* plus *bonds outstanding.*

capitalization of earnings. The process of estimating the economic worth of a firm by computing the *net present value* of the predicted *net income* (not *cash flows*) of the firm for the future.

capitalization rate. An *interest rate* used to convert a series of payments or receipts or earnings into a single *present value.*

capitalize. To record an *expenditure* that may benefit a future period as an *asset* rather than to treat the expenditure as an *expense* of the period of its occurrence. Whether or not expenditures for advertising or for research and development should be capitalized is controversial, but *SFAS No. 2* requires expensing of *R&D* costs. We believe expenditures should be capitalized if they lead to future benefits and thus meet the criterion to be an asset.

carryback, carryforward, carryover. The use of losses or tax credits in one period to reduce income taxes payable in other periods. There are two common kinds of carrybacks: for net operating losses and for *capital losses*. They are applied against taxable income. In general, carrybacks are for three years with the earliest year first. Operating losses can be carried forward for fifteen years. Corporate capital loss carryforwards are for five years. The capital loss for individuals can be carried forward indefinitely.

carrying cost. Costs (such as property taxes and insurance) of holding, or storing, *inventory* from the time of purchase until the time of sale or use.

carrying value (amount). *Book value.*

CASB. Cost Accounting Standards Board. A board of five members authorized by the U.S. Congress to "promulgate cost-accounting standards designed to achieve uniformity and consistency in the cost-accounting principles followed by defense contractors and subcontractors under federal contracts." The *principles* promulgated by the CASB are likely to have considerable weight in practice where the *FASB* has not established a standard. Although the Congress allowed the CASB to go out of existence in 1980, its standards have the same force as before.

cash. Currency and coins, negotiable checks, and balances in bank accounts. For the *statement of cash flows*, "cash" also includes *marketable securities* held as *current assets.*

cash basis of accounting. In contrast to the *accrual basis of accounting*, a system of accounting in which *revenues* are recognized when *cash* is received and *expenses* are recognized as *disbursements* are made. No attempt is made to *match revenues* and *expenses* in determining *income*. See *modified cash basis.*

cash budget. A schedule of expected cash *receipts* and *disbursements.*

cash collection basis. The *installment method* for recognizing *revenue*. Not to be confused with the *cash basis of accounting.*

cash conversion cycle. *Cash cycle.*

cash cycle. The period of time that elapses during which *cash* is converted into *inventories*, inventories are converted into *accounts receivable*, and receivables are converted back into cash. *Earnings cycle.*

cash disbursements journal. A specialized *journal* used to record *expenditures* by *cash* and by *check*. If a *check register* is also used, a cash disbursements journal records only expenditures of currency and coins.

cash discount. A reduction in sales or purchase price allowed for prompt payment.

cash dividend. See *dividend*.

cash equivalent value. A term used to describe the amount for which an *asset* could be sold. *Market value. Fair market price (value).*

cash flow. Cash *receipts* minus *disbursements* from a given *asset*, or group of assets, for a given period.

cash flow statement. *Statement of cash flows.*

cash provided by operations. An important subtotal in the *statement of cash flows*. This amount is the total of revenues producing *cash* less *expenses* requiring cash. Often, the amount is shown as *net income* plus expenses not requiring cash (such as depreciation charges) minus revenues not producing cash (such as revenues recognized under the *equity method* of accounting for a long-term investment). The statement of cash flows maintains the same distinctions between *continuing operations, discontinued operations*, and *income* or *loss* from *extraordinary items* as does the *income statement*.

cash receipts journal. A specialized *journal* used to record all *receipts* of *cash*.

cash (surrender) value of life insurance. An amount equal, not to the face value of the policy to be paid in event of death, but to the amount that could be realized if the policy were immediately canceled and traded with the insurance company for cash. If a firm owns a life insurance policy, the policy is reported as an asset at an amount equal to this value.

cash yield. See *yield*.

cashier's check. A bank's own *check* drawn on itself and signed by the cashier or other authorized official. It is a direct obligation of the bank. Compare with *certified check*.

catch-up depreciation. *Backlog depreciation.*

CCA. *Current cost accounting; current value accounting.*

central corporate expenses. General *overhead expenses* incurred in running the corporate headquarters and related supporting activities of a corporation. These expenses are treated as *period expenses*. Contrast with *manufacturing overhead*. A major problem in *line of business reporting* is the treatment of these expenses.

certificate. The document that is the physical embodiment of a *bond* or a *share of stock*. A term sometimes used for the *auditor's report*.

Certificate in Management Accounting. *CMA.*

certificate of deposit. Federal law constrains the *rate of interest* that banks can pay. Under current law banks are allowed to pay a rate higher than the one allowed on a *time deposit* if the depositor promises to leave funds on deposit for several months or more. When the bank receives such funds, it issues a certificate of deposit. The depositor can withdraw the funds before maturity if a penalty is paid.

certified check. The *check* of a depositor drawn on a bank on the face of which the bank has inserted the words "accepted" or "certified" with the date and signature of a bank official. The check then becomes an obligation of the bank. Compare with *cashier's check*.

certified financial statement. A financial statement attested to by an independent *auditor* who is a *CPA*.

certified internal auditor. See *CIA*.

certified public accountant. CPA. An accountant who has satisfied the statutory and administrative requirements of his or her jurisdiction to be registered or licensed as a public accountant. In addition to passing the Uniform CPA Examination administered by the *AICPA*, the CPA must meet certain educational, experience, and moral requirements that differ from jurisdiction to jurisdiction. The jurisdictions are the 50 states, the District of Columbia, Guam, Puerto Rico, and the Virgin Islands.

chain discount. A series of *discount* percentages; for example, if a chain discount of 10 and 5 percent is quoted, then the actual, or *invoice*, price is the nominal, or list, price times .90 times .95, or 85.5 percent of invoice price.

change fund. Coins and currency issued to cashiers, delivery drivers, and so on.

changes, accounting. See *accounting changes*.

changes in financial position. See *statement of cash flows*.

charge. As a noun, a *debit* to an account; as a verb, to debit.

charge off. To treat as a *loss* or *expense* an amount originally recorded as an *asset*; use of this term implies that the charge is not in accord with original expectations.

chart of accounts. A list of names and numbers, systematically organized, of *accounts*.

charter. Document issued by a state government authorizing the creation of a corporation.

chartered accountant. CA. The title used in Australia, Canada, and the United Kingdom for an accountant who has satisfied the requirements of the institute of his or her jurisdiction to be qualified to serve as a *public accountant*. In Canada, each provincial institute or order has the right to administer the examination and set the standards of performance and ethics for Chartered Accountants in its province. For a number of years, however, the provincial organizations have pooled their rights to qualify new members through the Inter-provincial Education Committee and the result is that there are nationally set and graded examinations given in English and French. The pass/fail grade awarded by the Board of Examiners (a subcommittee of the Inter-provincial Education Committee) is rarely deviated from.

check. You know what a check is. The Federal Reserve Board defines a check as "a *draft* or order upon a bank or banking house purporting to be drawn upon a deposit of funds for the payment at all events of a certain sum of money to a certain person therein named or to him or his order or to bearer and payable instantly on demand." It must contain the phrase "pay to the order of." The amount shown on the check's face must be clearly readable and it must have the signature of the drawer. Checks need not be dated, although they usually are. The *balance* in the *cash account* is usually reduced when a check is issued, not later when it clears the bank and reduces cash in bank. See *remittance advice*.

check register. A *journal* to record *checks* issued.

CIA. Certified Internal Auditor. One who has satisfied certain requirements of the *Institute of Internal Auditors* including experience, ethics, education, and passing examinations.

CICA. *Canadian Institute of Chartered Accountants.*

CIF. Cost, insurance, and freight; a term used in contracts along with the name of a given port to indicate that the quoted price includes insurance, handling, and freight charges up to delivery by the seller at the given port.

circulating capital. *Working capital.*

clean opinion. See *auditor's report*.

clean surplus concept. The notion that the only entries to the *retained earnings* account are to record *net income* and *dividends*. See *comprehensive income*. Contrast with *current operating performance concept*. This concept, with minor exceptions, is now controlling in *GAAP*. (See *APB Opinions* Nos. 9 and 30.)

clearing account. An account containing amounts to be transferred to another account(s) before the end of the *accounting period*. Examples are the *income summary* account (whose balance is transferred to *retained earnings*) and the purchases account (whose balance is transferred to *inventory* or to *cost of goods sold*).

close. As a verb, to transfer the *balance* of a *temporary* or *contra* or *adjunct* account to the main account to which it relates; for example, to transfer *revenue* and *expense* accounts directly, or through the *income summary* account, to an *owner's equity* account, or to transfer *purchase discounts* to purchases.

closed account. An *account* with equal *debits* and *credits*, usually as a result of a *closing entry*. See *ruling an account*.

closing entries. The *entries* that accomplish the transfer of balances in *temporary accounts* to the related *balance sheet accounts*. See *work sheet*.

closing inventory. *Ending inventory*.

CMA. Certificate in Management Accounting. Awarded by the Institute of Certified Management Accountants of the *National Association of Accountants* to those who pass a set of examinations and meet certain experience and continuing education requirements.

CoCoA. *Continuously contemporary accounting.*

coding of accounts. The numbering of *accounts*, as for a *chart of accounts*, which is necessary for computerized accounting.

coinsurance. Insurance policies that protect against hazards such as fire or water damage often specify that the owner of the property may not collect the full amount of insurance for a loss unless the insurance policy covers at least some specified "coinsurance" percentage, usually about 80 percent, of the *replacement cost* of the property. Coinsurance clauses induce the owner to carry full, or nearly full, coverage.

COLA. Cost-of-living adjustment. See *indexation*.

collateral. *Assets* pledged by a *borrower* that will be given up if the *loan* is not paid.

collectible. Capable of being converted into *cash*; now, if due; later, otherwise.

combination. See *business combination*.

commercial paper. *Short-term notes* issued by corporate borrowers.

commission. Remuneration, usually expressed as a percentage, to employees based upon an activity rate, such as sales.

committed costs. *Capacity costs*.

Committee on Accounting Procedure. CAP. Predecessor of the *APB*. The *AICPA's* principles-promulgating body from 1939 through 1959. Its 51 pronouncements are called *Accounting Research Bulletins*.

common cost. *Cost* resulting from use of *raw materials*, a facility (for example, plant or machines), or a service (for example, fire insurance) that benefits several products or departments and must be allocated to those products or departments. Common costs result when multiple products are produced together although they could be produced separately; joint costs occur when multiple products are of necessity produced together. Many writers use common costs and *joint costs* synonymously. See *joint costs*, *indirect costs*, and *overhead*. See *sterilized allocation*.

common dollar accounting. *Constant dollar accounting.*

common monetary measuring unit. For U.S. corporations, the dollar. See also *stable monetary unit assumption* and *constant dollar accounting.*

common shares. *Shares* representing the class of owners who have residual claims on the *assets* and *earnings* of a *corporation* after all *debt* and *preferred shareholders'* claims have been met.

common stock equivalent. A *security* whose primary value arises from its ability to be exchanged for *common shares*; includes *stock options, warrants,* and also *convertible bonds* or *convertible preferred stock* whose *effective interest rate* is at the time of issue is less than two-thirds the average Aa corporate bond yield. See *bond ratings.*

common size statement. A *percentage statement* usually based on total *assets* or *net sales* or *revenues.*

company wide control. See *control system.*

comparative (financial) statements. *Financial statements* showing information for the same company for different times, usually two successive years. Nearly all published financial statements are in this form. Contrast with *historical summary.*

compensating balance. When a bank lends funds to a customer, it often requires that the customer keep on deposit in his or her checking account an amount equal to some percentage—say, 20 percent—of the loan. The amount required to be left on deposit is the compensating balance. Such amounts effectively increase the *interest rate.* The amounts of such balances must be disclosed in *notes* to the *financial statements.*

completed contract method. Recognizing *revenues* and *expenses* for a job or order only when it is finished, except that when a loss on the contract is expected, revenues and expenses are recognized in the period when the loss is first forecast. This term is generally used only for long-term contracts. It is otherwise equivalent to the *sales basis* of *revenue recognition.*

completed sales basis. See *sales basis of revenue recognition.*

compliance audit. Objectively obtaining and evaluating evidence regarding assertions, actions, and events to ascertain the degree of correspondence between them and established performance criteria.

composite cost of capital. See *cost of capital.*

composite depreciation. *Group depreciation* of dissimilar items.

composite life method. *Group depreciation,* which see, for items of unlike kind. The term may be used when a single item, such as a crane, which consists of separate units with differing service lives, such as the chassis, the motor, the lifting mechanism, and so on, is depreciated as a whole rather than treating each of the components separately.

compound entry. A *journal entry* with more than one *debit* or more than one *credit,* or both. See *trade-in transaction* for an example.

compound interest. *Interest* calculated on *principal* plus previously undistributed interest.

compound interest depreciation. A method designed to hold the *rate of return* on an asset constant. First find the *internal rate of return* on the cash inflows and outflows of the asset. The periodic depreciation charge is the cash flow for the period less the internal rate of return multiplied by the asset's book value at the beginning of the period. When the cash flows from the asset are constant over time, the method is sometimes called the "annuity method" of depreciation.

compounding period. The time period for which *interest* is calculated. At the end of the period, the interest may be paid to the lender or added (that is, converted) to principal for the next interest-earning period, which is usually a year or some portion of a year.

comprehensive budget. *Master budget.*

comprehensive income. Defined in *SFAS No. 3* as "the change in equity (net assets) of an entity during a period from transactions and other events and circumstances from nonowner sources. It includes all changes in equity during a period except those resulting from investments by owners and distributions to owners." In this definition, "equity" means *owners' equity.*

comptroller. Same meaning and pronunciation as *controller.*

conceptual framework. A coherent system of interrelated objectives and fundamentals, promulgated by the *FASB* primarily through its *SFAC* publications, expected to lead to consistent standards for *financial accounting* and reporting.

confirmation. A formal memorandum delivered by the customers or suppliers of a company to its independent *auditor* verifying the amounts shown as receivable or payable. The confirmation document is originally sent by the auditor to the customer. If the auditor asks that the document be returned whether the *balance* is correct or incorrect, then it is called a "positive confirmation." If the auditor asks that the document be returned only if there is an error, it is called a "negative confirmation."

conglomerate. *Holding company.* This term is used when the owned companies are in dissimilar lines of business.

conservatism. A *reporting objective* that calls for anticipation of all *losses* and *expenses* but defers recognition of *gains* or *profits* until they are *realized* in *arm's-length* transactions. In the absence of certainty, events are to be reported in a way that tends to minimize cumulative income.

consignee. See *on consignment.*

consignment. See *on consignment.*

consignor. See *on consignment*.

consistency. Treatment of like *transactions* in the same way in consecutive periods so that financial statements will be more comparable than otherwise. The reporting policy implying that procedures, once adopted, should be followed from period to period by a reporting *entity*. See *accounting changes* for the treatment of inconsistencies.

consol. A *bond* that never matures; a *perpetuity* in the form of a bond. Originally issued by Great Britain after the Napoleonic wars to consolidate debt issues of that period. The term arose as an abbreviation for "consolidated annuities."

consolidated financial statements. Statements issued by legally separate companies that show financial position and income as they would appear if the companies were one economic *entity*.

constant dollar. A hypothetical unit of *general purchasing power*, denoted "C$" by the *FASB*.

constant dollar accounting. Accounting where items are measured in *constant dollars*. See *historical cost/constant dollar accounting* and *current cost/constant dollar accounting*.

constant dollar date. The time at which the *general purchasing power* of one *constant dollar* is exactly equal to the *general purchasing power* of one *nominal dollar*; that is, the date when C$1 = $1. When the constant dollar date is mid-period, then the nominal amounts of *revenues* and *expenses* spread evenly throughout the period are equal to their constant dollar amounts, but end-of-period *balance sheet* amounts measured in constant mid-period dollars differ from their nominal dollar amounts. When the constant dollar date is at the end of the period, then the constant dollar and nominal dollar amounts on a balance sheet for that date are identical.

constructive receipt. An item is included in taxable income when the taxpayer can control funds whether or not cash has been received. For example, *interest* added to *principal* in a savings account is deemed by the *IRS* to be constructively received.

Consumer Price Index. CPI. A *price index* computed and issued monthly by the Bureau of Labor Statistics of the U.S. Department of Labor. The index attempts to track the price level of a group of goods and services purchased by the average consumer. The CPI is used in *constant dollar accounting*. Contrast with *GNP Implicit Price Deflator*.

contingency. A potential *liability*; if a specified event were to occur, such as losing a lawsuit, a liability would be recognized. The contingency is merely disclosed in notes, rather than shown in the balance sheet. *SFAS No. 5* requires treatment as a contingency until the outcome is "probable" and the amount of payment can be reasonably estimated, perhaps within a range. When the outcome becomes probable (the future event is "likely" to occur) and the amount can be reasonably estimated (using the lower end of a range if only a range can be estimated), then the

liability is recognized in the accounts, rather than being disclosed in the notes. A *material* contingency may lead to a qualified, "*subject to*," auditor's opinion. *Gain* contingencies are not recorded in the accounts, but are merely disclosed in notes.

contingent annuity. An *annuity* whose number of payments depends upon the outcome of an event whose timing is uncertain at the time the annuity is set up; for example, an annuity payable until death of the *annuitant*. Contrast with *annuity certain*.

contingent issue (securities). Securities issuable to specific individuals upon the occurrence of some event, such as the firm's attaining a specified level of earnings.

contingent liability. *Contingency*. This term is to be avoided because it refers to something that is not a *liability* on the *balance sheet*.

continuing appropriation. A governmental *appropriation* automatically renewed without further legislative action until it is altered or revoked or expended.

continuing operations. See *income from continuing operations*.

continuity of operations. The assumption in accounting that the business *entity* will continue to operate long enough for current plans to be carried out. The *going-concern assumption*.

continuous budget. A *budget* that perpetually adds a period in the future as the period just ended is dropped.

continuous compounding. *Compound interest* where the *compounding period* is every instant of time. See *e* for the computation of the equivalent annual or periodic rate.

continuous inventory method. The *perpetual inventory* method.

Continuously Contemporary Accounting. CoCoA. A name coined by the Australian theorist, Raymond J. Chambers, to indicate a combination of *current value accounting* where amounts are measured in *constant dollars* and based on *exit values*.

contra account. An *account*, such as *accumulated depreciation*, that accumulates subtractions from another account, such as machinery. Contrast with *adjunct account*.

contributed capital. The sum of the balances in *capital stock* accounts plus *capital contributed in excess of par (or stated) value* accounts. Contrast with *donated capital*.

contributed surplus. An inferior term for *capital contributed in excess of par value*.

contribution approach. Method of preparing *income statements* that separates *variable costs* from *fixed costs* in order to emphasize the importance of cost behavior patterns for purposes of planning and control.

contribution margin. *Revenue* from *sales* less all variable *expenses*. See *gross margin*.

contribution margin ratio. *Contribution margin* divided by *net sales*; usually measured from the price and cost of a single unit.

contribution per unit. Selling price less *variable costs* per unit.

contributory. Said of a *pension plan* where employees, as well as employers, make payments to a pension *fund*. Note that the provisions for *vesting* are applicable only to the employer's payments. Whatever the degree of vesting of the employer's payments, the employee typically gets back all of his or her payments, with interest, in case of death, or other cessation of employment, before retirement.

control (controlling) account. A summary *account* with totals equal to those of entries and balances that appear in individual accounts in a *subsidiary ledger*. Accounts Receivable is a control account backed up with an account for each customer. The balance in a control account should not be changed unless a corresponding change is made in one of the subsidiary accounts.

control system. A device for ensuring that actions are carried out according to plan or for safeguarding *assets*. A system for ensuring that actions are carried out according to plan can be designed for a single function within the firm, called "operational control," for autonomous segments within the firm that generally have responsibility for both revenues and costs, called "divisional control," or for activities of the firm as a whole, called "company-wide control." Systems designed for safeguarding *assets* are called "internal control" systems.

controllable cost. A *cost* whose amount can be influenced by the way in which operations are carried out, such as advertising costs. These costs can be *fixed* or *variable*. See *programmed costs* and *managed costs*.

controlled company. A company, a majority of whose voting shares is held by an individual or corporation. Effective control can sometimes be exercised when less than 50 percent of the shares is owned.

controller. The title often used for the chief accountant of an organization. Often spelled *comptroller*.

conversion. The act of exchanging a convertible security for another security.

conversion cost. *Direct labor* costs plus factory *overhead* costs incurred in producing a product. That is, the cost to convert raw materials to finished products. *Manufacturing cost*.

conversion period. *Compounding period*. Also, period during which a *convertible bond* or *convertible preferred stock* can be converted into *common stock*.

convertible bond. A *bond* that may be converted into a specified number of shares of *capital stock* during the *conversion period*.

convertible preferred stock. *Preferred shares* that may be converted into a specified number of shares of *common stock*.

co-product. A product sharing production facilities with another product. For example, if an apparel manufacturer produces shirts and jeans on the same line, these are co-products. Co-products are distinguished from *joint products* and *by-products* which, by their very nature, must be produced together, such as the various grades of wood produced in a lumber factory.

copyright. Exclusive right granted by the government to an individual author, composer, playwright, and the like for the life of the individual plus 50 years. If the copyright is granted to a firm, then the right extends 75 years after the original publication. The *economic life* of a copyright may be considerably less than the legal life as, for example, the copyright of this book.

corporation. A legal entity authorized by a state to operate under the rules of the entity's *charter*.

correcting entry. An *adjusting entry* where an improperly recorded *transaction* is properly recorded. Not to be confused with entries that correct *accounting errors*.

correction of errors. See *accounting errors*.

cost. The sacrifice, measured by the *price* paid or required to be paid, to acquire *goods* or *services*. See *acquisition cost* and *replacement cost*. The term "cost" is often used when referring to the valuation of a good or service acquired. When "cost" is used in this sense, a cost is an *asset*. When the benefits of the acquisition (the goods or services acquired) expire, the cost becomes an *expense* or *loss*. Some writers, however, use cost and expense as synonyms. Contrast with *expense*.

cost accounting. Classifying, summarizing, recording, reporting, and allocating current or predicted *costs*. A subset of *managerial accounting*.

Cost Accounting Standards Board. See *CASB*.

cost accumulation. Bringing together, usually in a single *account*, all *costs* of a specified activity. Contrast with *cost allocation*.

cost allocation. Assigning *costs* to individual products or time periods. Contrast with *cost accumulation*.

cost-based transfer price. A *transfer price* based on *historical costs*.

cost behavior. The functional relation between changes in activity and changes in *cost*. For example, *fixed* versus *variable costs*; linear versus curvilinear cost.

cost/benefit criterion. Some measure of *costs* compared to some measure of *benefits* for a proposed undertaking. If the costs exceed the benefits, then the undertaking is judged not worthwhile. This criterion will not give good decisions unless all costs and benefits flowing from the undertaking are estimated.

cost center. A unit of activity for which *expenditures* and *expenses* are accumulated.

cost effective. Among alternatives, the one whose benefit, or payoff, per unit of cost is highest. Sometimes said of an action whose expected benefits exceed expected costs whether or not there are other alternatives with larger benefit/cost ratios.

cost estimation. The process of measuring the functional relation between changes in activity levels and changes in cost.

cost flow assumption. See *flow assumption*.

cost flows. Costs passing through various classifications within an entity. See *flow of costs* for a diagram.

cost method (for investments). Accounting for an investment in the *capital stock* or *bonds* of another company where the investment is shown at *acquisition cost*, and only *dividends* declared or *interest receivable* is treated as *revenue*.

cost method (for treasury stock). The method of showing *treasury stock* in a *contra account* to all other items of *shareholders' equity* in an amount equal to that paid to reacquire the stock.

cost objective. Any activity for which a separate measurement of *costs* is desired. Examples include departments, products, and territories.

cost of capital. *Opportunity cost* of funds invested in a business. The rate of return required to be earned on an asset before the rational owner will devote that asset to a particular purpose. Sometimes measured as the average rate per year a company must pay for its *equities*. In efficient capital markets, the *discount rate* that equates the expected *present value* of all future cash flows to common shareholders with the market value of common stock at a given time.

The cost of capital is often measured by taking a *weighted average* of the firm's *debt* and various *equity securities*. The measurement so derived is sometimes called the "composite cost of capital," and some analysts confuse this measurement of the cost of capital with the cost of capital itself. For example, if the equities of a firm include substantial amounts for the *deferred income tax liability*, the composite cost of capital will underestimate the true cost of capital, the required rate of return on a firm's assets, because the deferred income tax liability has no explicit cost.

cost of goods manufactured. The sum of all costs allocated to products completed during a period; includes materials, labor, and *overhead*.

cost of goods purchased. Net purchase price of goods acquired plus costs of storage and delivery to the place where the items can be productively used.

cost of goods sold. Inventoriable *costs* that are *expensed* because the units are sold; equals *beginning inventory* plus *cost of goods purchased* or *manufactured* minus *ending inventory*.

cost of sales. Generally refers to *cost of goods sold*; occasionally, to *selling expenses*.

cost or market, whichever is lower. See *lower of cost or market*.

cost percentage. One less *markup percentage*. *Cost* of *goods available for sale* divided by selling prices of goods available for sale (when FIFO is used). With *LIFO*, *cost* of *purchases* divided by selling price of purchases. See *markup* for further detail on inclusions in calculation of cost percentage.

cost pool. *Indirect cost pool*.

cost principle. The *principle* that requires reporting *assets* at *historical* or *acquisition cost*, less accumulated *amortization*. This principle is based on the assumption that cost is equal to *fair market value* at the date of acquisition and subsequent changes are not likely to be significant.

cost-recovery-first method. A method of *revenue* recognition that *credits inventory* as collections are received until all costs are recovered. Only after costs are completely recovered is *income* recognized. To be used in financial reporting only when the total amount of collections is highly uncertain. Can never be used in income tax reporting. Contrast with the *installment method* where *constant* proportions of each collection are credited both to cost and to income.

cost sheet. Statement that shows all the elements comprising the total cost of an item.

cost terminology. The word "cost" appears in many accounting terms. The accompanying exhibit classifies some of these by the distinctions the terms are used to make.

cost-to-cost. The *percentage-of-completion method* where the estimate of completion is the ratio of costs incurred to date divided by total costs expected to be incurred for the entire project.

cost-volume-profit analysis. A study of the sensitivity of *profits* to changes in units sold (or produced), assuming some *semivariable costs* in the cost structure.

cost-volume-profit graph (chart). A graph that shows the relation between *fixed costs, contribution per unit, breakeven point,* and *sales*. See *breakeven chart*.

costing. The process of calculating the cost of activities, products, or services. The British word for *cost accounting*.

coupon. That portion of a *bond* document redeemable at a specified date for *interest* payments. Its physical form is much like a ticket; each coupon is dated and is deposited at a bank, just like a check, for collection or is mailed to the issuer's agent for collection.

coupon rate. Of a *bond*, the amount of annual coupons divided by par value. Contrast with *effective rate*.

covenant. A promise with legal validity.

CPA. See *certified public accountant*. The *AICPA* suggests that no periods be shown in the abbreviation

Cost Terminology: Distinctions among Terms Containing the Word "Cost"

Terms (Synonyms Given in Parentheses)			Distinctions and Comments
			1. The following pairs of terms distinguish the basis measured in accounting.
Historical Cost (Acquisition Cost)	vs.	Current Cost	A distinction used in financial accounting. Current cost can be used more specifically to mean replacement cost, net realizable value, or present value of cash flows. "Current cost" is often used narrowly to mean replacement cost.
Historical Cost (Actual Cost)	vs.	Standard Cost	The distinction between historical and standard costs arises in product costing for inventory valuation. Some systems record actual costs while others record the standard costs.
			2. The following pairs of terms denote various distinctions among historical costs. For each pair of terms, the sum of the two kinds of costs equals total historical cost used in financial reporting.
Variable Cost	vs.	Fixed Cost (Constant Cost)	Distinction used in breakeven analysis and in designing cost accounting systems, particularly for product costing. See (4), below, for a further subdivision of fixed costs and (5), below, for an economic distinction closely paralleling this one.
Traceable Cost	vs.	Common Cost (Joint Cost)	Distinction arises in allocating manufacturing costs to product. Common costs are allocated to product, but the allocations are more-or-less arbitrary. The distinction also arises in segment reporting and in separating manufacturing from nonmanufacturing costs.
Direct Cost	vs.	Indirect Cost	Distinction arises in designing cost accounting systems and in product costing. Direct costs can be traced directly to a cost object (e.g., a product, a responsibility center), whereas indirect costs cannot.
Out-of-Pocket Cost (Outlay Cost; Cash Cost)	vs.	Book Cost	Virtually all costs recorded in financial statements require a cash outlay at one time or another. The distinction here separates expenditures to occur in the future from those already made and is used in making decisions. Book costs, such as for depreciation, reduce income without requiring a future outlay of cash. The cash has already been spent. See future vs. past costs in (5), below.
Incremental Cost (Marginal Cost; Differential Cost)	vs.	Unavoidable Cost (Inescapable Cost; Sunk Cost)	Distinction used in making decisions. Incremental costs will be incurred (or saved) if a decision is made to go ahead (or to stop) some activity, but not otherwise. Unavoidable costs will be reported in financial statements whether the decision is made to go ahead or not, because cash has already been spent or committed. Not all unavoidable costs are book costs, as, for example, a salary promised but not yet earned, that will be paid even if a no-go decision is made. The economist restricts the term marginal cost to the cost of producing one more unit. Thus the next unit has a marginal cost; the next week's output has an incremental cost. If a firm produces and sells a new product, the related new costs would properly be called incremental, not marginal. If a factory is closed, the costs saved are incremental, not marginal.
Escapable Cost	vs.	Inescapable Cost (Unavoidable Cost)	Same distinction as incremental vs. sunk costs, but this pair is used only when the decision maker is considering stopping something— ceasing to produce a product, closing a factory, or the like. See next pair.
Avoidable Cost	vs.	Unavoidable Cost	A distinction sometimes used in discussing the merits of variable and absorption costing. Avoidable costs are treated as product cost and unavoidable costs are treated as period expenses under variable costing.
Controllable Cost	vs.	Uncontrollable Cost	The distinction here is used in assigning responsibility and in setting bonus or incentive plans. All costs can be affected by someone in the entity; those who design incentive schemes attempt to hold a person responsible for a cost only if that person can influence the amount of the cost.
			3. In each of the following pairs, used in historical cost accounting, the word "cost" appears in one of the terms where "expense" is meant.
Expired Cost	vs.	Unexpired Cost	The distinction is between *expense* and *asset*.
Product Cost	vs.	Period Cost	The terms distinguish product cost from period expense. When a given asset is used, is its cost converted into work in process and then finished goods on the balance sheet until the goods are sold or is it an expense shown on this period's income statement? Product costs appear on the income statement as part of cost of goods sold in the pe-

Cost Terminology: Distinctions among Terms Containing the Word "Cost"

Terms (Synonyms Given in Parentheses)			Distinctions and Comments
			riod when the goods are sold. Period expenses appear on the income statement with an appropriate caption for the item in the period when the cost is incurred or recognized.
			4. The following subdivisions of fixed (historical) costs are used in analyzing operations. The relation between the components of fixed costs is:

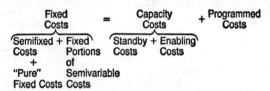

Terms (Synonyms Given in Parentheses)			Distinctions and Comments
Capacity Cost (Committed Cost)	vs.	Programmed Cost (Managed Cost; Discretionary Cost)	Capacity costs give a firm the capability to produce or to sell. Programmed costs, such as for advertising or research and development, may not be essential, but once a decision to incur them is made, they become fixed costs.
Standby Cost	vs.	Enabling Cost	Standby costs will be incurred whether capacity, once acquired, is used or not, such as property taxes and depreciation on a factory. Enabling costs, such as for security force, can be avoided if the capacity is unused.
Semifixed Cost	vs.	Semivariable Cost	A cost fixed over a wide range but that can change at various levels is a semifixed cost or "step cost." An example is the cost of rail lines from the factory to the main rail line where fixed cost depends on whether there are one or two parallel lines, but are independent of the number of trains run per day. Semivariable costs combine a strictly fixed component cost plus a variable component. Telephone charges usually have a fixed monthly component plus a charge related to usage.
			5. The following pairs of terms distinguish among economic uses or decision making uses or regulatory uses of cost terms.
Fully Absorbed Cost	vs.	Variable Cost (Direct Cost)	Fully absorbed costs refer to costs where fixed costs have been allocated to units or departments as required by generally accepted accounting principles. Variable costs, in contrast, may be more relevant for making decisions, such as in setting prices.
Fully Absorbed Cost	vs.	Full Cost	In full costing, all costs, manufacturing costs as well as central corporate express (including financing expenses) are allocated to product or divisions. In full absorption costing, only manufacturing costs are allocated to product. Only in full costing will revenues, expenses, and income summed over all products or divisions equal corporate revenues, expenses, and income.
Opportunity Cost	vs.	Outlay Cost (Out-of-Pocket Cost)	Opportunity cost refers to the economic benefit foregone by using a resource for one purpose instead of for another. The outlay cost of the resource will be recorded in financial records. The distinction arises because a resource is already in the possession of the entity with a recorded historical cost. Its economic value to the firm, opportunity cost, generally differs from the historical cost; it can be either larger or smaller.
Future Cost	vs.	Past Cost	Effective decision making analyzes only present and future outlay costs, or out-of-pocket costs. Opportunity costs are relevant for profit maximizing; past costs are used in financial reporting.
Short-Run Cost	vs.	Long-Run Cost	Short-run costs vary as output is varied for a given configuration of plant and equipment. Long-run costs can be incurred to change that configuration. This pair of terms is the economic analog of the accounting pair, see (2) above, variable and fixed costs. The analogy is not perfect because some short-run costs are fixed, such as property taxes on the factory, from the point of view of breakeven analysis.
Imputed Cost	vs.	Book Cost	In a regulatory setting some costs, for example the cost of owners' equity capital, are calculated and used for various purposes; these are imputed costs. Imputed costs are not recorded in the historical costs accounting records for financial reporting. Book costs are recorded.

Cost Terminology: Distinctions among Terms Containing the Word "Cost"

Terms (Synonyms Given in Parentheses)			Distinctions and Comments
Average Cost	vs.	Marginal Cost	The economic distinction equivalent to fully absorbed cost of product and direct cost of product. Average cost is total cost divided by number of units. Marginal cost is the cost to produce the next unit (or the last unit).
Incremental Cost	vs.	Variable Cost	Whether a cost changes or remains fixed depends on the activity basis being considered. Typically, but not invariably, costs are said to be variable or fixed with respect to an activity basis such as changes in production levels. Typically, but not invariably, costs are said to be incremental or not with respect to an activity basis such as the undertaking of some new venture. For example, consider the decision to undertake the production of food processors, rather than food blenders, which the manufacturer has been making. To produce processors requires the acquisition of a new machine tool. The cost of the new machine tool is incremental with respect to a decision to produce food processors instead of food blenders, but, once acquired, becomes a fixed cost of producing food processors. If costs of direct labor hours are going to be incurred for the production of food processors or food blenders, whichever is produced (in a scenario when not both are to be produced), such costs are variable with respect to production measured in units, but not incremental with respect to the decision to produce processors rather than blenders. This distinction is often blurred in practice, so a careful understanding of the activity basis being considered is necessary for understanding of the concepts being used in a particular application.

CPI. *Consumer price index.*

CPP. Current purchasing power; usually used as an adjective modifying the word "accounting" to mean the accounting that produces *constant dollar financial statements.*

Cr. Abbreviation for *credit.*

credit. As a noun, an entry on the right-hand side of an *account.* As a verb, to make an entry on the right-hand side of an account. Records increases in *liabilities, owner's equity, revenues* and *gains*; records decreases in *assets* and *expenses.* See *debit and credit conventions.* Also the ability or right to buy or borrow in return for a promise to pay later.

credit loss. The amount of *accounts receivable* that is, or is expected to become, *uncollectible.*

credit memorandum. A document used by a seller to inform a buyer that the buyer's *account receivable* is being credited (reduced) because of *errors, returns*, or *allowances.* Also, the document provided by a bank to a depositor to indicate that the depositor's balance is being increased because of some event other than a deposit, such as the collection by the bank of the depositor's *note receivable.*

creditor. One who lends.

cross-reference (index). A number placed by each *account* in a *journal entry* indicating the *ledger* account to which the entry is posted and placing in the ledger the page number of the journal where the entry was made.

cross-section analysis. Analysis of *financial statements* of various firms for a single period of time; contrast with time-series analysis where statements of a given firm are analyzed over several periods of time.

cumulative dividend. Preferred stock *dividends* that, if not paid, accrue as a commitment that must be paid before dividends to common shareholders can be declared.

cumulative preferred shares. *Preferred* shares with *cumulative dividend* rights.

current asset. *Cash* and other *assets* that are expected to be turned into cash, sold, or exchanged within the normal operating cycle of the firm, usually one year. Current assets include *cash, marketable securities, receivables, inventory*, and *current prepayments.*

current cost. *Cost* stated in terms of current values (of *productive capacity*) rather than in terms of *acquisition cost.* See *net realizable value, current selling price.*

current cost accounting. The *FASB's* term for *financial statements* where the *attribute measured* is *current cost.*

current cost/nominal dollar accounting. Accounting based on *current cost* valuations measured in *nominal dollars.* Components of *income* include an *operating margin* and *holding gains and losses.*

current exit value. *Exit value.*

current fund. In governmental accounting, a synonym for general fund.

current funds. *Cash* and other assets readily convertible into cash. In governmental accounting, funds spent for operating purposes during the current period. Includes *general, special revenue, debt service*, and *enterprise funds*.

current (gross) margin. See *operating margin (based on current costs)*.

current liability. A debt or other obligation that must be discharged within a short time, usually the *earnings cycle* or one year, normally by expending *current assets*.

current (gross) margin. See *operating margin (based on current costs)*.

current operating performance concept. The notion that reported *income* for a period ought to reflect only ordinary, normal, and recurring operations of that period. A consequence is that *extraordinary* and nonrecurring items are entered directly in the Retained Earnings account. Contrast with *clean surplus concept*. This concept is no longer acceptable. (See *APB Opinions Nos. 9* and *30*.)

current ratio. Sum of *current assets* divided by sum of *current liabilities*. See *ratio*.

current realizable value. *Realizable value*.

current replacement cost. Of an *asset*, the amount currently required to acquire an identical asset (in the same condition and with the same service potential) or an asset capable of rendering the same service at a current *fair market price*. If these two amounts differ, the lower is usually used. Contrast with *reproduction cost*.

current selling price. The amount for which an *asset* could be sold as of a given time in an *arm's-length* transaction, rather than in a forced sale.

current service costs. *Service costs* of a *pension plan*.

current value accounting. The form of accounting where all assets are shown at *current replacement cost (entry value)* or *current selling price* or *net realizable value (exit value)* and all *liabilities* are shown at *present value*. Entry and exit values may be quite different from each other so there is no general agreement on the precise meaning of current value accounting.

current yield. Of a *bond*, the annual amount of *interest coupons* divided by current market price of the bond. Contrast with *yield to maturity*.

currently attainable standard cost. *Normal standard cost*.

curvilinear (variable) cost. A continuous, but not necessarily linear (straight-line), functional relation between activity levels and *costs*.

customers' ledger. The *ledger* that shows accounts receivable of individual customers. It is the *subsidiary ledger* for the *controlling account*, Accounts Receivable.

cutoff rate. *Hurdle rate*.

D

days of average inventory on hand. See *ratio*.

DCF. *Discounted cash flow*.

DDB. *Double-declining-balance depreciation*.

debenture bond. A *bond* not secured with *collateral*.

debit. As a noun, an entry on the left hand side of an *account*. As a verb, to make an entry on the left hand side of an account. Records increases in *assets* and *expenses*; records decreases in *liabilities, owners' equity*, and *revenues*. See *debit and credit conventions*.

debit and credit conventions. The equality of the two sides of the *accounting equation* is maintained by recording equal amounts of *debits* and *credits* for each *transaction*. The conventional use of the *T-account* form and the rules for debit and credit in *balance sheet accounts* are summarized as follows.

Any Asset Account

Opening Balance Increase + Dr. Ending Balance	Decrease − Cr.

Any Liability Account

Decrease − Dr.	Opening Balance Increase + Cr. Ending Balance

Any Owners' Equity Account

Decrease − Dr.	Opening Balance Increase + Cr. Ending Balance

Revenue and expense accounts belong to the owners' equity group. The relationship and the rules for debit and credit in these accounts can be expressed as follows.

Owners' Equity

Decrease − Dr. Expenses		Increase + Cr. Revenues	
Dr. + *	Cr. −	Dr. −	Cr. + *

*Normal balance prior to closing

debit memorandum. A document used by a seller to inform a buyer that the seller is debiting (increasing) the amount of the buyer's *account receivable*. Also, the document provided by a bank to a depositor to indicate that the depositor's *balance* is being decreased because of some event other than payment for a *check*, such as monthly service charges or the printing of checks.

debt. An amount owed. The general name for *notes, bonds, mortgages*, and the like that are evidence of amounts owed and have definite payment dates.

debt-equity ratio. Total *liabilities* divided by total equities. See *ratio*. Sometimes the denominator is merely total shareholders' equity. Sometimes the numerator is restricted to *long-term debt*.

debt capital. *Noncurrent liabilities*. See *debt financing* and contrast with *equity financing*.

debt financing. Raising *funds* by issuing *bonds, mortgages*, or *notes*. Contrast with *equity financing*. *Leverage*.

debt guarantee. See *guarantee*.

debt ratio. *Debt-equity ratio*.

debt service fund. In governmental accounting, a *fund* established to account for payment of *interest* and *principal* on all general-obligation *debt* other than that payable from special *assessments*.

debt service requirement. The amount of cash required for payments of *interest*, current maturities of *principal* on outstanding *debt*, and payments to *sinking funds* (corporations) or to the *debt service fund* (governmental).

debtor. One who borrows.

decentralized decision making. A manager of a business unit is given responsibility for that unit's *revenues* and *costs*, being free to make decisions about prices, sources of supply, and the like, as though the unit were a separate business owned by the manager. See *responsibility accounting* and *transfer price*.

declaration date. Time when a *dividend* is declared by the *board of directors*.

declining balance depreciation. The method of calculating the periodic *depreciation* charge by multiplying the *book value* at the start of the period by a constant percentage. In pure declining-balance depreciation the constant percentage is $1 - \sqrt[n]{s/c}$, where n is the *depreciable life*, s is *salvage value*, and c is *acquisition cost*. See *double-declining balance depreciation*.

deep discount bonds. Said of *bonds* selling much below (exactly how much is not clear) *par value*.

defalcation. Embezzlement.

default. Failure to pay *interest* or *principal* on a *debt* when due.

defeasance. *Interest rates* have increased over the past several decades. Consequently, the *market value* of *debt* outstanding is substantially less than its *book value* for many firms. In *historical cost accounting* for debt retirements, retiring debt with a *cash* payment less than the book value of the debt results in a gain (generally, an *extraordinary item*). Many firms would like to retire the outstanding debt issues and report the gain. Two factors impede doing so: (1) the gain can be a taxable event generating adverse *income tax* consequences; and (2) the transactions costs in retiring all of the debt can be large, in part because not all debt holders can easily be located or persuaded to sell back their bonds to the issuer. The process of "defeasance" is the economic equivalent to retiring a debt issue that saves the issuer from adverse tax consequences and actually having to locate and retire the bonds. The process works as follows. The debt issuing firms turns over to an independent trustee, such as bank, amounts of cash or low risk government bonds sufficient to make all debt service payments on the outstanding debt, including bond retirements, in return for the trustee's commitment to make all debt service payments. The debt issuer effectively retires the outstanding debt. It debits the liability account, credits Cash or Marketable Securities, as appropriate, and credits Extraordinary Gain on Debt Retirement. The trustee is free to retire debt or make debt service payments, whichever it chooses. For income tax purposes, however, the firm's debt is still outstanding. The firm will have taxable interest *deductions* for its still outstanding debt and taxable interest *revenue* on the investments held by the trustee for debt service. In law, the term "defeasance" means "a rendering null and void." This process described here renders the outstanding debt economically null and void, without causing a taxable event.

defensive interval. A financial *ratio* equal to the number of days of normal cash *expenditures* covered by *quick assets*. It is defined as

$$\frac{\text{Quick Assets}}{\text{(All Expenses Except Amortization and Others Not Using Funds/365)}}$$

The denominator of the ratio is the cash expenditure per day. This ratio has been found useful in predicting *bankruptcy*.

deferral. The accounting process concerned with past *cash receipts* and *payments*; in contrast to *accrual*. Recognizing a liability resulting from a current cash receipt (as for magazines to be delivered) or recognizing an asset from a current cash payment (or for prepaid insurance or a long-term depreciable asset).

deferral method. See *flow-through method* (of accounting for the *investment credit*) for definition and contrast.

deferred annuity. An *annuity* whose first payment is made sometime after the end of the first period.

deferred asset. *Deferred charge*.

deferred charge. *Expenditure* not recognized as an *expense* of the period when made but carried forward as an *asset* to be *written off* in future periods, such as for advance rent payments or insurance premiums. See *deferral*.

deferred cost. *Deferred charge.*

deferred credit. Sometimes used to indicate *advances from customers*.

deferred debit. *Deferred charge.*

deferred expense. *Deferred charge.*

deferred gross margin. *Unrealized gross margin.*

deferred income. *Advances from customers.*

deferred income tax (liability). An *indeterminate term liability* that arises when the pretax income shown on the tax return is less than what it would have been had the same *accounting principles* and *cost basis* for *assets* and *liabilities* been used in tax returns as used for financial reporting. The *FASB* requires that the firm debit income tax *expense* and credit deferred income tax with the amount of the taxes delayed by using different accounting principles in tax returns from those used in financial reports. See *temporary difference*, *timing difference*, and *permanent difference*. See *installment sales*. If, as a result of temporary differences, cumulative taxable income exceeds cumulative reported income before taxes, the deferred income tax account will have a *debit* balance and will be reported as a *deferred charge*.

deferred revenue. Sometimes used to indicate *advances from customers*.

deferred tax. See *deferred income tax*.

deficit. A *debit balance* in the Retained Earnings account; presented on the balance sheet in a *contra account* to shareholders' equity. Sometimes used to mean negative *net income* for a period.

defined-benefit plan. A *pension plan* where the employer promises specific dollar amounts to each eligible employee; the amounts usually depend on a formula which takes into account such things as the employee's earnings, years of employment, and age. The employer's cash contributions and pension expense are adjusted in relation to *actuarial* experience in the eligible employee group and investment performance of the pension *fund*. Sometimes called a "fixed-benefit" pension plan. Contrast with *money purchase plan*.

defined contribution plan. A *money purchase (pension) plan* or other arrangement, based on formula or discretion, where the employer makes cash contributions to eligible individual employee *accounts* under the terms of a written plan document. Profit-sharing pension plans are of this type.

deflation. A period of declining *general price changes*.

demand deposit. *Funds* in a *checking account* at a bank.

demand loan. See *term loan* for definition and contrast.

denominator volume. Capacity measured in expected number of units to be produced this period; divided into *budgeted fixed costs* to obtain fixed costs applied per unit of product.

dependent variable. See *regression analysis*.

depletion. Exhaustion or *amortization* of a *wasting asset*, or natural resource. Also see *percentage depletion*.

depletion allowance. See *percentage depletion*.

deposit method (of revenue recognition). This method of *revenue* recognition does not differ from the *completed sale* or *completed contract method*. In some contexts such as retail land sales, the customer must make substantial payments while still having the right to back out of the deal and receive a refund. When there is uncertainty about whether the deal will be completed but a cash collection is made by the seller, the seller must *credit* deposits, a *liability account*, rather than *revenue*. (In this regard, the accounting differs from the completed contract method where the account credited is offset against the *work-in-process inventory* account.) When the *sale* becomes complete, a revenue account is credited and the deposit account is *debited*.

deposit, sinking fund. Payments made to a *sinking fund*.

deposits (by customers). A *liability* arising upon receipt of *cash* (as in a bank, or in a grocery store when the customer pays cash for sodapop bottles to be repaid when the bottles are returned).

deposits in transit. Deposits made by a firm but not yet reflected on the *bank statement*.

depreciable cost. That part of the *cost* of an asset, usually *acquisition cost* less *salvage value*, that is to be charged off over the life of the asset through the process of *depreciation*.

depreciable life. For an *asset*, the time period or units of activity (such as miles driven for a truck) over which *depreciable cost* is to be allocated. For tax returns, depreciable life may be shorter than estimated *service life*.

depreciation. *Amortization of plant assets*; the process of allocating the cost of an asset to the periods of benefit—the *depreciable life*. Classified as a *production cost* or a *period expense*, depending upon the asset and whether *absorption* or *variable costing* is used. Depreciation methods described in this glossary include the *annuity method*, *appraisal method*, *composite method*, *compound interest method*, *production method*, *replacement method*, *retirement method*, *straight line method*, *sinking fund method*, and *sum-of-the-years'-digits method*.

depreciation reserve. An inferior term for *accumulated depreciation*. See *reserve*. Do not confuse with a replacement *fund*.

Descartes' rule of signs. In a *capital budgeting* context, the rule says that a series of cash flows will have a nonnegative number of *internal rates of return*. The number is equal to the number of variations in the sign of the cash flow series or is less than that number by an even integer. Consider the following series of cash flows, the first occurring now and the others at subsequent yearly intervals: -100, -100, $+50$, $+175$, -50, $+100$. The internal rates of return are the numbers for r that satisfy the equation

$$-100 - \frac{100}{(1+r)} + \frac{50}{(1+r)^2} + \frac{175}{(1+r)^3} - \frac{50}{(1+r)^4} + \frac{100}{(1+r)^5} = 0.$$

The series of cash flows has three variations in sign: a change from minus to plus, a change from plus to minus, and a change from minus to plus. The rule says that this series must have either one or three internal rates of return; in fact, it has only one, about 12 percent. But also see *reinvestment rate*.

determination. See *determine*.

determine. The verb "determine" and the noun "determination" are often used (in our opinion, overused) by accountants and those who describe the accounting process. A leading dictionary associates the following meanings with the verb "determine": settle, decide, conclude, ascertain, cause, affect, control, impel, terminate, and decide upon. In addition, accounting writers can mean any one of the following: measure, allocate, report, calculate, compute, observe, choose, and legislate. In accounting, there are two distinct sets of meanings—those encompassed by the synonym "cause or legislate" and those encompassed by the synonym "measure." The first set of uses conveys the active notion of causing something to happen and the second set of uses conveys the more passive notion of observing something that someone else has caused to happen. An accountant who speaks of cost or income "determination" generally means measurement or observation, not causation; management and economic conditions cause costs and income to be what they are. One who speaks of accounting principles "determination" can mean choosing or applying (as in "determining depreciation charges" from an allowable set) or causing to be acceptable (as in the *FASB* "determining" the accounting for *leases*). In the long run, income is cash in less cash out, so management and economic conditions "determine" (cause) income to be what it is. In the short run, reported income is a function of accounting principles chosen and applied, so the accountant "determines" (measures) income. A question such as "Who determines income?" has, therefore, no unambiguous answer. The meaning of "an accountant determining acceptable accounting principles" is also vague. Does the clause mean merely choosing one from the set of generally acceptable principles, or does it mean using professional judgement to decide that some of the generally accepted principles are not correct under the current circumstances? We try never to use "determine" unless we mean "cause." Otherwise we use "measure," "report," "calculate," "compute," or whatever specific verb seems appropriate. We suggest that careful writers will always "determine" to use the most specific verb to convey meaning. "Determine" is seldom

the best choice of words to describe a process where those who make decisions often differ from those who apply technique.

development stage enterprise. As defined in *SFAS No. 7*, a firm whose planned principal *operations* have not commenced or having commenced, have not generated significant *revenue*. Such enterprises should be so identified, but no special *accounting principles* apply to them.

differential analysis. Analysis of *incremental costs*.

differential cost. *Incremental cost*. If a total cost curve is smooth (in mathematical terms, differentiable), then the curve graphing the derivative of the total cost curve is often said to show differential costs, the costs increments associated with infinitesimal changes in volume.

dilution. A potential reduction in *earnings per share* or *book value* per share by the potential *conversion* of securities or by the potential exercise of *warrants* or *options*.

dilutive. Said of a *security* that would reduce *earnings per share* if it were exchanged for *common stock*.

dipping into LIFO layers. See *LIFO inventory layer*.

direct cost. Cost of *direct material* and *direct labor* incurred in producing a product. See *prime cost*. In some accounting literature, this term is used to mean the same thing as *variable cost*.

direct costing. Another, less-preferred, term for *variable costing*.

direct labor (material) cost. Cost of labor (material) applied and assigned directly to a product; contrast with *indirect labor (material)*.

direct labor variance. *Price* and *quantity variances* for direct labor in *standard costs systems*.

direct method. See *statement of cash flows*.

direct posting. A method of bookkeeping where *entries* are made directly in *ledger accounts*, without the use of a *journal*.

direct write-off method. See *write-off method*.

disbursement. Payment by *cash* or by *check*. See *expenditure*.

DISC. Domestic International Sales Corporation. A U.S. *corporation*, usually a *subsidiary*, whose *income* is primarily attributable to exports. *Income tax* on 50 percent of a DISC's income is usually deferred for a long period. Generally, this results in a lower overall corporate tax for the *parent* than would otherwise be incurred.

disclaimer of opinion. An *auditor's report* stating that an opinion cannot be given on the *financial statements*. Usually results from *material* restrictions on the scope of the audit or from material uncertainties about the accounts which cannot be resolved at the time of the audit.

disclosure. The showing of facts in *financial statements, notes* thereto, or the *auditor's report*.

discontinued operations. See *income from discontinued operations*.

discount. In the context of *compound interest, bonds* and *notes*, the difference between *face* or *future value* and *present value* of a payment. In the context of *sales* and *purchases*, a reduction in price granted for prompt payment. See also *chain discount, quantity discount*, and *trade discount*.

discount factor. The reciprocal of one plus the *discount rate*. If the discount rate is 10 percent per period, the discount factor for three periods is $1/(1.10)^3 = (1.10)^{-3} = 0.75131$.

discount rate. *Interest rate* used to convert future payments to *present values*.

discounted bailout period. In a *capital budgeting* context, the total time that must elapse before discounted value of net accumulated cash flows from a project, including potential *salvage value* at various times of assets, equals or exceeds the *present value* of net accumulated cash outflows. Contrast with *discounted payback period*.

discounted cash flow. DCF. Using either the *net present value* or the *internal rate of return* in an analysis to measure the value of future expected cash *expenditures* and *receipts* at a common date. In discounted cash flow analysis, choosing the alternative with the largest *internal rate of return* may give wrong answers when there are *mutually exclusive projects* and the amounts of initial investment are quite different for two of the projects. Consider, to take an unrealistic example to illustrate the point, a project involving an initial investment of $1, with an *IRR* of 60 percent and another project involving an initial investment of $1 million with an IRR of 40 percent. Under most conditions, most firms will prefer the second project to the first, but choosing the project with the larger IRR will lead to undertaking the first, not the second. This shortcoming of choosing between alternatives based on the magnitude of the internal rate or return, rather than based on the magnitude of the *net present value* of the cash flows, is called the "scale effect."

discounted payback period. The shortest amount of time which must elapse before the discounted present value of cash inflows from a project, excluding potential *salvage value*, equals the discounted *present value* of the cash outflows.

discounting a note. See *note receivable discounted* and *factoring*.

discounts lapsed (lost). The sum of *discounts* offered for prompt payment that were not taken (or allowed) because of expiration of the discount period. See *terms of sale*.

discovery value accounting. See *reserve recognition accounting*.

discretionary costs. *Programmed costs*.

Discussion Memorandum. A neutral discussion of all the issues concerning an accounting problem of current concern to the *FASB*. The publication of such a document usually implies that the FASB is considering issuing an *SFAS* or *SFAC* on this particular problem. The discussion memorandum brings together material about the particular problem to facilitate interaction and comment by those interested in the matter. It may lead to an *Exposure Draft*.

dishonored note. A *promissory note* whose maker does not repay the loan at *maturity* for a *term loan*, or on demand, for a *demand loan*.

disintermediation. Federal law regulates the maximum *interest rate* that both banks and savings and loan associations can pay for *time deposits*. When free-market interest rates exceed the regulated interest ceiling for such time deposits, some depositors withdraw their funds and invest them elsewhere at a higher interest rate. This process is known as "disintermediation."

distributable income. The portion of conventional accounting net income that can be distributed to owners (usually in the form of *dividends*) without impairing the physical capacity of the firm to continue operations at current levels. Pretax distributable income is conventional pretax income less the excess of *current cost* of goods sold and *depreciation* charges based on the replacement cost of *productive capacity* over cost of goods sold and depreciation on an *acquisition cost basis*. Contrast with *sustainable income*. See *inventory profit*.

distribution expense. *Expense* of selling, advertising, and delivery activities.

dividend. A distribution of assets generated from *earnings* to owners of a corporation; it may be paid in cash (cash dividend), with stock (stock dividend), with property, or with other securities (dividend in kind). Dividends, except stock dividends, become a legal liability of the corporation when they are declared. Hence, the owner of stock ordinarily recognizes *revenue* when a dividend, other than a stock dividend, is declared. See also *liquidating dividend* and *stock dividend*.

dividend yield. *Dividends* declared for the year divided by market price of the stock as of a given time of the year.

dividends in arrears. Dividends on *cumulative preferred stock* that have not been declared in accordance with the preferred stock contract. Such arrearages must usually be cleared before dividends on *common stock* can be declared.

dividends in kind. See *dividend*.

division. A more or less self-contained business unit which is part of a larger family of business units under common control.

divisional control. See *control system*.

divisional reporting. *Line-of-business reporting*.

dollar sign rules. In presenting accounting statements or schedules, place a dollar sign beside the first figure in each column and beside any figure below a horizontal line drawn under the preceding figure.

dollar-value LIFO method. A form of *LIFO* inventory accounting with inventory quantities (*layers*) measured in dollar, rather than physical, terms. Adjustments to account for changing prices are made by use of specific price indexes appropriate for the kinds of items in the inventory.

Domestic International Sales Corporation. See *DISC*.

donated capital. A *shareholders' equity* account credited when contributions, such as land or buildings, are freely given to the company. Do not confuse with *contributed capital*.

double entry. The system of recording transactions that maintains the equality of the accounting equation; each entry results in recording equal amounts of *debits* and *credits*.

double-declining-balance depreciation. DDB. *Declining-balance depreciation*, which see, where the constant percentage used to multiply by book value in computing the depreciation charge for the year is $2/n$ and n is the *depreciable life* in periods. *Salvage value* is omitted from the depreciable amount. Thus if the asset cost $100 and has a depreciable life of 5 years, the depreciation in the first year would be $40 = 2/5 x $100, in the second would be $24 = 2/5 x ($100 - $40), and in the third year would be $14.40 = 2/5 x ($100 - $40 - $24). By the fourth year, the remaining undepreciated cost could be depreciated under the straight line method at $10.80 = 1/2 x ($100 - $40 - $24 - $14.40) per year for tax purposes.

double T-account. *T-account* with an extra horizontal line showing a change in the account balance to be explained by the subsequent entries into the account, such as:

Plant

42,000	

This account shows an increase in the asset account, plant, of $42,000 to be explained. Such accounts are useful in preparing the *statement of cash flows*; they are not a part of the formal record-keeping process.

double taxation. Corporate income is subject to the corporate income tax and the aftertax income, when distributed to owners as dividends, is subject to the personal income tax.

doubtful accounts. *Accounts receivable* estimated to be *uncollectible*.

Dr. The abbreviation for *debit*.

draft. A written order by the first party, called the drawer, instructing a second party, called the drawee (such as a bank) to pay a third party, called the payee. See also *check, cashier's check, certified check, NOW account, sight draft,* and *trade acceptance*.

drawee. See *draft*.

drawer. See *draft*.

drawing account. A *temporary account* used in *sole proprietorships* and *partnerships* to record payments to owners or partners during a period. At the end of the period, the drawing account is closed by crediting it and debiting the owner's or partner's share of income or, perhaps, his or her capital account.

drawings. Payments made to a *sole proprietor* or to a *partner* during a period. See *drawing account*.

dry-hole accounting. See *reserve recognition accounting* for definition and contrast.

dual transactions assumption (fiction). In presenting the *statement of cash flows*, some transactions not involving *cash* accounts are reported as though cash was generated and then used. For example, the issue of *capital stock* in return for the *asset*, land, is reported in the statement of cash flows as though stock were issued for *cash* and cash were used to acquire land. Other examples of transactions that require the dual transaction fiction are the issue of the *mortgage* in return for a noncurrent asset and the issue of stock to bondholders on *conversion* of their *convertible bonds*.

dual transfer prices. The *transfer price charged* to the buying *division* differs from that *credited* to the selling division. Such prices make sense when the selling division has excess capacity and, as usual, the *incremental cost* to produce the goods or services being transferred is less than their *fair market value*.

duality. The axiom of *double entry* record keeping that every *transaction* is broken down into equal *debit* and *credit* amounts.

E

e. The base of natural logarithms; 2.718281828459045. . . . If *interest* is compounded continuously during a period at stated rate of r per period, then the effective *interest rate* is equivalent to interest compounded once per period at rate i where $i = e^r - 1$. Tables of e^r are widely available. If 12 percent annual interest is compounded continuously, the effective annual rate is $e^{.12} - 1 = 12.75$ percent.

earned surplus. A term once used, but no longer considered proper, for *retained earnings*.

earnings. *Income*, or sometimes *profit*.

earnings cycle. The period of time that elapses for a given firm, or the series of transactions, during which *cash* is converted into *goods* and *services*, goods and services are sold to customers, and customers pay for their purchases with cash. *Cash cycle*.

earnings per share (of common stock). *Net income* to common shareholders (net income minus *preferred dividends)* divided by the average number of *common shares* outstanding; see also *primary earnings per share* and *fully diluted earnings per share.* See *ratio.*

earnings, retained. See *retained earnings.*

earnings statement. *Income statement.*

earnings per share (of preferred stock). *Net income* divided by the average number of *preferred shares* outstanding during the period. This ratio indicates how well the preferred dividends are covered or protected; it does not indicate a legal share of *earnings.* See *ratio.*

earnings, retained. See *retained earnings.*

earn-out. An agreement between two merging firms under which the amount of payment by the acquiring firm to the acquired firm's shareholders depends on the future earnings of the acquired firm or, perhaps of the *consolidated entity.*

easement. The acquired right or privilege of one person to use, or have access to, certain property of another. For example, a public utility's right to lay pipes or lines under property of another and to service those facilities.

economic depreciation. Decline in *current cost* of an *asset* during a period.

economic entity. See *entity.*

economic life. The time span over which the benefits of an *asset* are expected to be received. The economic life of a *patent, copyright,* or *franchise* may be less than the legal life. *Service life.*

economic order quantity. In mathematical *inventory* analysis, the optimal amount of stock to order when inventory is reduced to a level called the "reorder point." If *A* represents the *incremental cost* of placing a single order, *D* represents the total demand for a period of time in units, and *H* represents the incremental holding cost during the period per unit of inventory, then the economic order quantity $Q = \sqrt{2AD/H}$. *Q* is sometimes called the "optimal lot size."

ED. *Exposure Draft.*

effective interest method. A systematic method for computing *interest expense* (or *revenue*) that makes the interest expense for each period divided by the amount of the net *liability (asset) at the beginning of the period equal to the yield rate* on the bond at the time of issue (acquisition). Interest for a period is yield rate (at time of issue) multiplied by the net liability (asset) at the start of the period. The *amortization* of discount or premium is the *plug* to give equal *debits* and *credits.* (Interest expense is a debit and the amount of coupon payments is a credit.)

effective (interest) rate. Of a bond, the *internal rate of return* or *yield to maturity* at the time of issue. Contrast

with *coupon rate.* If the bond is issued for a price below *par,* the effective rate is higher than the coupon rate; if it is issued for a price greater than par, then the effective rate is lower than the coupon rate. In the context of *compound interest,* when the *compounding period* on a *loan* is different from one year, such as a nominal interest rate of 12 percent compounded monthly, the single payment that could be made at the end of a year that is economically equivalent to the series of interest payments exceeds the quoted nominal rate multiplied by the *principal.* If 12 percent per year is compounded monthly, the effective annual interest rate is 12.683 percent. In general, if the nominal rate is *r* percent per year and is compounded *m* times per year, then the effective rate is $(1 + r/m)^m - 1$.

efficiency variance. A term used for the *quantity variance* for labor or *variable overhead* in a *standard cost system.*

efficient market hypothesis. The supposition in finance that securities' prices reflect all available information and react nearly instantaneously and in an unbiased fashion to new information.

EITF. *Emerging Issues Task Force.*

eliminations. *Work sheet* entries to prepare *consolidated statements* that are made to avoid duplicating the amounts of *assets, liabilities, owners' equity, revenues,* and *expenses* of the consolidated *entity* when the accounts of the *parent* and *subsidiaries* are summed.

Emerging Issues Task Force. EITF. A group convened by the *SEC* and the *FASB* to deal more rapidly with accounting issues than the FASB's due process procedures can allow. The task force comprises about 20 members from public accounting, industry, and several trade as,soci,ations. It meets every six weeks. Meetings are chaired by the FASB's director of research. Several FASB board members usually attend and participate. The chief accountant of the SEC has indicated that the SEC will require that published financial statements fol,low guidelines set by a consensus of the EITF. The EITF requires that nearly all of its members agree on a position before that position is given the label of "consensus." Since 1984, the EITF has become one of the promulgators of *GAAP.*

employee stock option. See *stock option.*

Employee Stock Ownership Trust (or Pian). See *ESOT.*

employer, employee payroll taxes. See *payroll.*

enabling costs. A type of *capacity cost* that will stop being incurred if operations are shut down completely but must be incurred in full if operations are carried out at any level. Costs of a security force or of a quality control inspector for an assembly line might be examples. Contrast with *standby costs.*

encumbrance. In governmental accounting, an anticipated *expenditure,* or *funds* restricted for anticipated expenditure, such as for outstanding purchase orders. *Appropriations* less expenditures less outstanding encumbrances yields unencumbered balance.

ending inventory. The *cost* of *inventory* on hand at the end of the *accounting period*, often called "closing inventory." The dollar amount of inventory to be carried to the subsequent period.

endorsee. See *endorser.*

endorsement. See *draft.* The *payee* signs the draft and transfers it to a fourth party, such as the payee's bank.

endorser. The *payee* of a *note* or *draft* signs it, after writing "Pay to the order of X," transfers the note to person X, and presumably receives some benefit, such as cash, in return. The payee who signs over the note is called the endorser and person X is called the endorsee. The endorsee then has the rights of the payee and may in turn become an endorser by endorsing the note to another endorsee.

engineering method (of cost estimation). Estimates of unit costs of product built up from study of the materials, labor and *overhead* components of the production process.

enterprise. Any business organization, usually defining the accounting *entity.*

enterprise fund. A *fund* established by a governmental unit to account for acquisition, operation, and maintenance of governmental services that are supposed to be self-supporting from user charges, such as for water or airports.

entity. A person, *partnership, corporation,* or other organization. The *accounting entity* for which accounting statements are prepared may not be the same as the entity defined by law. For example, a *sole proprietorship* is an accounting entity but the individual's combined business and personal assets are the legal entity in most jurisdictions. Several affiliated corporations may be separate legal entities while *consolidated financial statements* are prepared for the group of companies operating as a single economic entity.

entity theory. The view of the corporation that emphasizes the form of the *accounting equation* that says *assets = equities.* Contrast with *proprietorship theory.* The entity theory is less concerned with a distinct line between *liabilities* and *shareholders' equity* than is the proprietorship theory. Rather, all equities are provided to the corporation by outsiders who merely have claims of differing legal standings. The entity theory implies using a *multiple-step* income statement.

entry value. The *current cost* of acquiring an asset or service at a *fair market price. Replacement cost.*

EOQ. *Economic order quantity.*

EPS. *Earnings per share.*

EPVI. *Excess present value index.*

equalization reserve. An inferior title for the allowance or *estimated liability* account when the *allowance method* is used for such things as maintenance expenses. Periodically, maintenance *expense* is debited and the allowance is credited. As maintenance *expenditures* are actually incurred, the allowance is debited and cash or the other asset expended is credited.

equities. *Liabilities* plus *owners' equity.* See *equity.*

equity. A claim to *assets;* a source of assets. *SFAS No. 3* defines equity as "the residual interest in the assets of an entity that remains after deducting its liabilities." Usage may be changing so that "equity" will exclude liabilities. We prefer to keep the broader definition, including liabilities, because there is no other single word that serves this useful purpose.

equity financing. Raising *funds* by issuance of *capital stock.* Contrast with *debt financing.*

equity method. A method of accounting for an *investment* in the stock of another company in which the proportionate share of the earnings of the other company is debited to the investment account and credited to a *revenue* account as earned. When *dividends* are received, *cash* is debited and the investment account is credited. Used in reporting when the investor owns sufficient shares of stock of an unconsolidated company to exercise significant control over the actions of that company. One of the few instances where revenue is recognized without a change in *working capital.*

equity ratio. *Shareholders' equity* divided by total *assets.* See *ratio.*

equivalent production. *Equivalent units.*

equivalent units (of work). The number of units of completed output that would require the same costs as were actually incurred for production of completed and partially completed units during a period. Used primarily in *process costing* calculations to measure in uniform terms the output of a continuous process.

ERISA. Employee Retirement Income Security Act of 1974. The federal law that sets most *pension plan* requirements.

error accounting. See *accounting errors.*

escapable cost. *Avoidable costs.*

ESOP. Employee Stock Ownership Plan. See *ESOT.*

ESOT. Employee Stock Ownership Trust. A trust *fund* created by a corporate employer that can provide certain tax benefits to the corporation while providing for employee stock ownership. The corporate employer can contribute up to 25 percent of its payroll per year to the trust. The contributions are *deductions* from otherwise taxable income for federal *income tax* purposes. The assets of the trust must be used for the benefit of employees—for example, to fund death or retirement benefits. The assets of the trust are usually the *common stock*, sometimes nonvoting, of the corporate employer. As an example of the potential *tax shelter*, consider the case of a corporation with $1 million of *debt* outstanding, which it wishes to retire, and an annual payroll of $2 million. The corporation sells $1 million of common stock to the ESOT. The ESOT borrows $1 million with the loan guaranteed by, and therefore a *contingency* of, the corporation. The corporation uses the $1 million proceeds of the stock issue to retire its outstanding debt. (The debt of the corporation has been replaced with the debt of the ESOT.) The corporation can contribute $500,000 (= .25 x $2 million payroll) to the ESOT each year and treat the contribution as a deduction for tax purposes. After a little more than two years, the ESOT has received sufficient funds to retire its loan. The corporation has effectively repaid its original $1 million debt with pretax dollars. Assuming an income tax rate of 40 percent, it has saved $400,000 (= .40 x $1 million) of aftertax dollars *if* the $500,000 expense for the contribution to the ESOT for the pension benefits of employees would have been made, in one form or another, anyway. Observe that the corporation could use the proceeds ($1 million in the example) of the stock issued to the ESOT for any of several different purposes: financing expansion, replacing plant assets, or acquiring another company. Basically this same form of pretax dollar financing through pensions is "almost" available with any corporate pension plan, but with one important exception. The trustees of an ordinary pension trust must invest the assets "prudently" and if they do not, they are personally liable to employees. Current judgment about "prudent" investment requires diversification—pension trust assets should be invested in a wide variety of investment opportunities. (Not more than 10 percent of a pension trust's assets can ordinarily be invested in the parent's common stock.) Thus the ordinary pension trust cannot, in practice, invest all, or even most, of its assets in the parent corporation's stock. This constraint does not apply to the investments of an ESOT. All ESOT assets may be invested in the parent company's stock. The ESOT also provides a means for closely held corporations to achieve wider ownership of shares without *going public*. The laws enabling ESOT's provide for independent professional appraisal of shares not traded in public markets and for transactions between the corporation and the ESOT or between the ESOT and the employees to be based on the appraised values of the shares.

estimated expenses. See *after cost.*

estimated liability. The preferred terminology for estimated costs to be incurred for such uncertain things as repairs under *warranty*. An estimated liability appears on the *balance sheet*. Contrast with *contingency.*

estimated revenue. A term used in governmental accounting to designate revenue expected to accrue during a period whether or not it will be collected during the period. A *budgetary account* is usually established at the beginning of the budget period.

estimated salvage value. Synonymous with *salvage value* of an *asset* before its retirement.

estimates, changes in. See *accounting changes.*

except for. Qualification in *auditor's report*, usually caused by a change, approved by the auditor, from one acceptable accounting principle or procedure to another.

excess present value. In a *capital budgeting* context, *present value* of (anticipated net cash inflows minus cash outflows including initial cash outflow) for a project.

excess present value index. *Present value*, of future *cash* inflows divided by initial cash outlay.

exchange. The generic term for a transaction (or more technically, a reciprocal transfer) between one entity and another. In another context, the name for a market, such as the New York Stock Exchange.

exchange gain or loss. The phrase used by the *FASB* for *foreign exchange gain or loss.*

exchange rate. The *price* of one country's currency in terms of another country's currency. For example, the British pound sterling might be worth $1.60 at a given time. The exchange rate would be stated as "one pound is worth one dollar and sixty cents" or "one dollar is worth £.625 (= £1/$1.60)."

excise tax. Tax on the manufacture, sale, or consumption of a commodity.

ex-dividend. Said of a stock at the time when the declared *dividend* becomes the property of the person who owned the stock on the *record date*. The payment date follows the ex-dividend date.

executory contract. A mere exchange of promises. An agreement providing for payment by a payor to a payee upon the performance of an act or service by the payee, such as a labor contract. Obligations under such contracts generally are not recognized as *liabilities.*

exemption. A term used for various amounts subtracted from gross income in computing taxable income. Not all such subtractions are called "exemptions." See *tax deduction.*

exercise. When owners of an *option* or *warrant* purchase the security that the option entitles them to purchase, they have exercised the option or warrant.

exercise price. See *option.*

exit value. The proceeds that would be received if assets were disposed of in an *arm's-length transaction. Current selling price. Net realizable value.*

expected value. The mean or arithmetic *average* of a statistical distribution or series of numbers.

expected value of (perfect) information. Expected *net benefits* from an undertaking with (perfect) information minus expected net benefits of the undertaking without (perfect) information.

expendable fund. In governmental accounting, a *fund* whose resources, *principal*, and earnings may be distributed.

expenditure. Payment of *cash* for goods or services received. Payment may be made either at the time the goods or services are received or at a later time. Virtually synonymous with *disbursement* except that disbursement is a broader term and includes all payments for goods or services. Contrast with *expense*.

expense. As a noun, a decrease in *owners' equity* caused by the using up of *assets* in producing *revenue* or carrying out other activities that are part of the entity's *operations*. A "gone" asset; an expired cost. The amount is the *cost* of the assets used up. Do not confuse with *expenditure* or *disbursement*, which may occur before, when, or after the related expense is recognized. Use the word "cost" to refer to an item that still has service potential and is an asset. Use the word "expense" after the asset's service potential has been used. As a verb, to designate a past or current expenditure as a current expense.

expense account. An *account* to accumulate *expenses*; such accounts are closed at the end of the accounting period. A *temporary owners' equity* account. Also used to describe a listing of expenses by an employee submitted to the employer for reimbursement.

experience rating. A term used in insurance, particularly unemployment insurance, to denote changes from ordinary rates to reflect extraordinarily large or small amounts of claims over time by the insured.

expired cost. An *expense* or a *loss*.

Exposure Draft. ED. A preliminary statement of the *FASB* (or *APB* between 1962 and 1973) that shows the contents of a pronouncement the Board is considering making effective.

external reporting. Reporting to shareholders and the public, as opposed to internal reporting for management's benefit. See *financial accounting* and contrast with *managerial accounting*.

extraordinary item. A *material expense* or *revenue* item characterized both by its unusual nature and infrequency of occurrence that is shown along with its income tax effects separately from ordinary income and *income from discontinued operations* on the *income statement*. A *loss* from an earthquake would probably be classified as an extraordinary item. Gain (or loss) on retirement of *bonds* is treated as an extraordinary item under the terms of *SFAS No. 4*.

F

face amount (value). The nominal amount due at *maturity* from a *bond* or *note* not including contractual interest that may also be due on the same date. The corresponding amount of a stock certificate is best called the *par* or *stated value*, whichever is applicable.

factoring. The process of buying *notes* or *accounts receivable* at a *discount* from the holder to whom the debt is owed; from the holder's point of view, the selling of such notes or accounts. When a single note is involved, the process is called "discounting a note."

factory. Used synonymously with *manufacturing* as an adjective.

factory burden. Manufacturing *overhead*.

factory cost. *Manufacturing cost*.

factory expense. Manufacturing *overhead*. *Expense* is a poor term in this context because the item is a *product cost*.

factory overhead. Usually an item of *manufacturing cost* other than *direct labor* or *direct materials*.

fair market price (value). Price (value) negotiated at *arm's-length* between a willing buyer and a willing seller, each acting rationally in his or her own self interest. May be estimated in the absence of a monetary transaction.

fair presentation (fairness). When the *auditor's report* says that the *financial statements* "present fairly. . . ," the auditor means that the accounting alternatives used by the entity are all in accordance with *GAAP*. In recent years, however, courts are finding that conformity with *generally accepted accounting principles* may be insufficient grounds for an opinion that the statements are fair. *SAS No. 5* requires that the auditor judge the accounting principles used "appropriate in the circumstances" before attesting to fair presentation.

FASB. Financial Accounting Standards Board. An independent board responsible, since 1973, for establishing *generally accepted accounting principles*. Its official pronouncements are called "Statements of Financial Accounting Concepts" ("SFAC"), "Statements of Financial Accounting Standards" ("SFAS"), and "Interpretations of Financial Accounting Standards." See also *Discussion Memorandum* and *Technical Bulletin*.

FASB Interpretation. An official statement of the *FASB* interpreting the meaning of *Accounting Research Bulletins*, *APB Opinions*, and *Statements of Financial Accounting Standards*.

FASB Technical Bulletin. See *Technical Bulletin*.

favorable variance. An excess of actual *revenues* over expected revenues. An excess of *standard cost* over actual cost.

federal income tax. *Income tax* levied by the U.S. government on individuals and corporations.

Federal Insurance Contribution Act. See *FICA*.

Federal Unemployment Tax Act. See *FUTA*.

feedback. The process of informing employees about how their actual performance compares with the expected or desired level of performance in the hope that the information will reinforce desired behavior and reduce unproductive behavior.

FEI. *Financial Executives Institute.*

FICA. Federal Insurance Contributions Act. The law that sets "*Social Security*" *taxes* and benefits.

fiduciary. Someone responsible for the custody or administration of property belonging to another, such as an executor (of an estate), agent, receiver (in *bankruptcy*), or trustee (of a trust).

FIFO. First-in, first-out; the *inventory flow assumption* by which *ending inventory* cost is computed from most recent purchases and *cost of goods sold* is computed from oldest purchases including beginning inventory. See *LISH*. Contrast with *LIFO*.

finance. As a verb, to supply with *funds* through the *issue* of stocks, bonds, notes, or mortgages, or through the retention of earnings.

financial accounting. The accounting for *assets, equities, revenues*, and *expenses* of a business. Primarily concerned with the historical reporting of the *financial position* and operations of an *entity* to external users on a regular, periodic basis. Contrast with *managerial accounting*.

Financial Accounting Foundation. The independent foundation (committee) that raises funds to support the *FASB*.

Financial Accounting Standards Advisory Council. A committee giving advice to the *FASB* on matters of strategy and emerging issues.

Financial Accounting Standards Board. *FASB.*

Financial Executives Institute. An organization of financial executives, such as chief accountants, *controllers*, and treasurers, of large businesses.

financial expense. An *expense* incurred in raising or managing *funds*.

financial flexibilty. As defined by *SFAC No. 5*, "the ability of an entity to take effective actions to alter amounts and timing of cash flows so it can respond to unexpected needs and opportunities."

financial forecast. See *financial projection* for definition and contrast.

financial projection. An estimate of *financial position*, results of *operations*, and changes in cash flows for one or more future periods based on a set of assumptions. If the assumptions are not necessarily the most likely outcomes, then the estimate is called a "projection." If the assumptions represent the most probable outcomes, then the estimate is called a "forecast." "Most probable" means that the assumptions have been evaluated by management and that they are management's judgment of the most likely set of conditions and most likely outcomes.

financial leverage. See *leverage*.

financial position (condition). Statement of the *assets* and *equities* of a firm displayed as a *balance sheet*.

financial ratio. See *ratio*.

financial reporting objectives. FASB *Statement of Financial Accounting Concepts No. 1* sets out the broad objectives of financial reporting that are intended to guide the development of specific *accounting standards*.

Financial Reporting Release. Series of releases, issued by the SEC since 1982. Replaces the *Accounting Series Releases*. See *SEC*.

financial statements. The *balance sheet, income statement, statement of retained earnings, statement of cash flows*, statement of changes in *owners' equity accounts*, and *notes* thereto.

financial structure. *Capital structure.*

financial year. The term for *fiscal year* in Australia and Britain.

financing activities. Obtaining resources from (a) owners and providing them with a return on and a return of their *investment* and (b) *creditors* and repaying amounts borrowed (or otherwise settling the obligation). See *statement of cash flows*.

financing lease. *Capital lease.*

finished goods (inventory account). Manufactured product ready for sale; a *current asset (inventory) account*.

firm. Informally, any business entity. (Strictly speaking, a firm is a *partnership*.)

first-in, first-out. See *FIFO*.

fiscal year. A period of 12 consecutive months chosen by a business as the *accounting period* for annual reports. May or may not be a *natural business year* or a calendar year.

FISH. An acronym, conceived by George H. Sorter, for *first in, still here*. FISH is the same cost flow assumption as *LIFO*. Many readers of accounting statements find it easier to think about inventory questions in terms of items still on hand. Think of LIFO in connection with *cost of goods sold* but of FISH in connection with *ending inventory*. See *LISH*.

fixed assets. *Plant assets.*

fixed assets turnover. *Sales* divided by average total *fixed assets*.

fixed benefit plan. A *defined-benefit (pension) plan*.

fixed budget. A plan that provides for specified amounts of *expenditures* and *receipts* that do not vary with activity levels. Sometimes called a "static budget." Contrast with *flexible budget*.

fixed charges earned (coverage) ratio. *Income* before *interest expense* and *income tax expense* divided by interest expense.

fixed cost (expense). An *expenditure* or *expense* that does not vary with volume of activity, at least in the short run. See *capacity costs*, which include *enabling costs* and *standby costs*, and *programmed costs* for various subdivisions of fixed costs. See *cost terminology*.

fixed liability. *Long-term* liability.

fixed manufacturing overhead applied. The portion of *fixed manufacturing overhead cost* allocated to units produced during a period.

fixed overhead variance. Difference between *actual fixed manufacturing costs* and fixed manufacturing costs applied to production in a *standard costing system*.

flexible budget. *Budget* that projects receipts and expenditures as a function of activity levels. Contrast with *fixed budget*.

flexible budget allowance. With respect to manufacturing overhead, the total cost that should have been incurred at the level of activity actually experienced during the period.

float. *Checks* whose amounts have been *added* to the depositor's bank account, but not yet subtracted from the *drawer's* bank account.

flow. The change in the amount of an item over time. Contrast with *stock*.

flow assumption. When a *withdrawal* is made from *inventory*, the cost of the withdrawal must be computed by a flow assumption if *specific identification* of units is not used. The usual flow assumptions are *FIFO*, *LIFO*, and *weighted average*.

flow of costs. *Costs* passing through various classifications within an *entity*. See the accompanying diagram for a summary of *product* and *period cost* flows.

flow-through method. Accounting for the *investment credit* to show all income statement benefits of the credit in the year of acquisition, rather than spreading them over the life of the asset acquired, called the "deferral method." The *APB* preferred the deferral method in *Opinion No. 2* (1962) but accepted the flow-through method in *Opinion No. 4* (1964). The term is also used in connection with *depreciation* accounting where *straight-line method* is used for financial reporting and an *accelerated* method for tax reporting. Followers of the flow-through method would not recognize a *deferred tax liability*. *APB Opinion No. 11* prohibits the use of the flow-through approach in

Flow of Costs (and Sales Revenue)

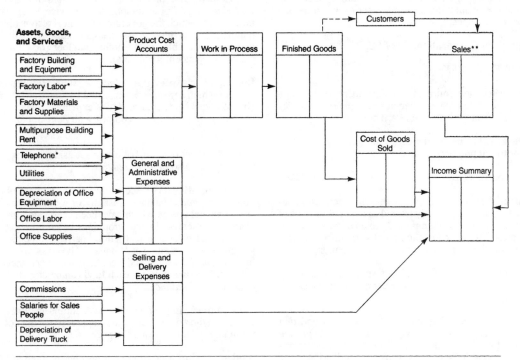

---

*The credit in the entry to record these items is usually to a payable; for all others, the credit is usually to an asset, or to an asset contra account.
**When sales to customers are recorded, the Sales account is credited. The debit is usually to Cash or Accounts Receivable.

financial reporting although it has been used by some regulatory commissions.

FOB. Free on board some location (for example, FOB shipping point; FOB destination); the *invoice* price includes delivery at seller's expense to that location. Title to goods usually passes from seller to buyer at the FOB location.

footing. Adding a column of figures.

footnotes. More detailed information than that provided in the *income statement, balance sheet, statement of retained earnings*, and *statement of cash flows*; these are considered an integral part of the statements and are covered by the *auditor's report*. Sometimes called "notes."

forecast. See *financial projection* for definition and contrast.

foreclosure. The borrower fails to make a required payment on a *mortgage*; the lender takes possession of the property for his or her own use or sale. Assume that the lender sells the property but the proceeds of sale are insufficient to cover the outstanding balance on the loan at the time of foreclosure. Under the terms of most mortgages, the lender becomes an unsecured creditor of the borrower for the still-unrecovered balance of the loan.

foreign currency. For *financial statements* prepared in a given currency, any other currency.

foreign exchange gain or loss. Gain or loss from holding *net* foreign *monetary items* during a period when the *exchange rate* changes.

Foreign Sales Corporation. See *FSC*.

Form 10-K. See *10-K*.

forward exchange contract. An agreement to exchange at a specified future date currencies of different countries at a specified rate call the "forward rate".

franchise. A privilege granted or sold, such as to use a name or to sell products or services.

free on board. *FOB*.

freight-in. The *cost* of freight or shipping incurred in acquiring *inventory*, preferably treated as a part of the cost of *inventory*. Often shown temporarily in an *adjunct account* that is closed at the end of the period with other purchase accounts to the inventory account by the acquirer.

freight-out. The *cost* of freight or shipping incurred in selling *inventory*, treated by the seller as a selling *expense* in the period of sale.

FSC. Foreign Sales Corporation. A foreign *corporation* engaging in certain export activities some of whose *income* is exempt from U.S. federal *income tax*. A U.S. corporation need pay no income taxes on *dividends* distributed by an FSC out of *earnings* attributable to certain foreign income.

full absorption costing. The method of *costing* which assigns all types of manufacturing costs (*direct material, direct labor, fixed* and *variable overhead*) to units produced; required by *GAAP*. Also called "absorption costing." Contrast with *variable costing*.

full costing. full costs. The total cost of producing and selling a unit. Full cost per unit equals *full absorption cost* per unit plus *marketing, administrative, interest*, and other *central corporate expenses*, per unit. The sum of full costs for all units equals total costs of the firm. Often used in *long-term* profitability and pricing decisions.

full disclosure. The reporting policy requiring that all significant or *material* information is to be presented in the financial statements. See *fair presentation*.

fully diluted earnings per share. Smallest *earnings per share* figure on *common stock* that can be obtained by computing an earnings per share for all possible combinations of assumed *exercise* or *conversion* of *potentially dilutive securities*. Must be reported on the *income statement* if it is less than 97 percent of earnings available to common shareholders divided by the average number of common shares outstanding during the period.

fully vested. Said of a *pension plan* when an employee (or his or her estate) has rights to all the benefits purchased with the employer's contributions to the plan even if the employee is not employed by this employer at the time of death or retirement.

function. In governmental accounting, said of a group of related activities for accomplishing a service or regulatory program for which the governmental unit is responsible. In mathematics, a rule for associating a number, called the dependent variable, with another number (or numbers), called independent variable(s).

functional classification. *Income statement* reporting form in which *expenses* are reported by functions, that is, cost of goods sold, administrative expenses, financing expenses, selling expenses; contrast with *natural classification*.

fund. An *asset* or group of assets set aside for a specific purpose. See also *fund accounting*.

fund accounting. The accounting for resources, obligations, and *capital* balances, usually of a not-for-profit or governmental *entity*, which have been segregated into *accounts* representing logical groupings based on legal, donor, or administrative restrictions or requirements. The groupings are described as "funds." The accounts of each fund are *self-balancing* and from them a *balance sheet* and an operating statement for each fund can be prepared. See *fund* and *fund balance*.

fund balance. In governmental accounting, the excess of assets of a *fund* over its liabilities and reserves; the not-for-profit equivalent of *owners' equity*.

funded. Said of a *pension plan* or other obligation when *funds* have been set aside for meeting the obligation when it becomes due. The federal law for pension plans requires that all *normal costs* be funded as recognized. In addition, *prior service cost* of pension plans must be funded over 30 or over 40 years, depending on the circumstances.

funding. Replacing *short-term* liabilities with *long-term* debt.

funds. Generally *working capital*; current assets less current liabilities. Sometimes used to refer to *cash* or to cash and *marketable securities*.

funds provided by operations. See *cash provided by operations*.

funds statement. An informal name often used for the *statement of cash flows*.

funny money. Said of securities such as *convertible preferred stock, convertible bonds, options*, and *warrants* that have aspects of *common stock* equity but that did not reduce reported *earnings per share* prior to the issuance of *APB Opinions No. 9* in 1967 and *No. 15* in 1969.

FUTA. Federal Unemployment Tax Act which provides for taxes to be collected at the federal level, to help subsidize the individual states' administration of their unemployment compensation programs.

future value. Value at a specified future date of a sum increased at a specified *interest rate*.

G

GAAP. *Generally accepted accounting principles*. A plural noun.

GAAS. *Generally accepted auditing standards*. A plural noun. Not to be confused with *GAS*.

gain. Increase in *owners' equity* caused by a transaction not part of a firm's typical, day-to-day operations and not part of owners' *investment* or *withdrawals*. The term "gain" (or "loss") is distinguished in two separate ways from related terms. First, gains (and losses) are generally used for nonoperating, incidental, peripheral, or nonroutine transactions: gain on sale of land in contrast to *gross margin* on *sale* of *inventory*. Second, gains and losses are *net* concepts, not gross concepts: gain or loss results from subtracting some measure of *cost* from the measure of inflow. *Revenues* and *expenses*, on the other hand, are gross concepts; their difference is a net concept. Gain is nonroutine and net, *profit* or *margin* is routine and net; revenue is routine and gross. Loss is net but can be either routine ("loss on sale of inventory") or not ("loss on disposal of segment of business").

gain contingency. See *contingency*.

GAS. *Goods available for sale*. Not to be confused with *GAAS*.

GASB. Government Accounting Standards Board. An independent body responsible, since 1982, for establishing accounting standards for state and local government units. It is part of the *Financial Accounting Foundation*, parallel to the *FASB*, and currently consists of five members.

gearing. British term for *financial leverage*.

gearing adjustment. Consider a firm, part of whose assets are *noncurrent liabilities* and who has experience *holding gains* on its *assets* during a period. All of the increase in wealth caused by the holding gains belongs to the owners; none typically belongs to the lenders. Some British accounting authorities believe that published *income statements* should show the part of the holding gain financed with debt in *income* for the period. That part is called the "gearing adjustment."

general debt. Debt of a governmental unit legally payable from general revenues and backed by the full faith and credit of the governmental unit.

general expenses. *Operating expenses* other than those specifically assigned to cost of goods sold, selling, and administration.

general fixed asset (group of accounts). Accounts showing those long-term assets of a governmental unit not accounted for in *enterprise, trust*, or intragovernmental service funds.

general fund. Assets and liabilities of a nonprofit entity not specifically earmarked for other purposes; the primary operating fund of a governmental unit.

general journal. The formal record where transactions, or summaries of similar transactions, are recorded in *journal entry* form as they occur. Use of the adjective "general" usually implies only two columns for cash amounts or that there are also various *special journals*, such as a *check register* or *sales journal*, in use.

general ledger. The name for the formal *ledger* containing all of the financial statement accounts. It has equal debits and credits as evidenced by the *trial balance*. Some of the accounts in the general ledger may be *controlling accounts*, supported by details contained in *subsidiary ledgers*.

general partner. Member of *partnership* personally liable for all debts of the partnership; contrast with *limited partner*.

general price index. A measure of the aggregate prices of a wide range of goods and services in the economy at one time relative to the prices during a base period. See *consumer price index* and *GNP Implicit Price Deflator*. Contrast with *specific price index*.

general price level-adjusted statements. See *constant dollar accounting*.

general price level changes. Changes in the aggregate prices of a wide range of goods and services in the economy. These price changes are measured using a *general price index*. Contrast with *specific price changes*.

general purchasing power. The command of the dollar over a wide range of goods and services in the economy. The general purchasing power of the dollar is inversely related to changes in a general price index. See *general price index.*

general purchasing power accounting. See *constant dollar accounting.*

generally accepted accounting principles. GAAP. As previously defined by the *APB* and now by the *FASB*, the conventions, rules, and procedures necessary to define accepted accounting practice at a particular time; includes both broad guidelines and relatively detailed practices and procedures.

generally accepted auditing standards. GAAS. The standards, as opposed to particular procedures, promulgated by the *AICPA* (in *Statements on Auditing Standards*) that concern "the auditor's professional quantities" and "the judgment exercised by him in the performance of his examination and in his report." Currently, there are ten such standards: three general ones (concerned with proficiency, independence, and degree of care to be exercised), three standards of field work, and four standards of reporting. The first standard of reporting requires that the *auditor's report* state whether or not the *financial statements* are prepared in accordance with *generally accepted accounting principles*. Thus the typical auditor's report says that the examination was conducted in accordance with generally accepted auditing standards and that the statements are prepared in accordance with generally accepted accounting principles. See *auditor's report.*

GNP Implicit Price Deflator (Index). A *price index* issued quarterly by the Office of Business Economics of the U.S. Department of Commerce. This index attempts to trace the price level of all *goods and services* comprising the *gross national product*. Contrast with *consumer price index.*

goal congruence. All members of an organization have incentives to perform for a common interest, *shareholder* wealth maximization for a *corporation.*

going-concern assumption. For accounting purposes, a business is assumed to remain in operation long enough for all its current plans to be carried out. This assumption is part of the justification for the *acquisition cost* basis, rather than a *liquidation* or *exit value* basis of accounting.

going public. Said of a business when its *shares* become widely traded, rather than being closely held by relatively few shareholders. Issuing shares to the general investing public.

goods. Items of merchandise, supplies, raw materials, or finished goods. Sometimes the meaning of "goods" is extended to include all *tangible* items, as in the phrase "goods and services."

goods available for sale. The sum of *beginning inventory* plus all acquisitions of merchandise or finished goods during an *accounting period.*

goods in process. *Work in process.*

goodwill. The excess of cost of an acquired firm (or operating unit) over the current *fair market value* of the separately identifiable *net assets* of the acquired unit. Before goodwill is recognized, all identifiable assets, whether or not on the books of the acquired unit, must be given a *fair market value*. For example, a firm has developed a *patent* which is not recognized on its books because of *SFAS No. 2*. If another company acquires the firm, the acquirer will recognize the patent at an amount equal to its estimated fair market value before computing goodwill. Informally, the term is used to indicate the value of good customer relations, high employee morale, a well-respected business name, and so on, that are expected to result in greater than that normal earning power.

goodwill method. A method of accounting for the *admission* of a new partner to a *partnership* when the new partner is to be credited with a portion of capital different from the value of the *tangible* assets contributed as a fraction of tangible assets on the partnership. See *bonus method* for a description and contrast.

Government Accounting Standards Advisory Committee. A group that consults with the *GASB* on agenda, technical issues, and the assignment of priorities to projects. It consists of mmore than a dozen members representing various areas of expertise.

Government Accounting Standards Board. *GASB.*

GPL. General price level; usually used as an adjective modifying the word "accounting" to mean *constant dollar accounting.*

GPLA. General price level-adjusted accounting; *constant dollar accounting.*

GPP. General purchasing power; usually used as an adjective modifying the word "accounting" to mean *constant dollar accounting.*

graded vesting. Said of a *pension plan* where not all employee benefits are currently *vested*. By law, the benefits must become vested according to one of several formulas as time passes.

grandfather clause. An exemption in new accounting *pronouncements* exempting transactions that occurred before a given date from the new accounting treatment. For example, *APB Opinion No. 17*, adopted in 1970, exempted *goodwill* acquired before 1970 from required *amortization*. The term "grandfather" appears in the title to *SFAS No. 10.*

gross. Not adjusted or reduced by deductions or subtractions. Contrast with *net.*

gross margin. *Net sales* minus *cost of goods sold.*

gross margin percent. $100 \times (1 - cost\ of\ goods\ sold/net\ sales) = 100 \times (gross\ margin/net\ sales)$.

gross national product. GNP. The market value within a nation for a year of all goods and services produced as measured by final sales of goods and services to individuals, corporations, and governments plus the excess of exports over imports.

gross price method (of recording purchase or sales discounts). The *purchase* (or *sale*) is recorded at its *invoice price*, not deducting the amounts of *discounts* available. Discounts taken are recorded in a *contra* account to purchases (or sales). Information on discounts lapsed is not made available, and for this reason, most firms prefer the *net price method* of recording purchase discounts.

gross profit. *Gross margin.*

gross profit method. A method of estimating *ending inventory* amounts. *Cost of goods sold* is measured as some fraction of sales; the *inventory equation* is then used to value *ending inventory*.

gross profit ratio. *Gross margin* divided by *net sales*.

gross sales. All *sales* at *invoice* prices, not reduced by *discounts*, *allowances*, *returns*, or other adjustments.

group depreciation. A method of calculating *depreciation* charges where similar assets are combined, rather than depreciated separately. No gain or loss is recognized on retirement of items from the group until the last item in the group is sold or retired. See *composite life method*.

guarantee. A promise to answer for payment of debt or performance of some obligation if the person liable for the debt or obligation fails to perform. A guarantee is a *contingency* of the *entity* making the promise. Often, the words "guarantee" and "warranty" are used to mean the same thing. In precise usage, however, "guarantee" means promise to fulfill the promise of some person to perform a contractual obligation such as to pay a sum of money, whereas "warranty" is most often used to refer to promises about pieces of machinery or other products. See *warranty*.

H

half-year convention. An assumption used in *tax accounting* under *ACRS*, and sometimes in *financial accounting*, that *depreciable assets* were acquired at mid-year of the year of acquisition. When this convention is used, the *depreciation charge* for the year is computed as one-half the charge that would be used if the assets had been acquired at the beginning of the year.

Hasselback. An annual directory of accounting faculty at colleges and universities, which gives information about the faculty's training and fields of specialization. The directory has been compiled for over a decade by James R. Hasselback of Florida State University and is distributed by Prentice-Hall of Englewood Cliffs, New Jersey.

hidden reserve. The term refers to an amount by which *owners' equity* has been understated, perhaps deliberately. The understatement arises from an undervaluation of *assets* or overvaluation of *liabilities*. By undervaluing assets on this period's *balance sheet*, *net income* in some future period can be made to look artificially high by disposing of the asset: actual *revenues* less artificially low cost of assets sold yields artificially high net income. There is no *account* that has this title.

historical cost. *Acquisition cost; original cost*; a *sunk cost*.

historical cost/constant dollar accounting. Accounting based on *historical cost* valuations measured in *constant dollars*. *Nonmonetary items* are restated to reflect changes in the *general purchasing power* of the dollar since the time the specific *assets* were acquired or *liabilities* were incurred. A *gain* or *loss* is recognized on *monetary items* as they are held over time periods when the general purchasing power of the dollar changes.

historical summary. A part of the *annual report* to shareholders that shows important items, such as *net income*, *revenues*, *expenses*, *asset* and *equity* totals, *earnings per share*, and the like, for five or ten periods including the current one. Usually not as much detail is shown in the historical summary as in *comparative statements*, which typically report as much detail for the two preceding years as for the current year. Annual reports may contain both comparative statements and a historical summary.

holding company. A company that confines its activities to owning *stock* in, and supervising management of, other companies. A holding company usually owns a controlling interest in, that is more than 50 percent of the voting stock of, the companies whose stock it holds. Contrast with *mutual fund*. See *conglomerate*. In British usage, the term refers to any company with controlling interest in another company.

holding gain or loss. Difference between end-of-period price and beginning-of-period price of an asset held during the period. Realized holding gains and losses are not ordinarily separately reported in financial statements. Unrealized gains are not usually reflected in income at all. Some unrealized losses, such as on inventory or marketable securities, are reflected in income or *owners' equity* as the losses occur; see *lower of cost or market*. See *inventory profit* for further refinement, including *gains* on *assets* sold during the period.

holding gain or loss net of inflation. Increase or decrease in the *current cost* of an asset while it is held measured in units of *constant dollars*.

horizontal analysis. *Time-series analysis.*

human resource accounting. A term used to describe a variety of proposals that seek to report and emphasize the importance of human resources—knowledgeable, trained, and loyal employees— in a company's earning process and total assets.

hurdle rate. Required rate of return in a *discounted cash flow* analysis.

hybrid security. *Security*, such as a *convertible bond*, containing elements of both *debt* and *owners' equity*.

hypothecation. The *pledging* of property, without transfer of title or possession, to secure a loan.

I

I. *Identity matrix.*

IAA. *Interamerican Accounting Association.*

ICMA. *Institute of Certified Management Accountants.* See *CMA* and *National Association of Accountants.*

ideal standard costs. *Standard costs* set equal to those that would be incurred under the best possible conditions.

identity matrix. A square *matrix* with ones on the main diagonal and zeros elsewhere; a matrix **I** such that for any other matrix **A, IA = AI = A**. The matrix equivalent to the number one.

IIA. *Institute of Internal Auditors.*

implicit interest. *Interest* not paid or received. See *interest, imputed.* All transactions involving the deferred payment or receipt of cash involved interest, whether explicitly stated or not. The implicit interest on a single-payment *note* is the difference between the amount collected at maturity less the amount lent at the start of the loan. The implicit *interest rate* per year can be computed from

$$\left[\frac{\text{Cash Received at Maturity}}{\text{Cash Lent}} \right]^{(1/t)} - 1.$$

where t is the term of the loan in years; t need not be an integer.

imprest fund. *Petty cash fund.*

improvement. An *expenditure* to extend the useful life of an *asset* or to improve its performance (rate of output, cost) over that of the original asset. Such expenditures are *capitalized* as part of the asset's cost. Sometimes called "betterment." Contrast with *maintenance* and *repair.*

imputed cost. A cost that does not appear in accounting records, such as the *interest* that could be earned on cash spent to acquire inventories rather than, say, government bonds. Or, consider a firm that owns the buildings it occupies. This firm has an imputed cost for rent in an amount equal to what it would have to pay to use similar buildings owned by another. *Opportunity cost.*

imputed interest. See *interest, imputed.*

incentive compatible compensation. Said of a compensation plan for managers that induces them to act for the interests of owners while acting in their own interests. For example, consider a time of rising prices and increasing inventories when using a *LIFO cost flow assumption* implies having to pay lower *income taxes* than would *FIFO.* A bonus scheme for managers based on accounting *net income* would not be incentive compatible, because the owners will be better off under LIFO, while managers will be better off if they report using FIFO. (See *LIFO conformity rule.*) See *goal congruence.*

income. *Excess of revenues* and *gains* over *expenses* and *losses* for a period; *net income.* Sometimes used with an appropriate modifier to refer to the various intermediate amounts shown in a *multiple-step income statement.* Sometimes used to refer to revenues, as in "rental income." See *comprehensive income.*

income accounts. *Revenue* and *expense accounts.*

income before taxes. On the *income statement*, the difference between all *revenues* and *expenses* except *income tax* expense. Contrast with *net income* and *taxable income.*

income determination. See *determine.*

income distribution account. *Temporary account* sometimes debited when *dividends* are declared; closed to *retained earnings.*

income from continuing operations. As defined by APB *Opinion No. 30*, all *revenues* less all *expenses* except for the following: results of operations (including *income tax* effects) that have been or will be discontinued; *gains* or *losses*, including income tax effects, on disposal of segments of the business; gains or losses, including income tax effects, from *extraordinary items*; and the cumulative effect of *accounting changes.*

income from discontinued operations. *Income*, net of tax effects, from parts of the business that have been discontinued during the period or are to be discontinued in the near future. Such items are reported on separate line of the *income statement* after *income from continuing operations* but before *extraordinary items.*

income (revenue) bond. See *special revenue debt.*

income smoothing. A method of timing business *transactions* or choosing *accounting principles* so that variations in reported *income* from year to year are reduced from what they would otherwise be. Although income smoothing is an objective of some managements, it is not an official *accounting principle* or *reporting objective.*

income statement. The statement of *revenues, expenses, gains*, and *losses* for the period ending with *net income* for the period. The *earnings-per-share* amount is usually shown on the income statement; the *reconciliation* of beginning and ending balances of *retained earnings* may also be shown in a combined statement of income and retained earnings. See *income from continuing operations, income* *from discontinued operations, extraordinary items, multiple-step, single-step.*

income summary. An *account* used in problem solving that serves as a surrogate for the *income statement*. All *revenues* are closed to the Income Summary as *credits* and all *expenses*, as *debits*. The *balance* in the account, after all other *closing entries* are made, is then closed to the retained earnings or other *owners' equity* account and represents *net income* for the period.

income tax. An annual tax levied by the federal and other governments on the income of an entity.

income tax allocation. See *deferred tax liability* and *tax allocation: intrastatement.*

incremental. An adjective used to describe the change in *cost, expense, investment, cash flow, revenue, profit,* and the like if one or more units are produced or sold or if an activity is undertaken.

incremental cost. See *incremental.*

indenture. See *bond indenture.*

independence. The mental attitude required of the *CPA* in performing the *attest* function. It implies impartiality and that the members of the auditing CPA firm own no stock in the corporation being audited.

independent accountant. The *CPA* who performs the *attest* function for a firm.

independent variable. See *regression analysis.*

indeterminate-term liability. A *liability* lacking the criterion of being due at a definite time. This term is our own coinage to encompass the *minority interest.*

indexation. An attempt by lawmakers or parties to a contract to cope with the effects of *inflation.* Amounts fixed in law or contracts are "indexed" when these amounts change as a given measure of price changes. For example, a so-called escalator clause (COLA—cost of living allowance or adjustment) in a labor contract might provide that hourly wages will be increased as the *Consumer Price Index* increases. Many economists have suggested the indexation of numbers fixed in the *income tax* laws. If, for example, the personal *exemption* is $1,000 at the start of the period, prices rise by 10 percent during the period, and the personal exemption is indexed, then the personal exemption would automatically rise to $1,100 (= $1,000 + .10 x $1,000) at the end of the period.

indirect cost pool. Any grouping of individual costs that is not identified with a *cost objective.*

indirect costs. Costs of production not easily associated with the production of specific goods and services; *overhead costs.* May be *allocated* on some arbitrary basis to specific products or departments.

indirect labor (material) cost. An *indirect cost* for labor (material) such as for supervisors (supplies).

indirect method. See *statement of cash flows.*

individual proprietorship. *Sole proprietorship.*

Industry Audit Guide. A series of publications by the *AICPA* providing specific accounting and *auditing principles* for specialized situations. Audit guides have been issued covering government contractors, state and local government units, investment companies, finance companies, brokers and dealers in securities, and many others.

inescapable cost. A *cost* that is not *avoidable.* A *cost* that is not *avoidable* because of an action. For example, if two operating rooms in a hospital are closed, but security is still employed, the security costs are "inescapable" with respect to the decision to close the operating rooms.

inflation. A time of generally rising prices.

inflation accounting. Strictly speaking, *constant dollar accounting.* Some writers use the term, incorrectly, to mean *current cost accounting.*

information system. A system, sometimes formal and sometimes informal, for collecting, processing, and communicating data that are useful for the managerial functions of decision making, planning, and control, and for financial reporting under the *attest* requirement.

insolvent. Unable to pay debts when due. Said of a company even though *assets* exceed *liabilities.*

installment. Partial payment of a debt or collection of a receivable, usually according to a contract.

installment contracts receivable. The name used for *accounts receivable* when the *installment method* of recognizing revenue is used. Its *contra account, unrealized gross margin,* is shown on the balance sheet as a subtraction from the amount receivable.

installment (sales) method. Recognizing *revenue* and *expense* (or *gross margin*) from a sales transaction in proportion to the fraction of the selling price collected during a period. Allowed by the *IRS* for income tax reporting, but acceptable in *GAAP (APB Opinion No. 10)* only when cash collections are uncertain. See *realized* (and *unrealized*) *gross margin.*

installment sales. Sales on account where the buyer promises to pay in several separate payments, called *installments.* Sometimes are, but need not be, accounted for on the *installment method.* If installment sales are accounted for with the sales *basis of revenue recognition* for financial reporting but with the installment method for income tax returns, then a *deferred income tax liability* arises.

Institute of Certified Management Accountants. See *ICMA.*

Institute of Internal Auditors. IIA. The national association of accountants who are engaged in internal auditing and are employed by business firms. Administers a comprehensive professional examination; those who pass qualify to be designated CIA, certified internal auditor.

insurance. A contract for reimbursement of specific losses; purchased with insurance premiums. Self-insurance is not insurance but merely the willingness to assume risk of incurring losses while saving the premium.

intangible asset. A nonphysical, *noncurrent* right that gives a firm an exclusive or preferred position in the marketplace. Examples are a *copyright, patent, trademark, goodwill, organization costs, capitalized* advertising cost, computer programs, licenses for any of the preceding, government licenses (e.g., broadcasting or the right to sell liquor), *leases,* franchises, mailing lists, exploration permits, import and export permits, construction permits, and marketing quotas.

Interamerican Accounting Association. An organization, headquartered in Mexico City, devoted to facilitating interaction between accounting practitioners in Central America, North America, and South America.

intercompany elimination. See *eliminations.*

intercompany profit. If one *affiliated company* sells to another, and the goods remain in the second company's *inventory* at the end of the period, then the first company's *profit* has not been realized by a sale to an outsider. That profit is called "intercompany profit" and is eliminated from net *income* in *consolidated income statements* or when the *equity method* is used.

intercompany transaction. *Transaction* between *parent company* and *subsidiary* or between subsidiaries in a *consolidated entity* whose effects are eliminated in preparing *consolidated financial statements.* See *intercompany profit.*

intercorporate investment. A given *corporation* owns *shares* or *debt* issued by another.

interdepartment monitoring. One of the advantages of allocating *service department costs* to *production departments* is that those charged with the costs will have an incentive to control the costs incurred in the service department.

interest. The charge or cost for using money; expressed as a rate per period, usually one year, called the "interest rate." See *effective interest rate* and *nominal interest rate.*

interest, imputed. If a borrower merely promises to pay a single amount, sometime later than the present, then the present value (computed at a *fair market* interest rate, called the "imputed interest rate") of the promise is less than the *face amount* to be paid at *maturity.* The difference between the face amount and the present value of a promise is called imputed interest. See also *imputed cost.*

interest factor. One plus the *interest* rate.

interest method. See *effective interest method.*

interest rate. See *interest.*

interfund accounts. In governmental accounting, the accounts that show transactions between funds, especially interfund receivables and payables.

interim statements. Statements issued for periods less than the regular, annual *accounting period.* Most corporations are required to issue interim statements on a quarterly basis. The basic issue in preparing interim reports is whether their purpose is to report on the interim period (1) as a self-contained accounting period or (2) as an integral part of the year of which they are a part so that forecasts of annual performance can be made. For example, assume that at the end of the first quarter, a retailer has depleted its *inventory* so that *LIFO cost of goods sold* is artificially low and *net income* is artificially high, relative to their amounts if purchases for inventory had been "normal" and equal to or greater than sales. The retailer expects to purchase inventory sufficiently large so that when cost of goods sold is computed for the year, there will be no *dips into old LIFO layers* and income will not be artificially high. Under the first approach, the quarterly income will be computed from cost of goods sold using data for the dips that have actually occurred by the end of the quarter. Under the second, quarterly income will be computed from cost of goods sold assuming that purchases were equal to "normal" amounts and that there are no dips into old LIFO layers. *APB Opinion No. 28* and the *SEC* require that interim reports be constructed largely to satisfy the second purpose.

internal audit. An *audit* conducted by employees to ascertain whether or not *internal control* procedures are working, as opposed to an external audit conducted by a *CPA.*

internal control. See *control system.*

internal rate of return. The discount rate that equates the net *present value* of a stream of cash outflows and inflows to zero.

internal reporting. Reporting for management's use in planning and control; contrast with *external reporting* for financial statement users.

Internal Revenue Service. IRS. Agency of the U.S. Treasury Department responsible for administering the Internal Revenue Code and collecting income, and certain other, taxes.

International Accounting Standards Committee. An organization that promotes the establishment of international accounting standards.

interperiod tax allocation. See *deferred income tax liability.*

interpolation. The estimation of an unknown number intermediate between two (or more) known numbers.

Interpretations of Statements of Financial Accounting Standards. See *FASB Interpretations.*

in the black (red). Operating at a profit (loss).

intrastatement tax allocation. See *tax allocation: intrastatement.*

inventoriable costs. *Costs* incurred that are added to the cost of manufactured products. *Product costs (assets)* as opposed to *period expenses.*

inventory. As a noun, the *balance* in an asset *account* such as raw materials, supplies, work in process, and finished goods. As a verb, to calculate the *cost* of goods on hand at a given time or to physically count items on hand.

inventory equation. *Beginning inventory* + net additions − withdrawals = ending inventory. Ordinarily, additions are net purchases and withdrawals are *cost of goods sold.* Notice that ending inventory, to be shown on the balance sheet, and cost of goods sold, to be shown on the income statement, are not independent of each other. The larger is one, the smaller must be the other. In valuing inventories, beginning inventory and net purchases are usually known. In some inventory methods (for example, some applications of the *retail inventory method*), costs of goods sold is measured and the equation is used to find the cost of ending inventory. In most methods, cost of ending inventory is measured and the equation is used to find the cost of goods sold (withdrawals). In *current cost* (in contrast to *historical cost*) accounting *additions* (in the equation) include holding gains, whether realized or not. Thus the current cost inventory equation is: Beginning Inventory (at Current Cost) + Purchases (where Current Cost is Historical Cost) + Holding Gains (whether Realized or Not) − Ending Inventory (at Current Cost) = Cost of Goods Sold (Current Cost).

inventory holding gains. See *inventory profit.*

inventory layer. See *LIFO inventory layer.*

inventory profit. This term has several possible meanings. Consider the data in the accompanying illustration. The *historical cost* data are derived in the conventional manner; the firm uses a *FIFO cost flow assumption.* The *current cost* data are assumed, but are of the kind that the FASB suggests in *SFAS No. 89.* The term *income from continuing operations* refers to revenues less expenses based on current, rather than historical, costs. To that subtotal add realized holding gains to arrive at realized (conventional) income. To that, add unrealized holding gains to arrive at *economic income.* The term "inventory profit" often refers (for example in some *SEC* releases) to the realized holding gain, $110 in the illustration. The amount of inventory profit will usually be material when FIFO is used and prices are rising. Others, including us, prefer to use the term "inventory profit" to refer to the total *holding gain,* $300 (= $110 + $190, both realized and unrealized), but this appears to be a lost cause. In periods of rising prices and increasing inventories, the realized holding gains under a FIFO cost flow assumption will be substantially larger than under LIFO. In the illustration, for example, assume under LIFO that the historical cost of goods sold is $4,800, that historical LIFO cost of beginning inventory is $600, and that historical LIFO cost of ending inventory is $800. Then income from continuing operations, based on current costs, remains $350 (= $5,200 −

Inventory Profit Illustration

	(Historical) Acquisition Cost Assuming FIFO	Current Cost
Assumed Data		
Inventory, 1/1	$ 900	$1,100
Inventory, 12/31	1,160	1,550
Cost of Goods Sold for Year.	4,740	4,850
Sales for Year.	$5,200	$5,200
INCOME STATEMENT FOR YEAR		
Sales	$5,200	$5,200
Cost of Goods Sold.	4,740	4,850
(1) Income from Continuing Operations		$ 350
Realized Holding Gains		110[a]
(2) Realized Income = Conventional Net Income (under FIFO)	$ 460	$ 460
Unrealized Holding Gain		190[b]
(3) Economic income		$ 650

[a]Realized holding gain during a period is current cost of goods sold less historical cost of goods sold; the realized holding gain for the year under FIFO is $110 = $4,850 − $4,740. Some refer to this as "inventory profit."

[b]The total unrealized holding gain at any time is current cost of inventory on hand at that time less historical cost of that inventory. The unrealized holding gain during a period is unrealized holding gain at the end of the period less the unrealized holding gain at the beginning of the period. Unrealized holding gain prior to this year is $200 = $1,000 − $900. Unrealized holding gain during this year = ($1,550 − $1,160) − ($1,100 − $900) = $390 − $200 = $190.

$4,850), realized holding gains are $50 (= $4,850 − $4,800), realized income is $400 (= $350 + $50), the unrealized holding gain for the year is $250 = ($1,550 − $800) − ($1,100 − $600), and economic income is $650 (= $350 + $50 + $250). Because the only real effect of the cost flow assumption is to split the total holding gain into realized and unrealized portions, economic income is the same, independent of the cost flow assumption. The total of holding gains is $300 in the illustration. The choice of cost flow assumption merely determines the portion reported as realized.

inventory turnover. Number of times the average *inventory* has been sold during a period; *cost of goods sold* for a period divided by average inventory for the period. See *ratio.*

invested capital. *Contributed capital.*

investee. A company whose *stock* is owned by another.

investing activities. Lending money and collecting *principal* (but not *interest*, which is an *operating activity*) on those loans; acquiring and selling *securities* or productive *assets* expected to produce *revenue* over several *periods*.

investment. An *expenditure* to acquire property or other assets in order to produce *revenue*; the *asset* so acquired; hence a *current* expenditure made in anticipation of future income. Said of *securities* of other companies held for the long term and shown in a separate section of the *balance sheet*; in this context, contrast with *marketable securities*.

investment center. A *responsibility center*, with control over *revenues, costs*, and *assets*.

investment credit. A reduction in income tax liability sometimes granted by the federal government to firms that buy new equipment. This item is a credit, in that it is deducted from the tax bill, not from pretax income. The tax credit has been a given percentage of the purchase price of certain assets purchased. The actual rules and rates have changed over the years. As of 1988, there is no investment credit. See *flow-through method* and *carryforward*.

investment tax credit. *Investment credit.*

investment turnover ratio. This term means the same thing as *total assets turnover ratio*, but is sometimes used for a *division*.

invoice. A document showing the details of a sale or purchase transaction.

IRR. *Internal rate of return.*

IRS. *Internal Revenue Service.*

isoprofit line. On a graph delimiting feasible production possibilities of two products that require the use of the same, limited resources, a line showing all feasible production possibility combinations with the same *profit* or, perhaps, *contribution margin*.

issue. When a corporation exchanges its stock (or bonds) for cash or other assets, the corporation is said to issue, not sell, that stock (or bonds). Also used in the context of withdrawing supplies or materials from inventory for use in operations and drawing of a *check*.

issued shares. Those shares of *authorized capital stock* of a *corporation* that have been distributed to the shareholders. See *issue*. Shares of *treasury stock* are legally issued but are not considered to be *outstanding* for the purpose of voting, *dividend declarations,* and *earnings-per-share* calculations.

J

job cost sheet. A schedule showing actual or budgeted inputs for a special order.

job development credit. The name used for the *investment credit* in the 1971 tax law, since repealed, on this subject.

job (-order) costing. Accumulation of *costs* for a particular identifiable batch of product, known as a job, as it moves through production.

joint cost. Cost of simultaneously producing or otherwise acquiring two or more products, called joint products, that must, by the nature of the process, be produced or acquired together, such as the cost of beef and hides of cattle. Generally, the joint costs of production are allocated to the individual products in proportion to their respective sales value at the *splitoff* point. Other examples include central *corporate expenses, overhead* of a department when several products are manufactured, and *basket purchases.* See *common cost.* See *sterilized allocation.*

joint cost allocation. See *joint cost.*

joint product. One of two or more outputs with significant value produced by a process that must be produced or acquired simultaneously. See *by-product* and *joint cost.*

journal. The place where transactions are recorded as they occur. The book of original entry.

journal entry. A recording in a *journal*, of equal *debits* and *credits*, with an explanation of the *transaction*, if necessary.

***Journal of Accountancy*.** A monthly publication of the *AICPA*.

***Journal of Accounting and Economics*.** Scholarly journal published three times a year by the Graduate School of Management of the University of Rochester.

***Journal of Accounting Research*.** Scholarly journal containing articles on theoretical and empirical aspects of accounting. Published three times a year by the Graduate School of Business of the University of Chicago.

journal voucher. A *voucher* documenting (and sometimes authorizing) a transaction, leading to an entry in the *journal.*

journalize. To make an entry in a *journal.*

just-in-time inventory (production); JIT. System of managing *inventory* for manufacturing where each component is purchased or manufactured just before it is used. Contrast with systems where many parts are acquired or manufactured in advance of needs. JIT systems have much smaller, ideally no, carrying costs for inventory, but run higher risks of incurring *stockout* costs.

K

kiting. This term means slightly different things in banking and auditing contexts. In both, however, it refers to the wrongful practice of taking advantage of the *float*, the time that elapses between the deposit of a *check* in one bank and its collection at another. In the banking context, an individual deposits in Bank A a check written on Bank B. He (or she) then writes checks against the deposit created in Bank A. Several days later, he deposits in Bank B a check written on Bank A, to cover the original check written on Bank B. Still later, he deposits in Bank A a check written on Bank B. The process of covering the deposit in Bank A with a check written on Bank B and vice versa is continued until an actual deposit of cash can be arranged. In the auditing context, kiting refers to a form of *window dressing* where the amount of the account Cash in Bank is made to appear larger than it actually is by depositing in Bank A a check written on Bank B without recording the check written on Bank B in the *check register* until after the close of the *accounting period*.

know-how. Technical or business information of the type defined under *trade secret*, but that is not maintained as a secret. The rules of accounting for this asset are the same as for other *intangibles*.

L

labor variances. The *price* (or *rate*) and *quantity* (or *usage*) *variances* for *direct labor* inputs in a *standard cost system*.

land. An *asset shown at acquisition cost* plus the *cost* of any nondepreciable *improvements*. In accounting, implies use as a plant or office site, rather than as a *natural resource*, such as timberland or farm land.

lapping (accounts receivable). The theft, by an employee, of cash sent in by a customer to discharge the latter's *payable*. The theft from the first customer is concealed by using cash received from a second customer. The theft from the second customer is concealed by using the cash received from a third customer, and so on. The process is continued until the thief returns the funds or can make the theft permanent by creating a fictitious *expense* or receivable write-off, or until the fraud is discovered.

lapse. To expire; said of, for example, an insurance policy or discounts made available for prompt payment that are not taken.

last-in, first-out. See *LIFO*.

layer. See *LIFO inventory layer*.

lead time. The time that elapses between placing an order and receipt of the *goods or services* ordered.

learning curve. A mathematical expression of the phenomenon that incremental unit costs to produce decrease as managers and labor gain experience from practice.

lease. A contract calling for the lessee (user) to pay the lessor (owner) for the use of an asset. A cancelable lease is one the lessee can cancel at any time. A noncancelable

lease requires payments from the lessee for the life of the lease and usually has many of the economic characteristics of *debt financing*. Most long-term noncancelable leases meet the usual criteria to be classified as a *liability* but some leases entered into before 1977 need not be shown as a liability. *SFAS No. 13* and the *SEC* require disclosure in notes to the financial statements of the commitments for long-term noncancelable leases. See *capital lease* and *operating lease*.

leasehold. The *asset* representing the right of the *lessee* to use leased property. See *lease* and *leasehold improvement*.

leasehold improvement. An *improvement* to leased property. Should be *amortized* over *service life* or the life of the lease, whichever is shorter.

least and latest rule. Pay the least amount of taxes as late as possible within the law to minimize the *present value* of tax payments for a given set of operations.

ledger. A book of accounts. See *general ledger* and *subsidiary ledger*; contrast with *journal*. Book of final entry.

legal capital. The amount of *contributed capital* that, according to state law, must remain permanently in the firm as protection for creditors.

legal entity. See *entity*.

lender. See *loan*.

lessee. See *lease*.

lessor. See *lease*.

letter stock. Privately placed *common shares*; so called because the *SEC* requires the purchaser to sign a letter of intent not to resell the shares.

leverage. "Operating leverage" refers to the tendency of *net income* to rise at a faster rate than sales when there are *fixed costs*. A doubling of sales, for example, usually implies a more than doubling of net income. "Financial leverage" (or "capital leverage") refers to the increased rate of return on *owners' equity* (see *ratio*) when an investment earns a return larger than the aftertax *interest rate* paid for *debt* financing. Because the interest charges on debt are usually fixed, any *incremental* income benefits owners and none benefits debtors. When "leverage" is used without a qualifying adjective, it usually refers to financial leverage and means the use of *long-term* debt in securing *funds* for the *entity*.

leveraged lease. A special form of lease involving three parties a *lender*, a *lessor*, and a *lessee*. The lender, such as a bank or insurance company, lends a portion, say 80 percent, of the cash required for acquiring the *asset*. The lessor puts up the remainder, 20 percent, of the cash required. The lessor acquires the asset with the cash, using the asset as security for the loan and leases it to the lessee on a *noncancelable* basis. The lessee makes periodic lease payments to the lessor, who in turn makes payments on the loan to the lender. Typically, the lessor has no obligation for the debt to the lender other than transferring a portion of the receipts from the lessee. If the lessee should default on required lease payments, then the lender can repossess the leased asset. The lessor is usually entitled to deductions for tax purposes for *depreciation* on the asset, for *interest expense* on the loan from the lender, and for any *investment credit*. The lease is leveraged in the sense that the lessor, who enjoys most of the risks and rewards of ownership, usually borrows most of the funds needed to acquire the asset. *See leverage.*

liability. An obligation to pay a definite (or reasonably definite) amount at a definite (or reasonably definite) time in return for a past or current benefit. That is, the obligation arises from other than an *executory contract*. A probable future sacrifice of economic benefits arising from present obligations of a particular *entity* to *transfer assets* or to provide services to other entities in the future as a result of past *transactions* or events. *SFAC No. 6* says that "probable" refers to that which can reasonably be expected or believed but is neither certain nor proved. A liability has three essential characteristics: (1) an obligation to transfer assets or services at a specified or determinable date, (2) the entity has little or no discretion to avoid the transfer, and (3) the event causing the obligation has already happened; that is, is not executory.

lien. The right of person A to satisfy a claim against person B by holding B's property as security or by seizing B's property.

life annuity. A *contingent annuity* in which payments cease at death of a specified person(s), usually the *annuitant(s)*.

LIFO. *Last-in, first-out.* An *inventory* flow assumption where the *cost of goods sold* is the cost of the most recently acquired units and the *ending inventory cost* is computed from costs of the oldest units; contrast with *FIFO*. In periods of rising prices and increasing inventories, LIFO leads to higher reported expenses and therefore lower reported income and lower balance sheet inventories than does FIFO. See also *FISH* and *inventory profit*.

LIFO conformity rule. The *IRS* requires that companies which use a *LIFO cost flow assumption for income taxes* also use LIFO in computing *income* reported in *financial statements* and forbids disclosure of *pro forma* results from using any other cost flow assumption.

LIFO, dollar-value method. See *dollar-value LIFO method*.

LIFO inventory layer. The *ending inventory* for a period is likely to be larger than the *beginning inventory*. Under a *LIFO cost flow assumption*, this increase in physical quantities is assigned a cost computed from the prices of the earliest purchases during the year. The LIFO inventory then consists of layers, sometimes called "slices," which typically consist of relatively small amounts of physical quantities from each of the past several years. Each layer carries the prices from near the beginning of the period when it was acquired. The earliest layers will typically (in periods of rising prices) have prices much less than current prices. If inventory quantities should decline in a subsequent period, the latest layers enter cost of goods sold first.

LIFO reserve. *Unrealized holding gain* in *ending inventory*: current or *FIFO historical* cost of ending inventory less LIFO *historical cost*. See *reserve*; a better term for this concept is "excess of current cost over LIFO historical cost."

limited liability. Shareholders of corporations are not personally liable for debts of the company.

limited partner. Member of a *partnership* not personally liable for debts of the partnership; every partnership must have at least one *general partner* who is fully liable.

line of business reporting. See *segment reporting*.

line of credit. An agreement with the bank or set of banks for short-term borrowings on demand.

linear programming. A mathematical tool for finding profit maximizing (or cost minimizing) combinations of products to produce when there are several products that can be produced but there are linear constraints on the resources available in the production processes or on maximum and minimum production requirements.

line-of-business reporting. See *segment reporting*.

liquid. Said of a business with a substantial amount (the amount is unspecified) of *working capital*, especially *quick assets*.

liquid assets. *Cash, current marketable securities*, and, sometimes, *current receivables*.

liquidating dividend. *Dividend* declared in the winding up of a business to distribute the assets of the company to the shareholders. Usually treated by recipient as a return of *investment*, not as *revenue*.

liquidation. Payment of a debt. Sale of assets in closing down a business or a segment thereof.

liquidation value per share. The amount each *share* of stock will receive if the corporation is dissolved. For *preferred stock* with a liquidation preference, a stated amount per share.

liquidity. Refers to the availability of *cash*, or near cash resources, for meeting a firm's obligations.

LISH. An acronym, conceived by George H. Sorter, for *last in, still here*. LISH is the same cost flow assumption as *FIFO*. Many readers of accounting statements find it easier to think about inventory questions in terms of items still on hand. Think of FIFO in connection with *cost of goods sold* but of LISH in connection with *ending inventory*. See *FISH*.

list price. The published or nominally quoted price for goods.

list price method. See *trade-in transaction*.

loan. An arrangement where the owner of property, called the lender, allows someone else, called the borrower, the use of the property for a period of time that is usually specified in the agreement setting up the loan. The borrower promises to return the property to the lender and, often, to make a payment for use of the property. Generally used when the property is *cash* and the payment for its use is *interest*.

long-lived (term) asset. An asset whose benefits are expected to be received over several years. A *noncurrent* asset, usually includes *investments*, *plant assets*, and *intangibles*.

long-run. long-term. A term denoting a time or time periods in the future. How far in the future depends on context. For some securities traders, "long-term" can mean anything beyond the next hour or two. For most managers, it means anything beyond the next year or two. For government policy makers, it can mean anything beyond the next decade or two.

long-term (construction) contract accounting. The *percentage of completion method* of *revenue* recognition. Sometimes used to mean the *completed contract method*.

long-term debt ratio. *Noncurrent liabilities* divided by total *assets*.

long-term liability (debt). *Noncurrent liability*.

long-term solvency risk. The risk that a firm will not have sufficient *cash* to pay its *debts* sometime in the *long-run*.

loophole. Imprecise term meaning a technicality allowing a taxpayer (or *financial statements*) to circumvent a law's (or *GAAP*'s) intent without violating its letter.

loss. Excess of *cost* over net proceeds for a single transaction; negative *income* for a period. A cost expiration that produced no *revenue*. See *gain* for a discussion of related and contrasting terms.

loss contingency. See *contingency*.

lower of cost or market. A basis for valuation of *inventory* or *marketable equity securities*. The inventory value is set at the lower of *acquisition cost* or *current replacement cost* (market), subject to the following constraints: First, the market value of an item used in the computation cannot exceed its *net realizable value*—an amount equal to selling price less reasonable costs to complete production and to sell the item. Second, the market value of an item used in the computation cannot be less than the net realizable value minus the normal *profit* ordinarily realized on disposition of completed items of this type. The lower-of-cost-or-market valuation is chosen as the lower of acquisition *cost* or replacement cost *(market)* subject to the upper and lower bounds on replacement cost established in the first two steps. Thus,

Market Value = Midvalue of (Replacement Cost, Net Realizable Value, Net Realizable Value less Normal Profit Margin)

Lower-of-Cost or-Market Valuation = Minimum (Acquisition Cost, Market Value).

The accompanying exhibit illustrates the calculation of the lower-of-cost-or-market valuation for four inventory items. Notice that each of the four possible outcome occurs once in determining lower of cost or market. Item 1 uses acquisition cost; item 2 uses net realizable value; item 3 uses replacement cost; and item 4 uses net realizable value less normal profit.

	Item			
	1	**2**	**3**	**4**
Calculation of Market Value				
(a) Replacement Cost	$92	$96	$92	$96
(b) Net Realizable Value	95	95	95	95
(c) Net Realizable Value Less Normal Profit Margin [= (b) − $9]	86	86	86	86
(d) Market = Midvalue [(a), (b), (c)]	92	95	92	95
Calculation of Lower of Cost or Market				
(e) Acquisition Cost.	90	97	96	90
(f) Market [= (d)].	92	95	92	95
(g) Lower of Cost or Market = Minimum [(e), (f)]	90	95	92	90

Lower of cost or market cannot be used for inventory on tax returns in a combination with a *LIFO cost flow assumption*. In the context of inventory, once the asset is written down, a new "original cost" basis is established and subsequent increases in market value are ignored in the accounts.

In the context of *marketable equity securities* the method is applied separately to short-term and long-term portfolios of securities. Losses in market value on the short-term portfolio (and any subsequent recoveries in value up to original cost) are reported as part of *income from continuing operations* for the period. For the long-term portfolio, the losses (and subsequent recoveries, if any) are *debited* (or *credited*) directly to an *owners' equity contra account*.

Note that hyphens are not used when the term is used as a noun but hyphens are used when the term is used as an adjectival phrase.

lump-sum acquisition. *Basket purchase*.

M

MD&A. *Management discussion and analysis* section of *financial statements*.

maintenance. *Expenditures* undertaken to preserve an *asset's* service potential for its originally intended life; these expenditures are treated as *period expenses* or *product costs*; contrast with *improvement*. See *repair*.

make-or-buy decision. A managerial decision about whether the firm should produce a product internally or purchase it from others. Proper make-or-buy decisions in the short run result when *incremental costs* are the only costs considered in decision making.

maker (of note) (of check). One who signs a *note* to borrow. One who signs a *check*; in this context synonymous with drawer; see *draft*.

management. Executive authority that operates a business.

management accounting. See *managerial accounting*.

Management Accounting. Monthly publication of the *NAA*.

management audit. An audit conducted to ascertain whether the objectives, policies, and procedures for a firm or one of its operating units are properly carried out. Generally applies only to activities for which qualitative standards can be specified. See *audit* and *internal audit*.

management by exception. A principle of management where attention is focused on performance only if it differs significantly from that expected.

management discussion and analysis. A discussion of management's views of the company's performance required by the *SEC* since 1980 to be included in the *10-K* and in the *annual report* to shareholders. The information typically contains discussion of such items and liquidity, results of *operations*, *segments*, and the effects of *inflation*.

managerial (management) accounting. Reporting designed to enhance the ability of management to do its job of decision making, planning, and control; contrast with *financial accounting*.

manufacturing cost. Cost of producing goods, usually in a factory.

manufacturing expense. An imprecise, and generally incorrect, alternative title for *manufacturing overhead*.

manufacturing overhead. General manufacturing *costs* incurred in providing a capacity to carry on productive activities but that are not directly associated with identifiable units of product. *Fixed* manufacturing overhead costs are treated as a *product cost* under *absorption costing* but as an *expense* of the period under *direct costing*.

margin. *Revenue* less specified expenses. See *contribution margin*, *gross margin*, and *current margin*.

margin of safety. Excess of actual, or budgeted, sales over *breakeven* sales. Usually expressed in dollars; may be expressed in units of product.

marginal cost. The *incremental cost* or *differential cost* of the last unit added to production or the first unit subtracted from production. See *cost terminology*.

marginal costing. *Direct costing*.

marginal revenue. The increment in *revenue* from sale of one additional unit of product.

marginal tax rate. The tax imposed on the next dollar of taxable income generated; contrast with *average tax rate*.

markdown. See *markup* for definition and contrast.

markdown cancellation. See *markup* for definition and contrast.

market-based transfer price. A *transfer price* based on external market, rather than internal company, data.

market price. See *fair market price*.

market rate. The rate of *interest* a company must pay to borrow *funds* currently. See *effective rate*.

marketable equity securities. *Marketable securities* representing *owners' equity* interest in other companies, rather than *loans* to them.

marketable securities. *Stocks* and *bonds* of other companies held that can be readily sold on stock exchanges or over-the-counter markets and that the company plans to sell as cash is needed. Classified as *current assets* and as part of "cash" in preparing the *statement of cash flows*. The same securities held for *long-term* purposes would be classified as *noncurrent assets*. SFAS No. 12 requires the *lower-of-cost-or-market* valuation basis for all marketable equity securities but different accounting treatments (with differing effect on income) depending upon whether the security is a *current* or a *noncurrent asset*.

markon. See *markup* for definition and contrast.

markup. When a retailer acquires items for *inventory*, the items are given a selling price. The difference between the original selling price and cost is most precisely called "markon," although many business people use the term "markup," and because of confusion of this use of "markup" with its precise definition (see below), "original markup" is sometimes used. If the originally established retail price is increased, the precise term for the amount of price increase is "markup," although "additional markup" is sometimes used. If a selling price is lowered, the terms "markdown" and "markup cancellation" are used. "Markup cancellation" refers to reduction ir price following "additional markups" and can, by definition, be no more than the amount of the additional markup; "cancellation of additional markup," although not used, is descriptive. "Markdown" refers to price reductions from the original retail price. A price increase after a markdown is a "markdown cancellation." If original cost is $12 and original selling price is $20, then markon (original markup) is $8; if the price is later increased to $24, the $4 increase is markup (additional markup); if the price is later lowered to $21, the $3 reduction is markup cancellation; if price is lowered further to $17, the $4 reduction comprises $1 markup cancellation and $3 markdown; if price is later increased to $22, the $5 increase comprises $3 of markdown cancellation and $2 of markup (additional markup). Markup cancellations and markdowns are separately counted because the former are deducted (while the latter are not) in computing the selling prices of goods available for sale for the denominator of the *cost percentage* used in the conventional *retail inventory method*.

markup cancellation. See *markup* for definition and contrast.

markup percentage. *Markup* divided by (acquisition cost plus *markup*).

master budget. A *budget* projecting all *financial statements* and their components.

matching convention. The concept of recognizing cost expirations *(expenses)* in the same accounting period when the related *revenues* are recognized. Combining or simultaneously recognizing the revenues and expenses that jointly result from the same *transactions* or other events.

material. As an adjective, it means relatively important. See *materiality*. Currently, no operational definition exists. As a noun, *raw material*.

material variances. *Price* and *quantity variances* for *direct materials* in *standard cost systems*. Sometimes used to mean variances that are significant; see *materiality*.

materiality. The concept that accounting should disclose separately only those events that are relatively important (no operable definition yet exists) for the business or for understanding its statements. *SFAC No. 2* suggests that accounting information is material if "the judgment of a reasonable person relying on the information would have been changed or influenced by the omission or misstatement."

matrix. A rectangular array of numbers or mathematical symbols.

matrix inverse. For a given square *matrix* **A**, *the square matrix inverse is the matrix*, A^{-1}, such that $AA^{-1} = A^{-1}A = I$, the *identity matrix*. Not all square matrices have inverses. Those that do not are called "singular"; those that do are nonsingular.

maturity. The date at which an obligation, such as the *principal* of a *bond* or a *note*, becomes due.

maturity value. The amount expected to be collected when a loan reaches *maturity*. Depending upon the context, the amount may be *principal* or principal and *interest*.

measuring unit. See *attribute measured* for definition and contrast.

merchandise. *Finished goods* bought by a retailer or wholesaler for resale; contrast with finished goods of a manufacturing business.

merchandise turnover. *Inventory turnover* for merchandise; see *ratio*.

merchandising business. As opposed to a manufacturing or service business, one that purchases (rather than manufactures) *finished goods* for resale.

merger. The joining of two or more businesses into a single *economic entity*. See *holding company*.

minority interest. A *balance sheet account* on *consolidated statements* showing the *equity* in a less-than-100-percent-owned *subsidiary* company allocable to those who are not part of the controlling (majority) interest. May be classified either as shareholders' equity or as a liability of *indeterminate term* on the consolidated balance sheet. On the *income statement*, the minority's interest in current period's income of the less-than-100-percent-owned subsidiary must be subtracted to arrive at consolidated *net income* for the period.

minority investment. A holding of less than 50 percent of the *voting stock* in another corporation. Accounted for with the *equity method* when sufficient shares are owned so that the investor can exercise "significant influence," and with the *lower-of-cost-or-market* otherwise. See *mutual fund*.

minutes book. A record of all actions authorized at corporate *board of director's* or shareholders' meetings.

mix variance. Many *standard cost* systems specify combinations of inputs, for example, labor of a certain skill and materials of a certain quality grade. Sometimes combinations of inputs used differ from those contemplated by the standard. The mix variance attempts to report the cost change caused by changing the combination of inputs.

mixed cost. A *semifixed* or a *semivariable* cost.

modified cash basis. The *cash basis of accounting* with long-term assets accounted for with the *accrual basis of accounting*. Most uses of the term "cash basis of accounting" actually mean "modified cash basis."

monetary assets and liabilities. See *monetary items*.

monetary gain or loss. The *gain* or *loss* in *general purchasing power* as a result of holding *monetary assets* or liabilities during a period when the *general purchasing power of the dollar* changes. During periods of *inflation*, holders of net monetary assets lose, and holders of net monetary liabilities gain, general purchasing power. During periods of *deflation*, holders of net monetary assets gain, and holders of net monetary liabilities lose, general purchasing power. Explicitly reported in *constant dollar accounting*.

monetary items. Amounts fixed in terms of dollars by statute or contract. *Cash, accounts receivable, accounts payable*, and *debt*. The distinction between monetary and nonmonetary items is important for *constant dollar accounting* and for *foreign exchange gain* or *loss* computations. In the foreign exchange context, account amounts denominated in dollars are not monetary items, whereas amounts denominated in any other currency are monetary.

money. A word seldom used with precision in accounting, at least in part because economists have not yet agreed on its definition. Economists use the term to refer to both a medium of exchange and a unit of value. See *cash* and *monetary items*.

money purchase plan. A *pension plan* where the employer contributes a specified amount of cash each year to each employee's pension fund. Benefits ultimately received by the employee are not specifically defined but depend on the rate of return on the cash invested. Sometimes called a "defined-contribution" pension plan; contrast with *defined-benefit plan*. As of the mid-1980's most corporate pension plans were defined-benefit plans because both the law and *generally accepted accounting principles* for pensions made defined-benefit plans more attractive than money purchase plans. *ERISA* makes money purchase plans relatively more attractive than they had been. We expect the relative number of money purchase plans to increase.

mortality table. Data of life expectancies or probabilities of death for persons of specified ages and sex.

mortgage. A claim given by the borrower (mortgagor) to the lender (mortgagee) against the borrower's property in return for a loan.

moving average. An *average* computed on observations over time. As a new observation becomes available, the oldest one is dropped so that the average is always computed for the same number of observations and only the most recent ones. Sometimes, however, this term is used synonymously with *weighted average*.

moving average method. *Weighted-average method.*

multiple-step. Said of an *income statement* where various classes of *expenses* and *losses* are subtracted from *revenues* to show intermediate items such as *operating income*, income of the enterprise (operating income plus *interest* income), income to investors (income of the enterprise less *income taxes*), net income to shareholders (income to investors less interest charges), and income retained (income to shareholders less dividends). See *entity theory*.

municipal bond. A *bond* issued by a village, town, or city. *Interest* on such bonds is generally exempt from federal *income taxes* and from some state income taxes. Because bonds issued by state and county governments often have these characteristics, such bonds are often called "municipals" as well. Sometimes referred to as "tax exempts."

mutual fund. An investment company that issues its own stock to the public and uses the proceeds to invest in securities of other companies. A mutual fund usually owns less than five or ten percent of the stock of any one company and accounts for its investments using current *market values*; contrast with *holding company*.

mutually exclusive projects. Competing investment projects, where accepting one project eliminates the possibility of undertaking the remaining projects.

N

NAARS. *National Automated Accounting Research System.*

NASDAQ. National Association of Securities Dealers Automated Quotation System; a computerized system to provide brokers and dealers with price quotations for securities traded *over the counter* as well as for some *NYSE* securities.

National Association of Accountants. NAA. A national society generally open to all engaged in activities closely associated with *managerial accounting*. Oversees the administration of the *CMA* Examinations through the *Institute of Certified Management Accountants*.

National Automated Accounting Research System. NAARS. A computer based information retrieval system containing, among other things, the complete text of most public corporate annual reports and *Forms 10-K*. The system is available to users through the *AICPA*.

natural business year. A 12-month period chosen as the reporting period so that the end of the period coincides with a low point in activity or inventories. See *ratio* for a discussion of analyses of financial statements of companies using a natural business year.

natural classification. *Income statement* reporting form in which *expenses* are classified by nature of items as acquired, that is, materials, wages, salaries, insurance, and taxes, as well as depreciation; contrast with *functional classification*.

natural resources. Timberland, oil and gas wells, ore deposits, and other products of nature that have economic value. The cost of natural resources is subject to *depletion*. Natural resources are "nonrenewable" (for example, oil, coal, gas, ore deposits) or "renewable" (timberland, sod fields); the former are often called "wasting assets." See also *reserve recognition accounting* and *percentage depletion*.

negative confirmation. See *confirmation*.

negative goodwill. Refer to *goodwill*. When the purchase price of the company acquired is less than the sum of the *fair market value* of the *net assets* acquired, *APB Opinion No. 16* requires that the valuation of noncurrent assets (except *investments* in *marketable securities*) acquired be reduced until the purchase price equals the adjusted valuation of the fair market value of net assets acquired. If, after the adjusted valuation of noncurrent assets is reduced to zero, the purchase price is still less than the net assets acquired, then the difference is shown as a credit balance in the balance sheet as negative goodwill and is amortized to income over a period not to exceed forty years. For negative goodwill to exist, someone must be willing to sell a company for less than the fair market value of net current assets and marketable securities. Because such a bargain purchase is rare, negative goodwill is rarely found in the financial statements; when it does appear, it generally signals un-recorded obligations, such as for *pensions* or contingent liability in a law suit.

negotiable. Legally capable of being transferred by endorsement. Usually said of *checks* and *notes* and sometimes of *stocks* and *bearer bonds*.

negotiated transfer price. A *transfer price* set jointly by the buying and selling divisions.

net. Reduced by all relevant deductions.

net assets. *Owners' equity*; total *assets* minus total *liabilities*.

net bank position. From a firm's point of view, *cash* in a specific bank less *loans* payable to that bank.

net current assets. *Working capital = current assets − current liabilities*.

net current asset value (per share). *Working capital* divided by the number of common shares outstanding. Many security analysts think that when a common share trades in the market for an amount less than net current asset value, then the shares are undervalued and should be purchased. We find this view naive because it ignores the efficiency of capital markets generally and, specifically, unrecorded obligations such as for some *pension plans*, not currently reported as liabilities in the *balance sheet* under *GAAP*.

net income. The excess of all *revenues* and *gains* for a period over all *expenses* and *losses* of the period. See *comprehensive income*.

net loss. The excess of all *expenses* and *losses* for a period over all *revenues* and *gains* of the period. Negative *net income*.

net markup. In the context of *retail inventory methods, markups* less markup cancellations; a figure that usually ignores *markdowns* and markdown cancellations.

net of tax method. A nonsanctioned method for dealing with the problem of *income tax allocation*; described in *APB Opinion No. 11*. Deferred tax items are subtracted from specific *asset* amounts rather than being shown as a *liability*.

net of tax reporting. Reporting, such as for *income from discontinued operations, extraordinary items*, and *prior-period adjustments*, where the amounts presented in *financial statements* have been adjusted for all income tax effects. For example, if an extraordinary loss amounted to $10,000 and the marginal tax rate were 40 percent, then the extraordinary item would be reported "net of taxes" as a $6,000 loss. Hence, all income taxes may not be reported on one line of the income statement. The taxes will be allocated to *income from continuing operations, income from discontinued operations, extraordinary items*, cumulative effects of *accounting changes*, and *prior-period adjustments*.

net operating profit. Income from *continuing operations*.

net present value. Discounted or *present value* of all cash inflows and outflows of a project or from an *investment* at a given *discount rate*.

net price method (of recording purchase or sales discounts). The *purchase* (or *sale*) is recorded at its *invoice* price less all *discounts* made available under the assumption that nearly all discounts will be taken. Discounts lapsed through failure to pay promptly are debited to an *expense* account. For purchases, management usually prefers to know about the amount of discounts lost because of inefficient operations, not the amounts taken, so that most managers prefer the net price method to the *gross price method*.

net realizable (sales) value. A method for *allocating joint costs* in proportion to *realizable values* of the joint products. For example, joint products A and B together cost $100 and A sells for $60 whereas B sells for $90. Then A would be allocated ($60/$150) x $100 = .40 x $100 = $40 of cost while B would be allocated ($90/$150) x $100 = $60 of cost.

net sales. Sales (at gross invoice amount) less *returns, allowances*, freight paid for customers, and *discounts* taken.

net working capital. *Working capital*; the "net" is redundant in accounting. Financial analysts sometimes mean *current assets* when they speak of working capital, so for them the "net" is not redundant.

net worth. A misleading term, to be avoided, that means the same as *owners' equity*.

New York Stock Exchange. NYSE. A public market where various corporate *securities* are traded.

next in, first out. See *NIFO*.

NIFO. *Next in, first out*. In making decisions, many managers consider *replacement costs* (rather than *historical costs*) and refer to them as NIFO costs.

no par. Said of *stock* without a *par value*.

nominal accounts. Temporary accounts, such as *revenue* and *expense* accounts, as opposed to *balance sheet accounts*. All nominal accounts are *closed* at the end of each accounting period.

nominal amount (value). An amount stated in dollars, in contrast to an amount stated in *constant dollars*. Contrast with *real amount (value)*.

nominal dollars. The measuring unit giving no consideration to differences in the *general purchasing power of the dollar* over time. The face amount of currency or coin, a *bond*, an *invoice*, a *receivable* is a nominal dollar amount. When that amount is adjusted for changes in *general purchasing power*, it is converted into a *constant dollar* amount.

nominal interest rate. A rate specified on a *debt* instrument, which usually differs from the market or *effective* *rate.* Also, a rate of *interest* quoted for a year. If the interest is compounded more often than annually, then the *effective interest rate* is higher than the nominal rate.

noncancelable. See *lease.*

nonconsolidated subsidiary. An *intercorporate investment* where more than 50 percent of the shares of the *subsidiary* are owned but the investment is accounted for with the *cost method* or *lower-of-cost-or-market method.*

noncontributory. Said of a *pension plan* where only the employer makes payments to a pension *fund*; contrast with *contributory.*

noncontrollable cost. A cost that is not *controllable* by a particular manager.

noncurrent. Due more than one year (or more than one *operating cycle*) hence.

nonexpendable fund. A governmental fund, whose *principal*, and sometimes earnings, may not be spent.

non-interest-bearing note. A *note* that bears no explicit interest. The *present value* of such a note at any time before *maturity* is less than the *face value* so long as *interest rates* are positive. *APB Opinion No. 21* requires that the present value, not face value, of long-term non-interest-bearing notes be reported as the *asset* or *liability* amount in financial statements. For this purpose, the *historical interest rate* is used. See *interest, imputed.*

nonmanufacturing costs. All *costs* incurred other than those to produce goods.

nonmonetary items. All items that are not monetary; see *monetary items.*

nonoperating. In the *income statement* context, said of revenues and expenses arising from transactions incidental to the company's main line(s) of business. In the *statement of cash flows* context, said of all sources or uses of cash other than cash provided by operations. See *operations.*

nonprofit corporation. An incorporated *entity*, such as a hospital, with owners who do not share in the earnings. It usually emphasizes providing services rather than maximizing income.

nonrecurring. Said of an event that is not expected to happen often for a given firm. Under *APB Opinion No. 30*, the effects of such events should be disclosed separately, but as part of *ordinary* items unless the event is also unusual. See *extraordinary* item.

normal cost. Former name for *service cost.*

normal costing. Method of charging costs to products using actual *direct materials*, actual *direct labor*, and predetermined *factory overhead* rates.

normal costing system. *Costing* based on *actual material* and *labor* costs, but using *predetermined overhead* rates

per unit of some *activity basis* (such as *direct labor hours* or machine hours) to apply overhead to production. This rate for overhead to be charged to production is decided at the start of the period. At the end of the period it is multiplied by the actual number of units of the base activity (such as actual direct labor hours worked or actual machine hours used during the period) to apply overhead to production.

normal spoilage. Costs incurred because of ordinary amounts of spoilage; such costs should be prorated to units produced as *product costs*; contrast with *abnormal spoilage.*

normal standard cost. normal standards. The *cost* expected to be incurred under reasonably efficient operating conditions with adequate provision for an average amount of rework, spoilage, and the like.

normal volume. The level of production over a time span, usually 1 year, that will satisfy demand by purchasers and provide for reasonable *inventory* levels.

note. An unconditional written promise by the maker (borrower) to pay a certain amount on demand or at a certain future time. See *footnotes* for another context.

note receivable discounted. A *note* assigned by the holder to another. The new holder of the note typically pays the old holder an amount less than the *face value* of the note; hence the word "discounted." But this word is used even if the payment by the new holder to the old is at or above face value. If the note is assigned with recourse, it is the *contingent liability* of the assignor until the debt is paid. See *factoring.*

NOW account. Negotiable order of withdrawal. A *savings account* on which orders to pay, much like *checks* but technically not checks, can be drawn and given to others who can redeem the order at the savings institution.

number of days sales in inventory (or receivables). Days of average inventory on hand (or average collection period for receivables). See *ratio.*

NYSE. *New York Stock Exchange.*

O

OASD(H)I. *Old Age, Survivors, Disability, and (Hospital) Insurance.*

objective. See *reporting objective* and *objectivity.*

objective function. In *linear programming*, the name of the profit or cost criterion to be optimized.

objectivity. The reporting policy implying that formal recognition will not be given to an event in financial statements until the magnitude of the events can be measured with reasonable accuracy and is subject to independent verification.

obsolescence. A decline in *market value* of an *asset* caused by improved alternatives becoming available that will be more *cost effective*; the decline in market value is unrelated to physical changes in the asset itself. See *partial obsolescence*.

Occupational Safety and Health Act. *OSHA*.

off-balance-sheet financing. A description often used for an obligation meeting all the tests to be a liability, except that the obligation arises from an *executory contract* and, hence, is not a *liability*. Consider the following example.

Miller Corporation desires to acquire land costing $25 million, on which it will build a shopping center. It could borrow the $25 million from its bank, paying interest at 12 percent, and buy the land outright from the seller. If so, both an asset and a liability will appear on the balance sheet. Instead, it borrows $5 million and purchases for $5 million from the seller an *option* to buy the land from the seller at any time within the next 6 years for a price of $20 million. The option costs Miller Corporation $5 million immediately and provides for continuing "option" payments of $2.4 million per year, which is just equal to Miller Corporation's borrowing rate multiplied by the remaining purchase price of the land: $2.4 million = .12 x $20 million. Although Miller Corporation need not continue payments and can let the option lapse at any time, it also has an obligation to begin developing on the site immediately. Because Miller Corporation has invested a substantial sum in the option, will invest more, and will begin immediately developing the land, Miller Corporation is almost certain to exercise its option before it expires. The seller of the land can take the option contract to the bank and borrow $20 million, paying interest at Miller Corporation's borrowing rate, 12 percent per year. The continuing option payments from Miller Corporation will be sufficient to enable the seller to make its payments to the bank. *Generally accepted accounting principles* view Miller Corporation as having acquired an option for $5 million, rather than having acquired land costing $25 million in return for $5 million of "debt" off the balance sheet until it borrows more funds to exercise the option.

Old Age, Survivors, Disability, and (Hospital) Insurance. The technical name for Social Security under the Federal Insurance Contribution Act (FICA).

on (open) account. Said of a *purchase* or *sale* when payment is expected sometime after delivery and no *note* evidencing the *debt* is given or received. The purchaser has generally signed an agreement sometime in the past promising to pay for such purchases according to an agreed time schedule. When a sale (purchase) is made on open account, *Accounts Receivable (Payable)* is *debited (credited)*.

on consignment. Said of goods delivered by the owner (the consignor) to another (the consignee) to be sold by the consignee; the owner is entitled to the return of the property or payment of an amount agreed upon in advance. The goods are assets of the consignor. Such arrangements provide the consignor with better protection than an outright *sale on account* to the consignee in case the consignee becomes bankrupt. In event of *bankruptcy*, the consignor can reclaim the goods, without going through lengthy bankruptcy proceedings from which the consignor might recover only a small percentage of the amounts owed to it.

one-line consolidation. Said of an *intercorporate investment* accounted for with the *equity method*. The effects of this method on reported *income* and *balance sheet* total *assets* and *equities* are identical to those that would appear if the investee firm were consolidated, even though the income from the investment appears on a single line of the income statement and the net investment appears on a single line in the assets section of the balance sheet.

open account. Any *account* with a nonzero *debit* or *credit* balance. See *on (open) account*.

operating. An adjective used to refer to *revenue* and *expense* items relating to the company's main line(s) of business. See *operations*.

operating accounts. *Revenue, expense,* and *production cost accounts*; contrast with *balance sheet accounts*.

operating activities. See *operations*. For purposes of the *statement of cash flows*, all *transactions* and *events* that are neither *financing activities* nor *investing activities*.

operating budget. A formal *budget* for the *operating cycle* or for a year.

operating cycle. *Earnings cycle*.

operating expenses. *Expenses* incurred in the course of *ordinary* activities of an *entity*. Frequently, a classification including only *selling, general,* and *administrative expenses*, thereby excluding *cost of goods sold, interest,* and *income tax* expenses. See *operations*.

operating lease. A *lease* accounted for by the *lessee* without showing an *asset* for the lease rights (*leasehold*) or a *liability* for the lease payment obligations. Rental payments of the lessee are merely shown as *expenses* of the period. The asset remains on the lessor's *books* where rental collections appear as *revenues*; contrast with *capital lease*.

operating leverage. Usually said of a firm with a large proportion of *fixed costs* in its *total costs*. Consider a book publisher or a railroad; the *incremental costs* of producing another book or transporting another freight car are much less than *average cost*, so the *gross margin* upon sale of the unit is relatively large. Contrast, for example, a grocery store, where the *contribution margin* is usually less than 5 percent of the selling price. For firms with equal profitability, however defined, the one with the larger percentage increase in income from a given percentage increase in unit sales is said to have the larger operating leverage. See *leverage* for contrast of this term with "financial leverage." See *cost terminology* for definition of terms involving the word "cost."

operating margin (based on current costs). *Revenues* from *sales* minus *current cost* of goods sold. A measure of operating efficiency that is independent of the *cost flow assumption* for *inventory*. Sometimes called "current (gross) margin.'' See *inventory profit* for illustrative computations.

operating ratio. See *ratio.*

operational control. See *control system.*

operations. A word not precisely defined in *accounting.* Generally, operating activities (producing and selling *goods* or *services*) are distinguished from financing activities (raising funds) and *investing activities.* Acquiring goods on account and then paying for them in one month, though generally classified as an operating activity, has the characteristics of a financing activity. Or consider the transaction of selling plant assets for a price in excess of book value. On the *income statement,* the gain is part of income from operations (continuing operations or discontinued operations, depending on the circumstances) but on the *statement of cash flows,* all of the funds received on disposition are reported below the ''cash from operations'' section, as a nonoperating source of cash, disposition of noncurrent assets. In income tax accounting an ''operating loss'' results whenever deductions are greater than taxable revenues.

opinion. The *auditor's report* containing an attestation or lack thereof. Also, *APB Opinion.*

opinion paragraph. Section of *auditor's report,* generally following the *scope paragraph,* giving the auditor's conclusion that the *financial statements* are (rarely, are not) in accordance with *GAAP* and present fairly the *financial position,* changes in financial position, and the results of *operations.*

opportunity cost. The *present value* of the *income* (or *costs)* that could be earned (or saved) from using an *asset* in its best alternative use to the one being considered.

option. The legal right to buy something during a specified period at a specified price, called the *exercise* price. Employee stock options should not be confused with *put* and *call* options traded in various public markets.

ordinary annuity. An *annuity in arrears.*

ordinary income. For income tax purposes, reportable *income* not qualifying as *capital gains.*

organization costs. The *costs* incurred in planning and establishing an *entity*; example of an *intangible* asset. Often, since the amounts are not *material,* the costs are treated as *expenses* in the period incurred even though the *expenditures* clearly provide future benefits and meet the test to be *assets.*

original cost. *Acquisition cost.* In public utility accounting, the acquisition cost of the *entity* first devoting the asset to public use. See *aboriginal cost.*

original entry. Entry in a *journal.*

OSHA. Occupational Safety and Health Act. The federal law that governs working conditions in commerce and industry.

outlay. The amount of an *expenditure.*

outlier. Said of an observation (or data point) which appears to differ significantly in some regard from other observations (or data points) of supposedly the same phenomenon. Often used in describing the results of a *regression analysis* when an observation is not ''near'' the fitted regression equation.

out-of-pocket. Said of an *expenditure* usually paid for with cash. An *incremental* cost.

out-of-stock cost. The estimated decrease in future *profit* as a result of losing customers because insufficient quantities of *inventory* are currently on hand to meet customers' demands.

output. Physical quantity or monetary measurement of *goods* and *services* produced.

outside director. A member of a corporate board of directors who is not a company officer and does not participate in the corporation's day-to-day management.

outstanding. Unpaid or uncollected. When said of *stock,* the shares issued less *treasury stock.* When said of checks, it means a check issued that did not clear the *drawer's* bank prior to the *bank statement* date.

over-and-short. Title for an *expense account* used to account for small differences between book balances of cash and actual cash and vouchers or receipts in *petty cash* or *change funds.*

overapplied (overabsorbed) overhead. An excess of costs applied, or *charged,* to product for a period over actual *overhead costs* during the period. A *credit balance* in an overhead account after overhead is assigned to product.

overdraft. A check written on a checking account that contains funds less than the amount of the check.

overhead costs. Any *cost* not directly associated with the production or sale of identifiable goods and services. Sometimes called ''burden'' or ''indirect costs'' and, in Britain, ''oncosts.'' Frequently limited to manufacturing overhead. See *central corporate expenses* and *manufacturing overhead.*

overhead rate. Standard, or other predetermined rate at which *overhead costs* are applied to products or to services.

over-the-counter. Said of a *security* traded in a negotiated transaction, rather than in an auctioned one on an organized stock exchange, such as the *New York Stock Exchange.*

owners' equity. *Proprietorship; assets* minus *liabilities; paid-in capital* plus *retained earnings* of a corporation; partners' capital accounts in a *partnership*; owner's capital account in a *sole proprietorship.*

P

P & L. Profit and loss statement; *income statement*.

paid-in capital. Sum of balances in *capital stock* and *capital contributed in excess of par (or stated) value* accounts. Same as *contributed capital* (minus *donated capital*). Some use the term to mean only *capital contributed in excess of par (or stated value)*.

paid-in surplus. See *surplus*.

paper profit. A *gain* not yet realized through a *transaction*. An *unrealized holding gain*.

par. See *at par* and *face amount*.

par value. *Face amount* of a *security*.

par value method. The method of accounting for *treasury stock* that *debits* a common stock account with the *par value* of the shares required and allocates the remaining debits between the *additional paid-in capital* and *retained earnings* accounts; contrast with *cost method*.

parent company. Company owning more than 50 percent of the voting shares of another company, called the *subsidiary*.

partial obsolescence. As technology improves, the economic value of existing *assets* declines. In many cases, however, it will not pay a firm to replace the existing asset with a new one even though the new type, rather than the old, would be acquired if a new acquisition were to be made currently. In these cases, the accountant should theoretically recognize a loss from partial obsolescence from the firm's owning an old, out-of-date asset, but *GAAP* does not permit recognition of partial obsolescence. The old asset will be carried at *cost* less *accumulated depreciation* until it is retired from service so long as the *undiscounted* future *cashflows* from the asset exceed its book value. See *obsolescence*.

partially funded. Said of a *pension plan* where not all earned benefits have been funded. See *funded* for funding requirements.

partially vested. Said of a *pension plan* where not all employee benefits are *vested*. See *graded vesting*.

participating dividend. *Dividend* paid to preferred shareholders in addition to the minimum preferred dividends when the *preferred stock* contract allows such sharing in earnings. Usually applied after dividends on *common stock* have reached a certain level.

participating preferred stock. *Preferred stock* with rights to *participating dividends*.

partner's drawing. A payment to a partner to be charged against his or her share of income or capital. The name of a *temporary account* to record such payments.

partnership. Contractual arrangement between individuals to share resources and operations in a jointly run business. See *general* and *limited partner* and *Uniform Partnership Act*.

patent. A right granted for up to 17 years by the federal government to exclude others from manufacturing, using or selling a claimed design, product or plant (e.g., a new breed of rose) or from using a claimed process or method of manufacture. An asset if acquired by purchase. If developed internally, the development costs are *expensed* when incurred under current *GAAP*.

payable. Unpaid but not necessarily due or past due.

pay as you go. Said of an *income tax* scheme where periodic payments of income taxes are made during the period when the income to be taxed is being earned; in contrast to a scheme where no payments are due until the end of, or after, the period whose income is being taxed. (Called PAYE—pay as you earn—in Britain.) Sometimes used to describe an *unfunded pension plan*, where payments to pension plan beneficiaries are made from general corporate funds, not from cash previously contributed to a pension fund. Not acceptable as a method of accounting for pension plans under *SFAS No. 87* nor as a method of *funding* under *ERISA*.

payback period. Amount of time that must elapse before the cash inflows from a project equal the cash outflows.

payback reciprocal. One divided by the *payback period*. This number approximates the *internal rate of return* on a project when the project life is more than twice the payback period and the cash inflows are identical in every period after the initial period.

PAYE. See *pay as you go*.

payee. The person or entity to whom a cash payment is made or who will receive the stated amount of money on a check. See *draft*.

payout ratio. *Common stock dividends* declared for a year divided by net *income* to common stock for the year. A term used by financial analysts; contrast with *dividend yield*.

payroll taxes. Taxes levied because salaries or wages are paid; for example, *FICA* and unemployment compensation insurance taxes. Typically, the employer pays a portion and withholds part of the employee's wage fund.

P/E ratio. *Price-earnings ratio*.

Pension Benefit Guarantee Corporation. PBGC. A federal corporation established under *ERISA* to guarantee basic pension benefits in covered pension plans by administering terminated pension plans and placing *liens* on corporate assets for certain unfunded pension liabilities.

pension fund. *Fund*, the assets of which are to be paid to retired ex-employees, usually as a *life annuity*. Usually held by an independent trustee and thus is not an *asset* of the employer.

pension plan. Details or provisions of employer's contract with employees for paying retirement *annuities* or other benefits. See *funded, vested, service cost, prior service cost, money purchase plan*, and *defined-benefit plan*.

per books. An expression used to refer to the *book value* of an item at a specific time.

percent. Any number, expressed as a decimal, multiplied by 100.

percentage depletion (allowance). Deductible *expense* allowed in some cases by the federal *income tax* regulations; computed as a percentage of gross income from a *natural resource* independent of the unamortized cost of the asset. Because the amount of the total deductions for tax purposes is usually greater than the cost of the asset being *depleted*, many people think the deduction is an unfair tax advantage or *loophole*.

percentage-of-completion method. Recognizing *revenues* and *expenses* on a job, order, or contract (a) in proportion to the *costs* incurred for the period divided by total costs expected to be incurred for the job or order ("cost to cost") or (b) in proportion to engineers' or architects' estimates of the incremental degree of completion of the job, order, or contract during the period. Contrast with *completed contract method.*

percentage statement. A statement containing, in addition to (or instead of) dollar amounts, ratios of dollar amounts to some base. In a percentage *income statement*, the base is usually either *net sales* or total *revenues* and in a percentage *balance sheet*, the base is usually total *assets*.

period. *Accounting period.*

period cost. An inferior term for *period expense.*

period expense (charge). *Expenditure*, usually based upon the passage of time, charged to operations of the accounting period rather than *capitalized* as an asset; contrast with *product cost.*

periodic inventory. A method of recording *inventory* that uses data on beginning inventory, additions to inventories, and ending inventory to find the cost of withdrawals from inventory. Contrast with *perpetual inventory.*

periodic procedures. The process of making *adjusting entries, closing entries*, and preparing the *financial statements*, usually by use of *trial balances* and *work sheets.*

permanent account. An account which appears on the *balance sheet*; contrast with *temporary account.*

permanent difference. Difference between reported income and taxable income that will never be reversed and, hence, requires no entry in the *deferred income tax liability* account. An example is the difference between taxable and reportable income from interest earned on state and municipal bonds; contrast with *timing difference* and see *deferred income tax liability.*

perpetual annuity. *Perpetuity.*

perpetual inventory. Records on quantities and amounts of *inventory* that are changed or made current with each physical addition to or withdrawal from the stock of goods; an inventory so recorded. The records will show the physical quantities and, frequently, the dollar valuations that should be on hand at any time. Because *cost of goods sold* is explicitly computed, the *inventory equation* can be used to compute an amount for what *ending inventory* should be. The computed amount of ending inventory can be compared to the actual amount of ending inventory as a *control* device. Contrast with *periodic inventory.*

perpetuity. An *annuity* whose payments continue forever. The *present value* of a perpetuity in *arrears* is p/r where p is the periodic payment and r is the *interest rate* per period. If $100 is promised each year, in arrears, forever and the interest rate is 8 percent per year, then the value of the perpetuity is $1,250 = $100/.08$.

personal account. *Drawing account.*

petty cash fund. Currency and coins maintained for expenditures that are made with cash on hand.

physical units method. A method of allocating a *joint cost* to the *joint products* based on a physical measure of the joint products. For example, allocating the cost of a cow to sirloin steak and to hamburger, based on the weight of the meat. This method usually provides nonsensical (see *sterilized allocation)* results unless the physical units of the joint products tend to have the same value.

physical verification. *Verification*, by an *auditor*, performed by actually inspecting items in *inventory, plant assets*, and the like; may be based on statistical sampling procedures; in contrast to mere checking of written records.

planning and control process. General name for the techniques of management comprising the setting of organizational goals and *strategic plans, capital budgeting, operations* budgeting, comparison of plans with actual results, performance evaluation and corrective action, and revisions of goals, plans, and budgets.

plant. *Plant assets.*

plant assets. Buildings, machinery, equipment, land, and natural resources. The phrase "property, plant and equipment" is, therefore, a redundancy. In this context, "plant" means buildings.

plant asset turnover. Number of dollars of *sales* generated per dollar of *plant assets*. Equal to sales divided by average *plant assets.*

pledging. The borrower assigns *assets* as security or *collateral* for repayment of a loan.

pledging of receivables. The process of using expected collections on accounts receivable as *collateral* for a loan. The borrower remains responsible for collecting the receivable but promises to use the proceeds for repaying the debt.

plow back. To retain assets generated by earnings for continued investment in the business.

plug. For any *account*, beginning balance + additions − deductions = ending balance; if any three of the four items are known, the fourth can be found by plugging. In making a *journal entry*, often all *debits* are known, as are all but one of the *credits* (or vice versa). Because *double-entry* bookkeeping requires equal debits and credits, the unknown quantity can be computed by subtracting the sum of the known credits from the sum of all the debits (or vice versa). This process is also known as plugging. The unknown found is called the plug. For example, if a *discount* on *bonds payable* is being *amortized* with the *straight-line method*, then *interest expense* is a plug: interest expense = interest payable + discount amortization. See *trade-in transaction* for an example. The term sometimes has a bad connotation for accountants because plugging occurs in a slightly different context: In preparing a *pre-closing trial balance* (or balance sheet), often the sum of the debits does not equal the sum of the credits. Rather than find the error, some accountants are tempted to force equality by changing one of the amounts, with a plugged debit or credit to an account such as Other Expenses. There is really nothing wrong with this procedure if the amount of the error is very small compared to asset totals because it is not cost effective to spend tens or hundreds of dollars in bookkeeper's or accountant's time to find an error of a few dollars. Still, most accounting teachers and auditors gravely frown on the process.

pooling-of-interests method. Accounting for a *business combination* by merely adding together the *book value* of the *assets* and *equities* of the combined firms. Contrast with *purchase method*. Generally leads to a higher reported *net income* for the combined firms than would be reported had the business combination been accounted for as a purchase because the *market values* of the merged assets are generally larger than their book values. *APB Opinion No. 16* states the conditions that, when met, require the pooling-of-interests treatment.

positive confirmation. See *confirmation*.

post. To record entries in an *account* in a *ledger*; usually the entries are transferred from a *journal*.

post-closing trial balance. *Trial balance* taken after all *temporary accounts* have been closed.

post-statement events. Events with *material* impact that occur between the end of the *accounting period* and the formal publication of the *financial statements*. Such events must be disclosed in notes for the auditor to give a *clean opinion*, even though the events are subsequent to the period being reported on.

potentially dilutive. A *security* that may be converted into, or exchanged for, common stock and thereby reduce reported *earnings per share: options, warrants, convertible bonds*, and *convertible preferred stock*.

PPB. *Program budgeting*; the second "P" means "plan".

practical capacity. Maximum level at which the plant or department can operate efficiently.

preclosing trial balance. *Trial balance* taken at the end of the period before *closing entries*. In this sense, an *adjusted trial balance*. Sometimes taken before *adjusting entries* and then is synonymous with *unadjusted trial balance*.

predetermined (factory) overhead rate. Rate used in applying *overhead* to products or departments developed at the start of a period by dividing estimated overhead cost by the estimated number of units of the overhead allocation base (or *denominator volume*) activity. See *normal costing*.

preemptive right. The privilege of a *shareholder* to maintain a proportionate share of ownership by purchasing a proportionate share of any new stock issues. Most state corporation laws allow corporations to pay shareholders to waive their preemptive rights or state that preemptive rights exist only if the *corporation charter* explicitly grants them. In practice, then, preemptive rights are the exception, rather than the rule.

preference as to assets. The rights of *preferred shareholders* to receive certain payments in case of dissolution before common shareholders receive payments.

preferred shares. *Capital stock* with a claim to *income* or *assets* after *bondholders* but before *common shares*. *Dividends* on preferred shares are *income distributions*, not *expenses*. See *cumulative preferred stock*.

premium. The excess of issue (or market) price over *par value*. For a different context, see *insurance*.

premium on capital stock. Alternative but inferior title for *capital contributed in excess of (par) or stated value*.

prepaid expense. An *expenditure* that leads to a *deferred charge* or *prepayment*; strictly speaking, a contradiction in terms because an *expense* is a gone asset and this title refers to past *expenditures*, such as for rent or insurance premiums, that still have future benefits and thus are *assets*.

prepaid income. An inferior alternative title for *advances from customers*. An item should not be called *revenue* or *income* until earned, when goods are delivered or services are rendered.

prepayments. *Deferred charges*. *Assets* representing *expenditures* for future benefits. Rent and insurance premiums paid in advance are usually classified as *current* prepayments.

present value. Value today (or at some specific date) of an amount or amounts to be paid or received later (or at other, different dates), discounted at some *interest* or *discount rate*.

price. The quantity of one *good* or *service*, usually *cash*, asked in return for a unit of another good or service. See *fair market price*.

price-earnings ratio. At a given time, the market value of a company's *common stock*, per share, divided by the *earnings per* common *share* for the past year. The denominator is usually based on *income from continuing operations* or, if the analyst thinks the current figure for that amount is not representative—such as when the number is negative—on some estimate of the number. See *ratio*.

price index. A series of numbers, one for each period, that purports to represent some *average* of prices for a series of periods, relative to a base period.

price level. The number from a *price index* series for a given period or date.

price level-adjusted statements. *Financial statements* expressed in terms of dollars of uniform purchasing power. *Nonmonetary* items are restated to reflect changes in general *price levels* since the time specific *assets* were acquired and *liabilities* were incurred. A *gain* or *loss* is recognized on *monetary items* as they are held over time periods when the general *price level changes*. Conventional financial statements show *historical costs* and ignore differences in purchasing power in different periods.

price variance. In accounting for *standard costs*, (actual cost per unit - standard cost per unit) times quantity purchased.

primary earnings per share. Net *income* to *common shareholders* plus *interest* (*net of tax* effects) or *dividends* paid on *common stock equivalents* divided by (weighted average of common share outstanding plus the net increase in the number of common shares that would become *outstanding* if all common stock equivalents were exchanged for common shares with cash proceeds, if any, used to retire common shares).

prime cost. Sum of *direct materials* plus *direct labor* costs assigned to product.

prime rate. The rate for loans charged by commercial banks to their creditworthy customers. Some customers pay even less than the prime rate and others, more. The *Federal Reserve Bulletin* is considered the authoritative source of information about historical prime rates.

principal. An amount in which *interest* is charged or earned. The *face amount* of a *loan*. Also, the absent owner (principal) who hires the manager or accountant (agent) in a "principal-agent" relationship.

principle. See *generally accepted accounting principles*.

prior-period adjustment. A *debit* or *credit* made directly to *retained earnings* (that does not affect *income* for the period) to adjust earnings as calculated for prior periods. Such adjustments are now extremely rare. Theory might suggest that corrections of errors in accounting estimates (such as the *depreciable life* or *salvage value* of an asset) should be treated as adjustments to retained earnings. But *GAAP* require that corrections of such estimates flow through current, and perhaps future, *income statements*. See *accounting changes* and *accounting errors*.

prior service cost. *Present value* at a given time of a *pension plan's* retroactive *benefits*. "Unrecognized prior service cost" refers to that portion of prior service cost not yet *debited* to *expense*. See *actuarial accrued liability* and *funded*; contrast with *normal cost*.

pro forma statements. Hypothetical statements. Financial statements as they would appear if some event, such as a *merger* or increased production and sales, had occurred or were to occur. Pro forma is often spelled as one word.

proceeds. The *funds* received from disposition of assets or from the issue of securities.

process costing. A method of *cost accounting* based on average costs (total cost divided by the *equivalent units* of work done in a period). Typically used for assembly lines or for products that are produced in a series of steps that are more continuous than discrete.

product. *Goods* or *services* produced.

product cost. Any *manufacturing cost* that can be inventoried. See *flow of costs* for example and contrast with *period expenses*.

production cost. *Manufacturing cost*.

production cost account. A *temporary account* for accumulating *manufacturing costs* during a period.

production department. A department producing salable *goods* or *services*; contrast with *service department*.

production method (depreciation). The depreciable asset (e.g., a truck) is given a *depreciable life* measured, not in elapsed time, but in units of output (e.g., miles) or perhaps in units of time of expected use. Then the *depreciation* charge for a period is a portion of depreciable cost equal to a fraction computed by dividing the actual output produced during the period by the expected total output to be produced over the life of the asset. Sometimes called the "units-of-production (or output) method."

production method (revenue recognition). *Percentage-of-completion method* for recognizing *revenue*.

production volume variance. Standard fixed *overhead* rate per unit of normal *capacity* (or base activity) times (units of base activity budgeted or planned for a period minus actual units of base activity worked or assigned to product during the period). Often called a "volume variance."

productive capacity. In computing *current cost* of *long-term assets*, we are interested in the cost of reproducing the productive capacity (for example, the ability to manufacture one million units a year), not the cost of reproducing the actual physical assets currently used (see *reproduction cost*). Replacement cost of productive capacity will be the same as reproduction cost of assets only in the unusual case when there has been no technological improvement in production processes and the relative prices of goods and services used in production have remained approximately the same as when the currently used ones were acquired.

profit. Excess of *revenues* over *expenses* for a *transaction*; sometimes used synonymously with *net income* for the period.

profit and loss sharing ratio. The fraction of *net income* or loss allocable to a partner in a *partnership*. Need not be the same fraction as the partner's share of capital.

profit and loss statement. *Income statement.*

profit center. A unit of activity for which both *revenue* and *expenses* are accumulated; contrast with *cost center.*

profit margin. Sales minus all expenses as a single amount. Frequently used to mean ratio of sales minus all *operating* expenses divided by sales.

profit margin percentage. *Profit margin* divided by *net sales.*

profit maximization. The doctrine that a given set of operations should be accounted for so as to make reported *net income* as large as possible; contrast with *conservatism.* This concept in accounting is slightly different from the profit-maximizing concept in economics where the doctrine states that operations should be managed to maximize the present value of the firm's wealth, generally by equating *marginal costs* and *marginal revenues.*

profit sharing plan. A *defined contribution plan*, where the employer contributes amounts based on *net income.*

profit variance analysis. Analysis of the causes of the difference between *budgeted profit* in the *master budget* and the profits earned.

profit-volume analysis (equation). See *breakeven analysis.*

profit-volume graph. See *breakeven chart.*

profit-volume ratio. *Net income* divided by net sales in dollars.

profitability accounting. *Responsibility accounting.*

program budgeting. Specification and analysis of inputs, outputs, costs, and alternatives that link plans to *budgets.*

programmed costs. A *fixed cost* not essential for carrying out operations. Research and development and advertising designed to generate new business are controllable, but once a commitment is made to incur them, they become fixed costs. Sometimes called *managed costs* or *discretionary costs*; contrast with *capacity costs.*

progressive tax. Tax for which the rate increases as the taxed base, such as income, increases; contrast with *regressive tax.*

project financing arrangement. As defined by *SFAS No. 47,* The financing of an investment project in which the lender looks principally to the *cash flows* and *earnings* of the project as the source of funds for repayment and to the *assets* of the project as *collateral* for the loan. The general *credit* of the project entity is usually not a significant factor, either because the entity is a *corporation* without other assets or because the financing is without direct *recourse* to the entity's owners.

projected benefit obligation. The *actuarial present value* at a given date of all pension benefits attributed by a *defined-benefit pension* formula to employee service rendered before that date. The obligation is measured using assumptions as to future compensation levels if the formula incorporates future compensation, as happens, for example, when the eventual pension benefit is based on wages of the last several years of employees' work lives. Contrast to "accumulated benefit obligation," where the obligation is measured using employee compensation levels at the time of the measurement date of the obligation.

projected financial statement. *Pro forma* financial statement.

projection. See *financial projection* for definition and contrast.

promissory note. An unconditional written promise to pay a specified sum of money on demand or at a specified date.

proof of journal. The process of checking arithmetic accuracy of *journal entries* by testing for the equality of all *debits* with all *credits* since the last previous proof.

property dividend. A *dividend in kind.*

proprietary accounts. See *budgetary accounts* for definition and contrast in context of governmental accounting.

proprietorship. *Assets* minus *liabilities* of an *entity*; equals *contributed capital* plus *retained earnings.*

proprietorship theory. The view of the corporation that emphasizes the form of the *accounting equation* that says *assets − liabilities = owners' equity*; contrast with *entity theory.* The major implication of a choice between these theories deals with the treatment of *subsidiaries.* For example, the view that *minority interest* is an *indeterminate term liability* is based on the proprietor,ship theory. The proprietorship theory implies using a *single-step income statement.*

prorate. To *allocate* in proportion to some base; for example, allocate *service department* costs in proportion to hours of service used by the benefited department. Or, to allocate *manufacturing variances* to product sold and to product added to *ending inventory.*

prorating variances. See *prorate.*

prospectus. Formal written document describing *securities* to be issued. See *proxy.*

protest fee. Fee charged by banks or other financial agencies when items (such as checks) presented for collection cannot be collected.

provision. Often the exact amount of an *expense* is uncertain, but must, nevertheless, be recognized currently. The entry for the estimated expense, such as for *income taxes* or expected costs under *warranty*, is:

Expense (Estimated)   X
   Liability (Estimated).   X

In American usage, the term "provision" is often used in the expense account title of the above entry. Thus, Provision for Income Taxes is used to mean the estimate of income tax expense. (In British usage, the term "provision" is used in the title for the estimated liability of the above entry, so that Provision for Income Taxes is a balance sheet account.)

proxy. Written authorization given by one person to another so that the second person can act for the first, such as to vote shares of stock. Of particular significance to accountants because the *SEC* presumes that financial information is distributed by management along with its proxy solicitations.

public accountant. Generally, this term is synonymous with *certified public accountant*. In some jurisdictions, individuals have been licensed as public accountants without being CPAs.

public accounting. That portion of accounting primarily involving the *attest* function, culminating in the *auditor's report*.

PuPU. An acronym for *pu*rchasing *p*ower *u*nit conceived by John C. Burton, former Chief Accountant of the SEC. Those who think *constant dollar accounting* not particularly useful poke fun at it by calling it "PuPU accounting."

purchase allowance. A reduction in sales *invoice price* usually granted because the *goods* received by the purchaser were not exactly as ordered. The goods are not returned to the seller, but are purchased at a price lower than originally agreed upon.

purchase discount. A reduction in purchase *invoice price* granted for prompt payment. See *sales discount* and *terms of sale*.

purchase method. Accounting for a *business combination* by adding the acquired company's assets at the price paid for them to the acquiring company's assets. Contrast with *pooling-of-interests method*. The acquired assets are put on the books at current values, rather than original costs; the subsequent *amortization expenses* are usually larger (and reported income, smaller) than for the same business combination accounted for as a pooling of interests. The purchase method is required unless all the criteria in *APB Opinion No. 16* to be a pooling are met.

purchase order. Document authorizing a seller to deliver goods with payment to be made later.

purchasing power gain or loss. *Monetary gain or loss.*

push-down accounting. Assume that Company A purchases substantially all of the *common shares* of Company B but that Company B must still issue its own *financial statements*. The question arises, shall the *basis* for Company B's *assets* and *equities* be changed on its own books to the same updated amounts at which they are shown on Company A's *consolidated* statements. When Company B shows the new asset and equity bases reflecting Company A's purchase, Company B is using "push-down accounting," because the new bases are "pushed down" from Company A (where they are required in *GAAP* to Company B (where the new bases would not appear in *historical cost accounting*). Since 1983, the *SEC* has required push-down accounting under some circumstances.

put. An option to sell *shares* of a publicly-traded corporation at a fixed price during a fixed time span. Contrast with *call*.

Q

qualified report (opinion). *Auditor's report* containing a statement that the auditor was unable to complete a satisfactory examination of all things considered relevant or that the auditor has doubts about the financial impact of some *material* item reported in the financial statements. See *except for* and *subject to*.

quantitative performance measure. A measure of output based on an objectively observable quantity, like units produced or *direct costs* incurred, rather than on an unobservable quantity or one observable only non-objectively, like quality of service provided.

quantity discount. A reduction in purchase price as quantity purchased increases; amount of the discount is constrained by law (Robinson-Patman Act). Not to be confused with *purchase discount*.

quantity variance. *Efficiency variance*. In *standard cost* systems, the standard price per unit times (actual quantity used minus standard quantity that should be used).

quasi-reorganization. A *reorganization* where no new company is formed or no court has intervened, as would happen in *bankruptcy*. The primary purpose is to absorb a *deficit* and get a "fresh start."

quick assets. *Assets* readily convertible into *cash*; includes cash, *current marketable securities* and *current receivables*.

quick ratio. Sum of (*cash, current marketable securities*, and *receivables*) divided by *current liabilities*. Some nonliquid receivables may be excluded from the numerator. Often called the "acid test ratio." See *ratio*.

R

R². The proportion of the statistical variance of a *dependent variable* explained by the equation fit to *independent variable(s)* in a *regression analysis*.

R & D. See *research and development*.

Railroad Accounting Principles Board. RAPB. A board brought into existence by the Staggers Rail Act of 1980 to advise the Interstate Commerce Commission on matters of accounting affecting railroads.

RAPB. *Railroad Accounting Principles Board.*

rate of return on assets. *Net income* plus aftertax *interest charges* plus *minority interest* in income divided by average total *assets*. Perhaps the single most useful ratio for assessing management's overall operating performance. See *ratio*.

rate of return on common stock equity. See *ratio*.

rate of return on shareholders' (owners') equity. See *ratio*.

rate of return (on total capital). See *ratio* and *rate of return on assets*.

rate variance. *Price variance*, usually for *direct labor costs*.

ratio. The number resulting when one number is divided by another. Ratios are generally used to assess aspects of profitability, solvency, and liquidity. The commonly used financial ratios are of three kinds: (1) those that summarize some aspect of *operations* for a period, usually a year, (2) those that summarize some aspect of *financial position* at a given moment—the moment for which a balance sheet has been prepared, and (3) those that relate some aspect of operations to some aspect of financial position.

The accompanying exhibit lists the most common financial ratios and shows separately both the numerator and denominator used to calculate each ratio.

For all ratios that require an average balance during the period, the average is most often derived as one half the sum of the beginning and ending balances. Sophisticated analysts recognize, however, that when companies use a fiscal year different from the calendar year, this averaging of beginning and ending balances may be misleading. Consider, for example, the *rate of return on assets* of Sears, Roebuck & Company whose fiscal year ends on January 31. Sears chooses a January 31 closing date at least in part because inventories are at a low level and are therefore easy to count—the Christmas merchandise has been sold and the Easter merchandise has not yet all been received. Furthermore, by January 31, most Christmas sales have been collected or returned, so receivable amounts are not unusually large. Thus at January 31, the amount of total assets is lower than at many other times during the year. Consequently, the denominator of the rate of return on assets, total assets, for Sears is more likely to represent the smallest amount of total assets on hand during the year than the average amount. The return on assets rate for Sears and other companies who choose a fiscal year-end to coincide with low points in the inventory cycle is likely to be larger than if a more accurate estimate of the average amounts of total assets were used.

raw material. Goods purchased for use in manufacturing a product.

reacquired stock. *Treasury stock*.

real accounts. *Balance sheet accounts*; as opposed to *nominal accounts*. See *permanent accounts*.

real amount (value). An amount stated in *constant dollars*. For example, if an investment costing $100 is sold for $130 after a period of 10 percent general *inflation*, the *nominal amount* of *gain* is $30 (= $130 - $100) but the real amount of gain is C$20 (= $130 - 1.10 x $100), where "C$" denotes constant dollars of purchasing power on the date of sale.

real estate. *Land* and its *improvements*, such as landscaping and roads, but not buildings.

realizable value. *Market value* or, sometimes, *net realizable value*.

realization convention. The accounting practice of delaying the recognition of *gains* and *losses* from changes in the market price of *assets* until the assets are sold. However, unrealized losses on *inventory* and *marketable securities* classified as *current assets* are recognized prior to sale when the *lower-of-cost-or-market* valuation basis is used.

realize. To convert into *funds*. When applied to a *gain* or *loss*, implies that an *arm's-length transaction* has taken place. Contrast with *recognize*; a loss (as for example on *marketable equity securities*) may be recognized in the financial statements even though it has not yet been realized in a transaction.

realized gain (or loss) on marketable equity securities. An income statement account title for the difference between the proceeds of disposition and the *original cost* of *marketable equity securities*.

realized holding gain. See *inventory profit* for definition and an example.

rearrangement costs. Costs of re-installing assets perhaps in a different location. May be *capitalized* as part of the assets cost, just as is original installation cost.

recapitalization. *Reorganization*.

recapture. Various provisions of the *income tax* rules require refund by the taxpayer (recapture by the government) of various tax advantages under certain conditions. For example, the tax savings provided by the *investment credit* or by *accelerated depreciation* must be repaid if the item providing the tax savings is retired prematurely.

Summary of Financial Statement Ratios

Ratio	Numerator	Denominator
Profitability Ratios		
Rate of Return on Assets . . .	Net Income + Interest Expense (net of tax effects)[a]	Average Total Assets During the Period
Profit Margin Ratio (before interest effects) . . .	Net Income + Interest Expense (net of tax effects)[a]	Revenues
Various Expense Ratios	Various Expenses	Revenues
Total Assets Turnover Ratio	Revenues	Average Total Assets During the Period
Accounts Receivable Turnover Ratio	Net Sales on Account	Average Accounts Receivable During the Period
Inventory Turnover Ratio. . . .	Cost of Goods Sold	Average Inventory During the Period
Plant Asset Turnover Ratio	Revenues	Average Plant Assets During the Period
Rate of Return on Common Shareholders' Equity	Net Income − Preferred Stock Dividends	Average Common Shareholders' Equity During the Period
Profit Margin Ratio (after interest expense and preferred dividends)	Net Income − Preferred Stock Dividends	Revenues
Leverage Ratio	Average Total Assets During the Period	Average Common Shareholders' Equity During the Period
Earnings per Share of Stock[b]	Net Income − Preferred Stock Dividends	Weighted-Average Number of Common Shares Outstanding During the Period
Short-Term Liquidity Ratios		
Current Ratio.	Current Assets	Current Liabilities
Quick or Acid Test Ratio	Highly Liquid Assets (ordinarily, cash, marketable securities, and receivables)[c]	Current Liabilities
Cash Flow from Operations to Current Liabilities Ratio	Cash Provided by Operations	Average Current Liabilities During the Period

[a]If a consolidated subsidiary is not owned entirely by the parent corporation, the minority interest share of earnings must also be added back to net income.

[b]This calculation can be more complicated when there are convertible securities, options, or warrants outstanding.

[c]Receivables could conceivably be excluded for some firms and inventories included for others. Such refinements are seldom employed in practice.

Summary of Financial Statement Ratios

Ratio	Numerator	Denominator
Working Capital Turnover Ratio	Revenues	Average Working Capital During the Period
Long-Term Liquidity Ratios		
Long-Term Debt Ratio	Total Long-Term Debt	Total Long-Term Debt Plus Shareholders' Equity
Debt-Equity Ratio	Total Liabilities	Total Equities (liabilities plus shareholders' equity)
Cash Flow from Operations to Total Liabilities Ratio	Cash Provided by Operations	Average Total Liabilities During the Period
Times Interest Charges Earned.	Net Income Before Interest and Income Taxes	Interest Expense

receipt. Acquisition of *cash.*

receivable. Any *collectible* whether or not it is currently due.

receivable turnover. See *ratio.*

reciprocal holdings. Company A owns stock of Company B and Company B owns stock of Company A.

recognize. To enter a transaction in the accounts. Not synonymous with *realize.*

reconciliation. A calculation that shows how one balance or figure is derived systematically from another, such as a *reconciliation of retained earnings* or a *bank reconciliation schedule.* See *articulate.*

record date. *Dividends* are paid on payment date to those who own the stock on the record date.

recourse. See *note receivable discounted.*

recovery of unrealized loss on marketable securities. An *income statement account title* for the *gain* during the current period on the *current asset* portfolio of *marketable equity securities.* This gain will be *recognized* only to the extent that net losses have been recognized in preceding periods in amounts no smaller than the current gain. (The Allowance for Declines in Marketable Equity Securities account can never have a *debit balance.*)

redemption. Retirement by the issuer, usually by a purchase or *call*, of *stocks* or *bonds.*

redemption premium. *Call premium.*

redemption value. The price to be paid by a corporation to retire *bonds* or *preferred stock* if called before *maturity.*

refunding bond issue. Said of a *bond* issue whose proceeds are used to retire bonds already *outstanding.*

register. Collection of consecutive entries, or other information, in chronological order, such as a check register or an insurance register, which lists all insurance policies owned. If entries are recorded, it may serve as a *journal.*

registered bond. *Principal* of such a *bond* and *interest*, if registered as to interest, is paid to the owner listed on the books of the issuer. As opposed to a bearer bond where the possessor of the bond is entitled to interest and principal.

registrar. An *agent*, usually a bank or trust company, appointed by a corporation to keep track of the names of shareholders and distributions of earnings.

registration statement. Statement required by the Securities Act of 1933 of most companies wishing to have its securities traded in public markets. The statement discloses financial data and other items of interest to potential investors.

regression analysis. A method of *cost estimation* based on statistical techniques for fitting a line (or its equivalent in higher mathematical dimensions) to an observed series of data points, usually by minimizing the sum of squared deviations of the observed data from the fitted line. The cost whose behavior is being explained is called the "dependent variable;" the variable(s) being used to estimate cost behavior are called "independent variable(s)." If there is more than one independent variable, the analysis is called "multiple regression analysis." See R^2, *standard error, t-value.*

regressive tax. Tax for which the rate decreases as the taxed base, such as income, increases. Contrast with *progressive tax.*

Regulation S-X. The *SEC*'s regulation specifying the form and content of financial reports to the SEC.

rehabilitation. The improving of a used *asset* via an extensive repair. Ordinary *repairs* and *maintenance* restore or maintain expected *service potential* of an asset and are treated as *expenses*. A rehabilitation improves the asset beyond its current service potential, enhancing the service potential to significantly higher level than before the rehabilitation. Once rehabilitated, the asset may be better, but need not be, than it was when new. *Expenditures* for rehabilitation, like those for *betterments* and *improvements*, are *capitalized*.

reinvestment rate. In a *capital budgeting* context, the rate at which cash inflows from a project occurring before the project's completion are invested. Once such a rate is assumed, there will never be multiple *internal rates of return*. See *Descartes' rule of signs*.

relative performance evaluation. Setting performance targets and, sometimes, compensation in relation to performance of others, perhaps in different firms or divisions, facing a similar environment.

relevant cost. *Incremental cost. Opportunity cost.*

relevant range. Activity levels over which costs are linear or for which *flexible budget* estimates and *breakeven charts* will remain valid.

relative sales value method. *Net realizable (sales) value method.*

remittance advice. Information on a *check stub*, or on a document attached to a check by the *drawer*, which tells the *payee* why a payment is being made.

rent. A charge for use of land, buildings, or other assets.

reorganization. A major change in the *capital structure* of a corporation that leads to changes in the rights, interests, and implied ownership of the various security owners. Usually results from a *merger* or agreement by senior security holders to take action to forestall *bankruptcy*.

repair. An *expenditure* to restore an *asset*'s service potential after damage or after prolonged use. In the second sense, after prolonged use, the difference between repairs and maintenance is one of degree and not of kind. Treated as an *expense* of the period when incurred. Because repairs and maintenance are treated similarly in this regard, the distinction is not important. A repair helps to maintain capacity intact at levels planned when the *asset* was acquired; contrast with *improvement*.

replacement cost. For an asset, the current fair market price to purchase another, similar asset (with the same future benefit or service potential). *Current cost*. See *reproduction cost* and *productive capacity*. See also *distributable income* and *inventory profit*.

replacement cost method of depreciation. The original cost *depreciation* charge is augmented by an amount based upon a portion of the difference between the *current replacement cost* of the asset and its *original cost*.

replacement system of depreciation. See *retirement method of depreciation* for definition and contrast.

report. *Financial statement; auditor's report.*

report form. This form of *balance sheet* typically shows *assets* minus *liabilities* as one total. Then, below that appears the components of *owners' equity* summing to the same total. Often, the top section shows *current* assets less current liabilities before *noncurrent assets* less noncurrent liabilities. Contrast with *account form*.

reporting objectives (policies). The general purposes for which *financial statements* are prepared. The *FASB* has discussed these in *SFAC No. 1*.

reproduction cost. The *cost* necessary to acquire an *asset* similar in all physical respects to another asset for which a *current value* is wanted. See *replacement cost* and *productive capacity* for further contrast.

required rate of return. *Cost of capital.*

requisition. A formal written order or request, such as for withdrawal of supplies from the storeroom.

resale value. *Exit value. Net realizable value.*

research and development. Research is activity aimed at discovering new knowledge in hopes that such activity will be useful in creating a new product, process, or service or improving a present product, process, or service. Development is the translation of research findings or other knowledge into a new or improved product, process, or service. *SFAS No. 2* requires that costs of such activities be *expensed* as incurred on the grounds that the future benefits are too uncertain to warrant *capitalization* as an asset. This treatment seems questionable to us because we wonder why firms would continue to undertake R&D if there were no expectation of future benefit; if future benefits exist, then its *costs* should be assets.

reserve. When properly used in accounting, the term refers to an account that appropriates *retained earnings* and restricts dividend declarations. Appropriating retained earnings is itself a poor and vanishing practice, so the word should seldom be used in accounting. In addition, used in the past to indicate an asset *contra account* (for example, "reserve for depreciation") or an *estimated liability* for example, "reserve for warranty costs"). In any case, reserve accounts have *credit* balances and are not pools of *funds* as the unwary reader might infer. If a company has set aside a pool of *cash* (or *marketable securities*) to serve some specific purpose such as paying for a new factory, then that cash will be called a *fund*. No other word in accounting is so misunderstood and misused by laymen and "experts" who should know better. A leading unabridged dictionary defines "reserve" as "Cash, or assets readily convertible into cash, held aside, as by a corporation, bank, state or national government, etc. to meet expected or unexpected demands." This definition is absolutely wrong in accounting. Reserves are not funds. For example, a contingency fund of $10,000 is created by depositing cash in a fund and this entry is made:

Dr. Contingency Fund	10,000	
Cr. Cash.		10,000

The following entry may accompany this entry, if retained earnings are to be appropriated:

Dr. Retained Earnings.	10,000	
Cr. Reserve for Contingencies		10,000

The transaction leading to the first entry is an event of economic significance. The second entry has little economic impact for most firms. The problem with the word "reserve" arises because the second entry can be made without the first—a company can create a reserve, that is appropriate retained earnings, without creating a fund. The problem is at least in part caused by the fact that in common usage, "reserve" means a pool of assets, as in the phrase "oil reserves." The *Internal Revenue Service* does not help in dispelling confusion about the term *reserves*. The federal *income tax* return for corporations uses the title "Reserve for Bad Debts" to mean to "Allowance for Uncollectible Accounts" and speaks of the "Reserve Method" in referring to the *allowance method* for estimating *revenue* or *income* reductions from estimated *uncollectibles*.

reserve recognition accounting. In exploration for natural resources, there is the problem of what to do with the expenditures for exploration. Suppose that $10 million is spent to drill 10 holes ($1 million each) and that nine of them are dry whereas one is a gusher containing oil with a *net realizable value* of $40 million. Dry hole, or *successful efforts*, accounting would expense $9 million and *capitalize* $1 million to be *depleted* as the oil was lifted from the ground. *SFAS No. 19*, now suspended, required successful efforts accounting. Full costing would expense nothing, but capitalize the $10 million of drilling costs to be depleted as the oil is lifted from the single productive well. Reserve recognition accounting would capitalize $40 million to be depleted as the oil is lifted, with a $30 million *credit* to *income* or *contributed capital*. The *balance sheet* shows the *net realizable value* of proven oil and gas reserves. The *income statement* has three sorts of items: (1) current income resulting from production or "lifting profit," which is the *revenue* from sales of oil and gas less the expense based on the current valuation amount at which these items have been carried on the balance sheet, (2) profit or loss from exploration efforts where the current value of new discoveries is revenue and all the exploration cost is expense, and (3) gain or loss on changes in current value during the year, which is in other contexts called a *holding gain or loss*.

residual income. In an external reporting context, this term refers to *net income* to *common shares* (= net income

less *preferred stock dividends*). In *managerial accounting*, this term refers to the excess of income for a *division* or *segment* of a company over the product of the *cost of capital* for the company multiplied by the average amount of capital invested in the division during the period over which the income was earned.

residual security. A *potentially dilutive security*. Options, warrants, convertible bonds, and convertible preferred stock.

residual value. At any time, the estimated or actual, *net realizable value* (that is, proceeds less removal costs) of an *asset*, usually a depreciable *plant asset*. In the context of depreciation accounting, this term is equivalent to *salvage value* and is preferable to *scrap value*, because the asset need not be scrapped. Sometimes used to mean net *book value*. In the context of a *noncancelable* lease, the estimated value of the leased asset at the end of the lease period. See *lease*.

responsibility accounting. Accounting for a business by considering various units as separate entities, or *profit centers*, giving management of each unit responsibility for the unit's *revenues* and *expenses*. Sometimes called "activity accounting." See *transfer price*.

responsibility center. Part or *segment* of an organization that is accountable for a specified set of activities. Also called "accountability center." See *cost center, investment center, profit center, revenue center.*

restricted assets. Governmental resources restricted by legal or contractual requirements for specific purpose.

restricted retained earnings. That part of *retained earnings* not legally available for *dividends*. See *retained earnings, appropriated*. Bond indentures and other loan contracts can curtail the legal ability of the corporation to declare dividends without formally requiring a retained earnings appropriation, but disclosure is required.

retail inventory method. Ascertaining cost amounts of *ending inventory* as follows (assuming FIFO): cost of ending inventory = (selling price of *goods available for sale* - sales) x *cost percentage*. Cost of goods sold is then computed from the inventory equation; costs of beginning inventory, purchases and ending inventory are all known. (When *LIFO* is used, the method is similar to the *dollar-value LIFO method*). See *markup*.

retail terminology. See *markup*.

retained earnings. Net *income* over the life of a corporation less all *dividends* (including capitalization through *stock dividends*); *owners' equity* less *contributed capital*.

retained earnings, appropriated. An *account* set up by crediting it and debiting *retained earnings*. Used to indicate that a portion of retained earnings is not available for dividends. The practice of appropriating retained earnings is misleading unless all capital is earmarked with its use, which is not practicable. Use of formal retained earnings appropriations is declining.

retained earnings statement. *Generally accepted accounting principles* require that whenever *comparative balance sheets* and an *income statement* are presented, there must also be presented a *reconciliation* of the beginning and ending balances in the *retained earnings account*. This reconciliation can appear in a separate statement, in a combined statement of income and retained earnings, or in the balance sheet.

retirement method of depreciation. No entry is recorded for *depreciation expense* until an *asset* is retired from service. Then, an entry is made *debiting* depreciation expense and *crediting* the asset account for the cost of the asset retired. If the retired asset has a *salvage value*, the amount of the debit to depreciation expense is reduced by the amount of salvage value with a corresponding debit to cash, receivables, or salvaged materials. The "replacement system of depreciation" is similar, except that the debit to depreciation expense equals the cost of the new asset less the salvage value, if any, of the old asset. These methods were used by some public utilities. For example, if ten telephone poles are acquired in Year 1 for $60 each and are replaced in Year 10 for $100 each when the salvage value of the old poles is $5 each, then the accounting would be as follows:

Retirement Method.	600	
Plant Assets.		
Cash		600
To acquire assets in Year 1.		
Depreciation Expense	550	
Salvage Receivable	50	
Plant Assets		600
To record retirement and depreciation in Year 10.		
Plant Assets.	1,000	
Cash		1,000
To record acquisition of new assets in Year 10.		
Replacement Method.	600	
Plant Assets.		
Cash		600
To acquire assets in Year 1.		
Depreciation Expense	950	
Salvage Receivable	50	
Cash		1,000
To record depreciation on old asset in amount quantified by net cost of replacement asset in Year 10.		

The retirement method is like *FIFO*, in that the cost of the first assets is recorded as depreciation and the cost of the second assets is put on the balance sheet. The replacement method is like *LIFO* in that the cost of the second assets

determines the depreciation expense and the cost of the first assets remains on the balance sheet.

retirement plan. *Pension plan.*

retroactive benefits. *Pension plan* benefits granted in initiating or amending a *defined-benefit* pension plan that are attributed by the benefit formula to employee services rendered in periods prior to the initiation or amendment. See *prior service costs.*

return. A schedule of information required by governmental bodies, such as the tax return required by the *Internal Revenue Service.* Also the physical return of merchandise. See also *return on investment.*

return of investment. return on capital. *Income* (before distributions to suppliers of capital) for a period. As a rate, this amount divided by average total assets. *Interest*, net of tax effects, should be added back to *net income* for the numerator. See *ratio.*

revenue. The increase in *owners' equity* caused by a service rendered or the sale of goods. The monetary measure of a service rendered. *Sales* of products, merchandise, and services, and earnings from *interest*, *dividends*, *rents*, and the like. The amount of revenue is the expected *net present value* of the net assets received. Do not confuse with *receipt* of *funds*, which may occur before, when, or after revenue is recognized. Contrast with *gain* and *income*. See also *holding gain*. Some writers use the term *gross income* synonymously with *revenue*; avoid such usage.

revenue center. A *responsibility center* within a firm that has control only over revenues generated; contrast with *cost center*. See *profit center.*

revenue expenditure. A phrase sometimes used to mean an *expense*, in contrast to a capital *expenditure* to acquire an *asset* or to discharge a *liability*. Avoid using this phrase; use *period expense* instead.

revenue received in advance. An inferior term for *advances from customers.*

reversal (reversing) entry. An *entry* in which all *debits* and *credits* are the credits and debits, respectively, of another entry, and in the same amounts. It is usually made on the first day of an *accounting period* to reverse a previous *adjusting entry*, usually an *accrual*. The purpose of such entries is to make the bookkeeper's tasks easier. Suppose that salaries are paid every other Friday, with paychecks compensating employees for the 2 weeks just ended. Total salaries accrue at the rate of $5,000 per 5-day work week. The bookkeeper is accustomed to making the following entry every other Friday:

(1)	Salary Expense	10,000	
	Cash.		10,000
To record salary expense and salary payments.			

If paychecks are delivered to employees on Friday, November 25, 1988, then the *adjusting entry* made on November 30 (or, perhaps, later) to record accrued salaries for November 28, 29, and 30 would be as follows:

(2)	Salary Expense	3,000	
	Salaries Payable		3,000

To charge November operations with all salaries earned in November.

The Salary Expense account would be closed as part of the November 30 closing entries. On the next pay day, December 9, the salary entry would have to be as follows:

(3)	Salary Expense	7,000	
	Salaries Payable.............	3,000	
	Cash		10,000

To record salary payments split between expense for December (7 days) and liability carried over from November.

To make entry (3), the bookkeeper must look back into the records to see how much of the debit is to Salaries Payable accrued from the previous year so that total debits are properly split between third quarter expense and the liability carried over from the second quarter. Notice that this entry forces the bookkeeper both (a) to refer to balances in old accounts and (b) to make an entry different from the one customarily made, entry (1). The reversing entry, made just after the books have been closed for the second quarter, makes the salary entry for December 9, 1988, the same as that made on all other Friday pay days. The reversing entry merely *reverses* the adjusting entry (2):

(4)	Salaries Payable.............	3,000	
	Salary Expense		3,000

To reverse the adjusting entry.

This entry results in a zero balance in the Salaries Payable account and a credit balance in the Salary Expense account. If entry (4) is made just after the books are closed for November, then the entry on December 9 will be the customary entry (1). Entries (4) and (1) together have exactly the same effect as entry (3).

The procedure for using reversal entries is as follows: The required adjustment to record an accrual (*payable* or *receivable*) is made at the end of an *accounting period*; the closing entry is made as usual; as of the first day of the following period, an entry is made reversing the adjusting entry; when a payment is made (or received), the entry is recorded as though no adjusting entry had been recorded. Whether or not reversal entries are used affects the record-keeping procedures, but not the financial statements.

Also used to describe the entry reversing an incorrect entry before recording the correct entry.

reverse stock split. A stock split in which the number of shares *outstanding* is decreased. See *stock split*.

revolving fund. A fund whose amounts are continually expended and then replenished; for example, a *petty cash fund*.

revolving loan. A *loan* that is expected to be renewed at *maturity*.

right. The privilege to subscribe to new *stock* issues or to purchase stock. Usually, rights are contained in securities called warrants and the *warrants* may be sold to others. See also *preemptive right*.

risk. A measure of the variability of the *return on investment*. For a given expected amount of return, most people prefer less risk to more risk. Therefore, in rational markets, investments with more risk usually promise, or are expected to yield, a higher rate of return than investments with lower risk. Most people use "risk" and "uncertainty" as synonyms. In technical language, however, these terms have different meanings. "Risk" is used when the probabilities attached to the various outcomes are known, such as the probabilities of heads or tails in the flip of a fair coin. "Uncertainty" refers to an event where the probabilities of the outcomes, such as winning or losing a lawsuit, can only be estimated.

risk adjusted discount rate. In a *capital budgeting* context, a decision maker compares projects by comparing their net *present values* for a given *interest* rate, usually the cost of capital. If a given project's outcome is considered to be much more or much less risky than the normal undertakings of the company, then the interest rate used in discounting will be increased (if the project is more risky) or decreased (if less risky) and the rate used is said to be "risk-adjusted."

risk premium. Extra compensation paid to an employee or extra *interest* paid to a lender, over amounts usually considered normal, in return for their undertaking to engage in activities more risky than normal.

ROI. *Return on investment*, but usually used to refer to a single project and expressed as a ratio: *income* divided by average *cost* of *assets* devoted to the project.

royalty. Compensation for the use of property, usually a patent, copyrighted material, or natural resources. The amount is often expressed as a percentage of receipts from using the property or as an amount per unit produced.

RRA. See *Reserve recognition accounting*.

RRR. Required rate of return.

rule of 69. An amount of money invested at r percent per period will double in $69/r + .35$ periods. This approximation is accurate to one tenth of a period for interest rates between 1/4 and 100 percent per period. For example, at 10 percent per period, the rule says that a given sum will double in 69/10 + .35 = 7.25 periods. At 10 percent per period, a given sum doubles in 7.27+ periods.

rule of 72. An amount of money invested at *r* percent per period will double in 72/*r* periods. A reasonable approximation but not nearly as accurate as the *rule of 69*. For example, at 10 percent per period, the rule says that a given sum will double in 72/10 = 7.2 periods.

rule of 78. The rule followed by many finance companies for allocating earnings on *loans* among the months of a year on the sum-of-the-months'-digits basis when equal monthly payments from the borrower are to be received. The sum of the digits from 1 through 12 is 78, so 12/78 of the year's earnings are allocated to the first month, 11/78 to the second month, and so on. See *sum-of-the-years'-digits depreciation*.

ruling (and balancing) an account. The process of summarizing a series of entries in an *account* by computing a new *balance* and drawing double lines to indicate the information above the double lines has been summarized in the new balance. The process is illustrated below. The steps are as follows. (1) Compute the sum of all *debit* entries including opening debit balance, if any—$1,464.16. (2) Compute the sum of all credit entries including opening credit balance, if any—$413.57. (3) If the amount in (1) is larger than the amount in (2), then write the excess as a credit with a check mark—$1,464.16 - $413.57 = $1,050.59. (4) Add both debit and credit columns, which should both now sum to the same amount, and show that identical total at the foot of both columns. (5) Draw double lines under those numbers and write the excess of debits over credits as the new debit balance with a check mark. (6) If the amount in (2) is larger than the amount in (1), then write the excess as a debit with a check mark. (7) Do steps (4) and (5) except that the excess becomes the new credit balance. (8) If the amount in (1) is equal to the amount in (2), then the balance is zero and only the totals with the double lines beneath them need be shown. This process is illustrated in the accompanying figure.

S

SAB. *Staff Accounting Bulletin* of the *SEC*.

safe-harbor lease. A form of *tax-transfer lease*.

salary. Compensation earned by managers, administrators, professionals, not based on an hourly rate. Contrast with *wage*.

sale. A *revenue* transaction where *goods* or *services* are delivered to a customer in return for cash or a contractual obligation to pay.

sale and leaseback. Describes a *financing* transaction where improved property is sold but is taken back for use on a long-term *lease*. Such transactions often have advantageous income tax effects, but usually have no effect on *financial statement income*.

sales allowance. A reduction in sales *invoice* price usually given because the *goods* received by the buyer are not exactly what was ordered. The amounts of such adjustments are often accumulated by the seller in a temporary *revenue contra account* having this, or a similar, title. See *sales discount*.

sales basis of revenue recognition. *Revenue* is recognized, not as goods are produced nor as orders are received, but only when the sale (delivery) has been consummated and cash or a *receivable* obtained. Most revenue is recognized on this basis. Compare with the *percentage-of-completion method* and the *installment method*. Identical with the *completed contract method* but this latter term is ordinarily used only for *long-term* construction projects.

sales contra, estimated uncollectibles. A title for the *contra-revenue account* to recognize estimated reductions in income caused by accounts receivable that will not be col-

An Open Account, Ruled and Balanced
(Steps indicated in parentheses correspond to steps described in ''ruling an account.'')

	Date 1987	Explanation	Ref.	Debit (1)		Date 1987	Explanation	Ref.	Credit (2)		
	Jan. 1	Balance	✔	100	00						
	Jan. 13		VR	121	37	Sept. 15		J		42	
	Mar. 20		VR	56	42	Nov. 12		J	413	15	
	June 5		J	1,138	09	Dec. 31	Balance	✔	1,050	59	(3)
	Aug. 18		J	1	21						
	Nov. 20		VR	38	43						
	Dec. 7		VR	8	64						
(4)				1,464	16				1,464	16	(4)
(5)	Jan. 1	Balance	✔	1,050	59						

lected. See *bad debt expense, allowance for uncollectibles,* and *allowance method.*

sales discount. Reduction in sales *invoice* price usually offered for prompt payment. See *terms of sale* and *2/10, n/30.*

sales return. The physical return of merchandise; the amounts of such returns are often accumulated by the seller in a temporary *revenue contra account.*

sales value method. *Relative sales value method.*

sales volume variance. *Budgeted contribution margin* per unit times (planned sales volume minus actual sales volume).

salvage value. Actual or estimated selling price, net of removal or disposal costs, of a used *plant asset* to be sold or otherwise retired. See *residual value.*

SAS. *Statement on Auditing Standards* of the *AICPA.*

scale effect. See *discounted cash flow.*

schedule. Supporting set of calculations that show how figures in a *financial statement* or tax return are derived.

scientific method. *Effective interest method* of *amortizing bond discount* or *premium.*

scrap value. *Salvage value* assuming item is to be junked. A *net realizable value. Residual value.*

SEC. Securities and Exchange Commission, an agency authorized by the U.S. Congress to regulate, among other things, the financial reporting practices of most public corporations. The SEC has indicated that it will usually allow the *FASB* to set accounting principles but it often requires more disclosure than required by the FASB. The SEC's accounting requirements are stated in its *Accounting Series Releases (ASR), Financial Reporting Releases (FRR),* Accounting and Auditing Enforcement Releases, *Staff Accounting Bulletins,* and *Regulation S-X.* See also *registration statement* and *10-K.*

secret reserve. *Hidden reserve.*

Securities and Exchange Commission. *SEC.*

security. Document that indicates ownership or indebtedness or potential ownership, such as an *option* or *warrant.*

segment (of a business). As defined by *APB Opinion No. 30,* "a component of an *entity* whose activities represent a separate major line of business or class of customer. . . . [It may be] a *subsidiary,* a division, or a department, . . . provided that its *assets,* results of *operations,* and activities can be clearly distinguished, physically and operationally for financial reporting purposes, from the other assets, results of operations, and activities of the entity." In *SFAS No. 14* a segment is defined as "A component of an enterprise engaged in promoting a product or service or a

group of related products and services primarily to unaffiliated customers . . . for a profit."

segment reporting. Reporting of *sales, income* and *assets* by *segments of a business,* usually classified by nature of products sold but sometimes by geographical area where goods are produced or sold or by type of customers. Sometimes called "line of business reporting." *Central corporate expenses* are not allocated to the segments.

self balancing. A set of records with equal *debits* and *credits* such as the *ledger* (but not individual accounts), the *balance sheet,* and a *fund* in nonprofit accounting.

self insurance. See *insurance.*

selling and administrative expenses. *Expenses* not specifically identifiable with, nor assigned to, production.

semifixed costs. *Costs* that increase with activity as a step function.

semivariable costs. *Costs* that increase strictly linearly with activity but that are positive at zero activity level. Royalty fees of 2 percent of sales are variable; royalty fees of $1,000 per year plus 2 percent of sales are semivariable.

senior securities. *Bonds* as opposed to *preferred stock; preferred stock* as opposed to *common stock.* The senior security has a claim against *earnings* or *assets* that must be met before the claim of less senior securities.

sensitivity analysis. Most decision making requires the use of assumptions. Sensitivity analysis is the study of how the outcome of a decision making process changes as one or more of the assumptions change.

serial bonds. An *issue* of *bonds* that mature in part at one date, another part on another date, and so on; the various maturity dates usually are equally spaced; contrast them with *term bonds.*

service basis of depreciation. *Production method.*

service cost. current service cost. *Pension plan expenses* incurred during an *accounting period* for employment services performed during that period; contrast with *prior service cost* and see *funded.*

service department. A department, such as the personnel or computer department, that provides services to other departments, rather than direct work on a salable product; contrast with *production department.* Costs of service departments whose services benefit manufacturing operations must be *allocated* as *product costs* under *absorption costing.*

service life. Period of expected usefulness of an asset; may not be the same as *depreciable life* for income tax purposes.

service potential. The future benefits embodied in an item that cause the item to be classified as an *asset.* Without service potential, there are no future benefits and the item should not be classified as an asset. *SFAS No. 6* suggests that the primary characteristic of service potential is the ability to generate future net cash inflows.

services. Useful work done by a person, a machine, or an organization. See *goods and services*.

setup. The time or costs required to prepare production equipment for doing a job.

SFAC. *Statement of Financial Accounting Concepts of the FASB.*

SFAS. *Statement of Financial Accounting Standards of the FASB.*

shadow price. One output of a *linear programming* analysis is the potential value of having available more of the scarce resources that constrain the production process; for example, the value of having more time available on a machine tool critical to the production of two products. This value is called a "shadow price" or the "dual value" of the scarce resource.

share. A unit of *stock* representing ownership in a corporation.

shareholders' equity. *Proprietorship* or *owners' equity* of a corporation. Because *stock* means inventory in Australian, British, and Canadian usage, the term "shareholders' equity" is usually used by Australian, British, and Canadian writers, who do not use the term "stockholders' equity."

short-run. short-term. The opposite of *long-run* or *long-term*. This pair of terms is equally imprecise.

short-term. Current; ordinarily, due within one year.

short-term liquidity risk. The risk that an *entity* will not have enough *cash* in the *short run* to pay its *debts*.

shrinkage. An excess of *inventory* shown on the *books* over actual physical quantities on hand. Can result from theft or shoplifting as well as from evaporation or general wear and tear.

sight draft. A demand for payment drawn by a person to whom money is owed. The *draft* is presented to the borrower's (the debtor's) bank in expectation that the borrower will authorize its bank to disburse the funds. Such drafts are often used when a seller sells goods to a new customer in a different city. The seller is not sure whether the buyer will pay the bill. The seller sends the *bill* of lading, or other evidence of ownership of the goods, along with a sight draft to the buyer's bank. Before the goods can be released to the buyer, the buyer must instruct its bank to honor the sight draft by withdrawing funds from the buyers' account. Once the sight draft is honored, the bill of lading or other document evidencing ownership is handed over to the buyer and the goods become the property of the buyer.

simple interest. *Interest* calculated on *principal* where interest earned during periods before maturity of the loan is neither added to the principal nor paid to the lender. *Interest = principal x interest rate x time.* Seldom used in economic calculations except for periods less than one year; contrast with *compound interest*.

single-entry accounting. Accounting that is neither *self-balancing* nor *articulated*; that is, it does not rely on equal *debits* and *credits*. *No journal entries* are made. *Plugging* is required to derive *owners' equity* for the *balance sheet*.

single proprietorship. *Sole proprietorship*.

single-step. Said of an *income statement* where *ordinary revenue* and *gain* items are shown first and totaled. Then all ordinary *expenses* and *losses* are totaled. Their difference, plus the effect of *income from discontinued operations* and *extraordinary items*, is shown as *net income*; contrast with *multiple-step* and see *proprietorship theory*.

sinking fund. *Assets* and their earnings earmarked for the retirement of bonds or other long-term obligations. Earnings of sinking fund investments are taxable income of the company.

sinking fund method of depreciation. The periodic charge is an amount so that when the charges are considered to be an *annuity*, the value of the annuity at the end of depreciable life is equal to the *acquisition cost* of the asset. In theory, the charge for a period ought also to include interest on the accumulated depreciation at the start of the period as well. A *fund* of cash is not necessarily, or even usually, accumulated. This method is rarely used.

skeleton account. *T-account*.

slide. The name of the error made by a bookkeeper in recording the digits of a number correctly with the decimal point misplaced; for example, recording $123.40 as $1,234.00 or as $12.34.

soak-up method. The *equity method*.

Social Security taxes. Taxes levied by the federal government on both employers and employees to provide *funds* to pay retired persons (or their survivors) who are entitled to receive such payments, either because they paid Social Security taxes themselves or because the Congress has declared them eligible. Unlike a *pension plan*, the Social Security system does not collect funds and invest them for many years. The tax collections in a given year are used primarily to pay benefits for that year. At any given time the system has a multi-trillion dollar unfunded obligation to current workers for their eventual retirement benefits. See *Old Age, Survivors, Disability*, and *(Hospital) Insurance*.

sole proprietorship. All *owners' equity* belongs to one person.

solvent. Able to meet debts when due.

SOP. *Statement of Position* (of *AcSEC* of the *AICPA*).

sound value. A phrase used mainly in appraisals of *fixed assets* to mean *fair market value* or *replacement cost* in present condition.

source of funds. Any *transaction* that increases *cash* and *marketable securities* held as *current assets*.

sources and uses statement. *Statement of cash flows.*

SOYD. *Sum-of-the years'-digits depreciation.*

special assessment. A compulsory levy made by a governmental unit on property to pay the costs of a specific improvement, or service, presumed not to benefit the general public but only the owners of the property so assessed. Accounted for in a special assessment fund.

special journal. A *journal*, such as a sales journal or cash disbursements journal, to record *transactions* of a similar nature that occur frequently.

special revenue debt. Debt of a governmental unit backed only by revenues from specific sources such as tolls from a bridge.

specific identification method. Method for valuing *ending inventory* and *cost of goods sold* by identifying actual units sold and in inventory and summing the actual costs of those individual units. Usually used for items with large unit value, such as precious jewelry, automobiles, and fur coats.

specific price changes. Changes in the market prices of specific *goods and services*; contrast with *general price level changes*.

specific price index. A measure of the price of a specific good or service, or a small group of similar goods or services, at one time relative to the price during a base period; contrast with *general price index*. See *dollar-value LIFO method*.

spending variance. In *standard cost systems*, the *rate* or *price variance* for *overhead* costs.

split. *Stock split.* Sometimes called "splitup."

splitoff point. The point where all costs are no longer *joint costs* but can be identified with individual products or perhaps with a smaller number of *joint products*.

spoilage. See *abnormal spoilage* and *normal spoilage*.

spread sheet. A *work sheet* organized like a *matrix* that provides a two-way classification of accounting data. The rows and columns are both labeled with *account* titles. An entry in a row represents a *debit* whereas an entry in a column represents a *credit*. Thus, the number "100" in the "cash" row and the "accounts receivable" column records an entry debiting cash and crediting accounts receivable for $100. A given row total indicates all debit entries to the account represented by that row and a given column total indicates the sum of all credit entries to the account represented by the column.

squeeze. A term sometimes used for *plug*.

SSARS. See *Statement on Standards for Accounting and Review Services*.

stabilized accounting. *Constant dollar accounting.*

stable monetary unit assumption. In spite of *inflation* that appears to be a way of life, the assumption that underlies *historical cost/nominal dollar accounting*—namely that current dollars and dollars of previous years can be meaningfully added together. No specific recognition is given to changing values of the dollar in the usual *financial statements*. See *constant dollar accounting*.

Staff Accounting Bulletin. An interpretation issued by the Staff of the Chief Accountant of the *SEC* "suggesting" how the various *Accounting Series Releases* should be applied in practice. The suggestions are effectively part of *GAAP*.

standard cost. Anticipated *cost* of producing a unit of output; a predetermined cost to be assigned to products produced. Standard cost implies a norm: what costs should be. Budgeted cost implies a forecast, something likely, but not necessarily a "should," as implied by a norm. Standard costs are used as the benchmark for gauging good and bad performance. While a budget may similarly be used, it need not. A budget may simply be a planning document, subject to changes whenever plans change, whereas standard costs are usually changed annually or when technology significantly changes or costs of labor and materials significantly change.

standard cost system. *Product costing* using *standard costs* rather than actual costs. May be based on either *absorption* or *direct costing* principles.

standard costing. *Costing* based on *standard costs*.

standard error (of regression coefficients). A measure of the uncertainty about the magnitude of the estimated parameters of an equation fit with a *regression analysis*.

standard manufacturing overhead. *Overhead* costs expected to be incurred per unit of time and per unit produced.

standard price (rate). Unit price established for materials or labor used in *standard cost systems*.

standard quantity allowed. The quantity of direct material or direct labor (inputs) that should have been used if the units of output had been produced in accordance with preset *standards*.

standby costs. A type of *capacity cost*, such as property taxes, incurred even if operations are shut down completely. Contrast with *enabling costs*.

stated capital. Amount of capital contributed by shareholders. Sometimes used to mean *legal capital*.

stated value. A term sometimes used for the *face amount of capital stock*, when no *par value* is indicated. Where there is stated value per share, it may be set by the directors (in which case, capital *contributed in excess of stated value* may come into being).

statement of affairs. A *balance sheet* showing immediate *liquidation* amounts, rather than *historical costs*, usually prepared when *insolvency* or *bankruptcy* is imminent. The *going-concern assumption* is not used.

statement of cash flows. The *FASB* requires that all for-profit companies present a schedule of *cash receipts* and *payments*, classified by *investing*, *financing*, and *operating activities*. Operating activities may be reported with either the direct method (where only receipts and payments of cash appear) or the indirect method (which starts with *net income* and shows adjustments for *revenues* not currently producing cash and for *expenses* not currently using cash). "Cash" includes cash equivalents such as Treasury bills, commercial paper and *marketable securities* held as *current assets*. Sometimes called the "funds statement." Before 1987, the FASB required the presentation of a similar statement called the *statement of changes in financial position*, which tended to emphasize *working capital*, not cash. See *dual transactions assumption*.

statement of changes in financial position. As defined by *APB Opinion No. 19*, a statement that explains the changes in *working capital* (or cash) balances during a period and shows the changes in the working capital (or cash) accounts themselves. This statement has been replaced with the *statement of cash flows*.

Statement of Financial Accounting Standards. SFAS. See *FASB*.

Statement of Financial Accounting Concepts. SFAC. One of a series of *FASB* publications in its *conceptual framework* for *financial accounting* and reporting. Such statements set forth objectives and fundamentals to be the basis for specific financial accounting and reporting standards.

statement of financial position. *Balance sheet*.

Statement of Position. SOP. A recommendation on an emerging accounting problem issued by the *AcSEC* of the *AICPA*. The AICPA's Code of Professional Ethics specifically states that *CPAs* need not treat *SOPs* as they do rules from the *FASB*, but a CPA would be wary of departing from the recommendations of a *SOP*.

statement of retained earnings (income). A statement that reconciles the beginning-of-period and end-of-period balances in the *retained earnings* account. It shows the effects of *earnings, dividend declarations*, and *prior-period adjustments*.

statement of significant accounting policies (principles). *APB Opinion No. 22* requires that every *annual report* summarize the significant *accounting principles* used in compiling the annual report. This summary may be a separate exhibit or the first *note* to the financial statements.

Statement on Auditing Standards. SAS. No. 1 of this series (1973) codifies all statements on auditing standards previously promulgated by the AICPA. Later numbers deal with specific auditing standards and procedures.

Statement on Standards for Accounting and Review Services. SSARS. Pronouncements issued by the *AICPA* on *unaudited financial statements* and unaudited financial information of nonpublic entities.

static budget. *Fixed budget*.

status quo. Events or costs incurrences that will happen or are expected to happen in the absence of taking some contemplated action.

statutory tax rate. The tax rate specified in the *income tax* law for each type of income (for example, *ordinary income, capital gain or loss*).

step allocation method. *Step-down method*.

step cost. *Semifixed cost*.

step-down method. The method for *allocating service department* costs that starts by allocating one service department's costs to *production departments* and to all other service departments. Then a second service department's costs, including costs allocated from the first, are allocated to production departments and to all other service departments except the first one. In this fashion, the costs of all service departments, including previous allocations, are allocated to production departments and to those service departments whose costs have not yet been allocated.

stepped cost. *Semifixed cost*.

sterilized allocation. Optimal decisions result from considering *incremental costs*, only. *Allocations* of *joint* or *common costs* are never required for optimal decisions. An allocation of these costs that causes the optimal decision choice not to differ from the one that occurs when joint or common costs are unallocated is "sterilized" with respect to that decision. The term was first used in this context by Arthur L. Thomas. Because *absorption costing* requires that all manufacturing costs be allocated to product, and because some allocations can lead to bad decisions, Thomas (and we) advocate that the allocation scheme chosen lead to sterilized allocations that do not alter the otherwise optimal decision. There is, however, no single allocation scheme that is always sterilized with respect to all decisions. Thus, Thomas (and we) advocate that decisions be made on the basis of incremental costs before any allocations.

stewardship. The function of management to be accountable for an *entity's* resources, for their efficient use, and for protecting them, as well as is practicable, from adverse impact. Some theorists believe that a primary goal of *accounting* is to aid users of *financial statements* in their assessment of management's performance in stewardship.

stock. *Inventory. Capital stock.* A measure of the amount of something on hand at a specific time; in this sense, contrast with *flow*.

stock appreciation rights. The employer promises to pay to the employee an amount of *cash* on a certain future date. The amount of cash is the difference between the *market value* of a certain number of *shares* of *stock* in the employer's company on a given future date and some base price set on the date the rights are granted. This form of compensation is sometimes used because both changes in tax laws in recent years have made *stock options* relatively less attractive. *GAAP* computes compensation based on the difference between market value of the shares and the base price set at the time of the grant. *Expense* is recognized as the holder of the rights performs the services required for the rights to be exercised.

stock dividend. A so-called *dividend* where additional *shares* of *capital stock* are distributed, without cash payments, to existing shareholders. It results in a *debit* to *retained earnings* in the amount of the market value of the shares issued and a *credit* to *capital stock* accounts. It is ordinarily used to indicate that earnings retained have been permanently reinvested in the business; contrast with a *stock split*, which requires no entry in the capital stock accounts other than a notation that the *par* or *stated value* per share has been changed.

stock option. The right to purchase a specified number of shares of *stock* for a specified price at specified times, usually granted to employees; contrast with *warrant*.

stockout. A unit of *inventory* is needed in production or to sell to a customer but is unavailable.

stockout costs. *Contribution margin* or other measure of *profits* not earned because a seller has run out of *inventory* and is unable to fill a customer's order. May be an extra cost incurred because of delay in filling an order.

stock right. See *right*.

stock split. Increase in the number of common shares outstanding resulting from the issuance of additional shares to existing shareholders without additional capital contributions by them. Does not increase the total *par* (or *stated) value of common stock* outstanding because par (or stated) value per share is reduced in inverse proportion. A three-for-one stock split reduces par (or stated) value per share to one third of its former amount. Stock splits are usually limited to distributions that increase the number of shares outstanding by 20 percent or more; compare with *stock dividend*.

stock subscriptions. See *subscription* and *subscribed stock*.

stock warrant. See *warrant*.

stockholders' equity. See *shareholders' equity*.

stores. *Raw materials*, parts, and supplies.

straight-debt value. An estimate of what the *market value* of a *convertible bond* would be if the bond did not contain a conversion privilege.

straight line depreciation. If the *depreciable life* is *n* periods, then the periodic *depreciation* charge is 1/*n* of the *depreciable cost*. Results in equal periodic charges and is sometimes called "straight time depreciation."

strategic plan. A statement of the method for achieving an organization's goals.

Subchapter S Corporation. A firm legally organized as a *corporation* but taxed as if it were a *partnership*. The corporations paying their own income taxes are called "C Corporations."

subject to. Qualifications in an *auditor's report* usually caused by a *material* uncertainty in the valuation of an item, such as future promised payments from a foreign government or outcome of pending litigation.

subordinated. Said of *debt* whose claim on income or assets is junior to, or comes after, claims of other debt.

subscribed stock. A *shareholders' equity* account showing the capital that will be contributed as soon as the subscription price is collected. A subscription is a legal contract so that an entry is made *debiting* an *owners' equity contra account* and *crediting* subscribed stock as soon as the stock is subscribed.

subscription. Agreement to buy a *security*, or to purchase periodicals, such as magazines.

subsequent events. *Post-statement events*.

subsidiary. Said of a company more than 50 percent of whose voting stock is owned by another.

subsidiary (ledger) accounts. The *accounts* in a *subsidiary ledger*.

subsidiary ledger. The *ledger* that contains the detailed accounts whose total is shown in a *controlling account* of the *general ledger*.

successful efforts accounting. In petroleum accounting, the *capitalization* of the drilling costs of only those wells that contain gas or oil. See *reserve recognition accounting* for an example.

sum-of-the-years'-digits depreciation. SYD. SOYD. An *accelerated depreciation* method for an asset with *depreciable life* of *n* years where the charge in period *i* ($i = 1, \ldots, n$) is the fraction $(n + 1 - i)/[n(n + 1)/2]$ of the *depreciable cost*. If an asset has a depreciable cost of $15,000 and a 5 year depreciable life, for example, the depreciation charges would be $5,000 (= 5/15 x $15,000) in the first year, $4,000 in the second, $3,000 in the third, $2,000 in the fourth, and $1,000 in the fifth. The name derives from the fact that the denominator in the fraction is the sum of the digits from 1 through *n*.

summary of significant accounting principles. *APB Opinion No. 22* requires that every *annual report* summarize the significant *accounting principles* used in compiling the annual report. This summary may be a separate exhibit or the first *note* to the financial statements.

sunk cost. *Costs* incurred in the past that cannot be affected by, and hence irrelevant for, current and future decisions, aside from *income tax* effects; contrast with *incremental costs* and *imputed costs*. For example, the *acquisition cost* of machinery is irrelevant to a decision of whether or not to scrap the machinery. The current *exit value* of the machine is the *opportunity cost* of continuing to own it and the cost of, say, electricity to run the machine is an incremental cost of its operation. Sunk costs become relevant for decision making when *income taxes (gain or loss* on disposal of asset) are taken into account because the cash payment for income taxes depends on the tax basis of the asset. The term should be avoided in careful writing because it is ambiguous. Consider, for example, a machine costing $100,000 with current *salvage* value of $20,000. Some (including us) would say that $100,000 is "sunk"; others would say that only $80,000 is "sunk."

supplementary statements (schedules). Statements (schedules) in addition to the four basic *financial statements* (including the *retained earnings* reconciliation as a basic statement).

surplus. A word once used but now considered poor terminology; prefaced by "earned" to mean *retained earnings* and prefaced by "capital" to mean *capital contributed in excess of par (or stated) value.*

surplus reserves. Of all the words in accounting, *reserve* is the most objectionable and *surplus* is the second most objectionable. This phrase, then, has nothing to recommend it. It means *appropriated retained earnings.*

suspense account. A *temporary account* used to record part of a transaction prior to final analysis of that transaction. For example, if a business regularly classifies all sales into a dozen or more different categories but wants to deposit the proceeds of cash sales every day, it may credit a sales suspense account pending detailed classification of all sales into sales, type 1; sales, type 2; and so on.

sustainable income. The part of *distributable income* (computed from *current cost* data) that the firm can be expected to earn in the next accounting period if operations are continued at the same levels as during the current period. *Income from discontinued operations*, for example, may be distributable but not sustainable.

S-X. See *Regulation S-X.*

SYD. *Sum-of-the-years'-digits depreciation. SOYD.*

T

T-account. Account form shaped like the letter T with the title above the horizontal line. *Debits* are shown to the left of the vertical line, *credits* to the right.

take-home pay. The amount of a paycheck; earned wages or *salary* reduced by deductions for *income taxes, Social Security taxes*, contributions to fringe benefit plans, union dues, and so on. Take home pay might be as little as half of earned compensation.

take-or-pay contract. As defined by *SFAS No. 47*, an agreement between a purchaser and a seller that provides for the purchaser to pay specified amounts periodically in return for products or services. The purchaser must make specified minimum payments even if it does not take delivery of the contracted products or services.

taking a bath. To incur a large loss. See *big bath.*

tangible. Having physical form. Accounting has never satisfactorily defined the distinction between tangible and intangible assets. Typically, intangibles are defined by giving an exhaustive list and everything not on the list is defined as tangible. See *intangible asset* for such a list.

target cost. *Standard cost.*

tax. A nonpenal, but compulsory, charge levied by a government on income, consumption, wealth, or other basis, for the benefit of all those governed. The term does not include fines or specific charges for benefits accruing only to those paying the charges, such as licenses, permits, special assessments, admissions fees, and tolls.

tax allocation: interperiod. See *deferred income tax liability.*

tax allocation: intrastatement. The showing of income tax effects on *extraordinary items, income from discontinued operations*, and *prior-period adjustments* along with these items, separately from income taxes on other income. See *net-of-tax reporting.*

tax avoidance. See *tax shelter* and *loophole.*

tax credit. A subtraction from taxes otherwise payable, contrast with *tax deduction.*

tax deduction. A subtraction from *revenues* and *gains* to arrive at taxable income. Tax deductions are technically different from tax *exemptions*, but the effect of both is to reduce gross income in computing taxable income. Both are different from *tax credits*, which are subtracted from the computed tax itself in determining taxes payable. If the tax rate is the fraction t of pretax income, then a *tax credit* of $1 is worth $1/t$ of *tax deductions.*

tax evasion. The fraudulent understatement of taxable revenues or overstatement of deductions and expenses or both; contrast with *tax shelter* and *loophole.*

tax exempts. See *municipal bonds.*

tax shelter. The legal avoidance of, or reduction in, *income taxes* resulting from a careful reading of the complex income tax regulations and the subsequent rearrangement of financial affairs to take advantage of the regulations.

Often the term is used pejoratively, but the courts have long held that an individual or corporation has no obligation to pay taxes any larger than the legal minimum. If the public concludes that a given tax shelter is "unfair," then the laws and regulations can be, and have been, changed. Sometimes used to refer to the investment that permits tax avoidance. See *loophole*.

tax shield. The amount of an *expense* that reduces taxable income but does not require *working capital*, such as *depreciation*. Sometimes this term is expanded to include expenses that reduce taxable income and use working capital. A depreciation deduction (or *R&D expense* in the expanded sense) of $10,000 provides a tax shield of $4,600 when the marginal tax rate is 46 percent.

taxable income. *Income* computed according to *IRS* regulations and subject to *income taxes*. Contrast with income, net income, income before taxes (in the *income statement*), and *comprehensive income* (a *financial reporting* concept). Use the term "pretax income" to refer to income before taxes on the income statement in financial reports.

tax-transfer lease. The Congress has in the past provided business with an incentive to invest in qualifying *plant and equipment* by granting an *investment credit*, which though it occurs as a reduction in *income taxes* otherwise payable, is effectively a reduction in the purchase price of the assets. Similarly, the Congress continues to grant an incentive to acquire such assets by allowing *Accelerated Cost Recovery* (*ACRS*, form of unusually *accelerated depreciation*). Accelerated depreciation for tax purposes allows a reduction of taxes paid in early years of an assets's life, which provides the firm with an increased *net present value* of *cash flows*. Both of these incentives are administered by the *IRS* through the income tax laws, rather than being granted as an outright cash payment by some other government agency. A business with no taxable income in many cases had difficulty reaping the benefits of the investment credit or of accelerated depreciation because the Congress had not provided for tax refunds to those who acquire qualifying assets but who have no taxable income. In principle, a company without taxable income could lease from another firm with taxable income an asset that would otherwise have been purchased by the first company. The second firm acquires the asset, gets the tax reduction benefits from the acquisition, and becomes a lessor, leasing the asset (presumably at a lower price reflecting its own costs lowered by the tax reductions) to the unprofitable company. Such leases were discouraged by the tax laws prior to 1981. That is, although firms could enter into such leases, the tax benefits could not be legally transferred. Under certain restrictive conditions, the tax law allows a profitable firm to earn tax credits and take deductions while leasing to the firm without tax liability in such leases. These leases have sometimes been called "safe-harbor leases."

Technical Bulletin. The *FASB* has authorized its staff to issue bulletins to provide guidance on financial accounting and reporting problems. Although the FASB does not formally approve the contents of the bulletins, their contents are presumed to be part of *GAAP*.

technology. The sum of a firm's technical *trade secrets* and *know-how*, as distinct from its *patents*.

temporary account. *Account* that does not appear on the *balance sheet*. Revenue and *expense* accounts, their adjuncts and contras, production cost accounts, dividend distribution accounts, and purchases-related accounts (which are closed to the various inventories). Sometimes called a "nominal account."

temporary difference. Temporary differences include *timing differences* and differences between *taxable income* and pretax income caused by different cost bases for assets. For example, a plant asset might have a cost of $10,000 for financial reporting, but a basis of $7,000 for income tax purposes; this creates a temporary difference which is not a timing difference.

temporary investments. Investments in *marketable securities* that the owner intends to sell within a short time, usually one year, and hence classified as *current assets*.

10-K. The name of the annual report required by the *SEC* of nearly all publicly held corporations.

term bonds. A *bond issue* whose component bonds all mature at the same time; contrast with *serial bonds*.

term loan. A loan with a *maturity* date, as opposed to a demand loan which is due whenever the lender requests payment. In practice, bankers and auditors use this phrase only for loans for a year or more.

terms of sale. The conditions governing payment for a sale. For example, the terms *2/10, n(et)/30* mean that if payment is made within 10 days of the invoice date, a *discount* of 2 percent from *invoice* price can be taken; the invoice amount must be paid, in any event, within 30 days or it becomes overdue.

throughput contract. As defined by *SFAS No. 47*, an agreement between a shipper (processor) and the owner of a transportation facility (such as an oil or natural gas pipeline or a ship) or a manufacturing facility that provides for the shipper (processor) to pay specified amounts periodically in return for the transportation (processing) of a product. The shipper (processor) is obligated to make cash payments even if it does not ship (process) the contracted quantities.

tickler file. A collection of *vouchers* or other memoranda arranged chronologically to remind the person in charge of certain duties to make payments (or to do other tasks) as scheduled.

time-adjusted rate of return. *Internal rate of return*.

time cost. *Period cost*.

time deposit. Cash in bank earning interest; contrast with *demand deposit*.

time-series analysis. See *cross-section analysis* for definition and contrast.

times-interest (charges) earned. Ratio of pretax *income* plus *interest* charges to interest charges. See *ratio.*

timing difference. The major type of *temporary difference.* A difference between taxable income and pretax income reported to shareholders that will be reversed in a subsequent period and requires an entry in the *deferred income tax* account. For example, the use of *accelerated depreciation* for tax returns and *straight line depreciation* for financial reporting. Contrast with *permanent difference.*

total assets turnover. *Sales* divided by average total *assets.*

traceable cost. A *cost* that can be identified with or assigned to a specific product; in contrast to a *joint cost.*

trade acceptance. A *draft* drawn by a seller which is presented for signature (acceptance) to the buyer at the time goods are purchased and which then becomes the equivalent of a *note receivable* of the seller and the *note payable* of the buyer.

trade credit. One business allows another to buy from it in return for a promise to pay later. As contrasted with consumer credit, where a business extends the privilege of paying later to a retail customer.

trade discount. A *discount* from *list price* offered to all customers of a given type; contrast with a *discount* offered for prompt payment and *quantity discount.*

trade payables (receivables). *Payables (receivables)* arising in the ordinary course of business transactions. Most accounts payable (receivable) are of this kind.

trade secret. Technical or business information such as formulas, recipes, computer programs, and marketing data not generally known by competitors and maintained by the firm as a secret. A famous example is the secret formula for *Coca-Cola* (a registered *trademark* of the company). Compare with *know-how.* Theoretically capable of having an infinite life, this intangible asset is capitalized only if purchased and then amortized over a period not to exceed 40 years. If it is developed internally, then no asset will be shown.

trade-in. Acquiring a new *asset* in exchange for a used one and perhaps additional cash. See *boot* and *trade- in transaction.*

trade-in transaction. The accounting for a trade-in depends whether or not the asset received is "similar" to the asset traded in and whether the accounting is for *financial statements* or for *income tax* returns. Assume that an old asset cost $5,000, has $3,000 of *accumulated depreciation* (after recording depreciation to the date of the trade-in), and hence has a *book value* of $2,000. The old asset appears to have a market value of $1,500, according to price quotations in used asset markets. The old asset is traded in on a new asset with a list price of $10,000. The old asset and $5,500 cash (*boot*) are given for the new asset. The generic entry for the trade in transaction is:

New Asset	A		
Accumulated Depreciation (Old Asset)	3,000		
Adjustment on Exchange of Asset	B	or	B
Old Asset			5,000
Cash			5,500

(1) The *list price* method of accounting for trade ins rests on the assumption that the list price of the new asset closely approximates its market value. The new asset is recorded at its list price (A = $10,000 in the example); B is a *plug* (= $2,500 credit in the example). If B requires a *debit* plug, the Adjustment on Exchange of Asset is a *loss*; if a *credit* plug is required (as in the example), the adjustment is a *gain.*

(2) Another theoretically sound method of accounting for trade-ins rests on the assumption that the price quotation from used-asset markets gives a more reliable measure of the market value of the old asset than is the list price a reliable measure of the market value of the new asset. This method uses the *fair market value* of the old asset, $1,500 in the example, to determine B (= $2,000 book value - $1,500 assumed proceeds on disposition = $500 debit or loss). The exchange results in a loss if the book value of the old asset exceeds its market value and in a gain if the market value exceeds the book value. The new asset is recorded on the books by plugging for A (= $7,000 in the example).

(3) For income tax reporting, no gain or loss may be recognized on the trade in. Thus the new asset is recorded on the books by assuming B is zero and plugging for A (= $7,500 in the example). In practice, firms that wish to recognize the loss currently will sell the old asset directly, rather than trading it in, and acquire the new asset entirely for cash.

(4) *Generally accepted accounting principles (APB Opinion No. 29)* require a variant of these methods. The basic method is (1) or (2), depending on whether the list price of the new asset (1) or the quotation of the old asset's market value (2) is the more reliable indication of market value. If, when applying the basic method, a debit entry, or loss, is required for the Adjustment on Exchange of Asset, then the trade-in is recorded as described in (1) or (2) and the full amount of the loss is recognized currently. If, however, a credit entry, or gain, is required for the Adjustment on Exchange of Asset, then the amount of gain recognized currently depends on whether or not the old asset and the new asset are "similar." If the assets are not similar, then the entire gain is recognized currently. If the assets are similar and cash is not received by the party trading in, then no gain is recognized and the treatment is like that in (3); that is B = 0, plug for A. If the assets are similar and cash is received by the party trading in—a rare case—then a portion of the gain recognized currently. The portion of the gain recognized currently is the fraction *cash received/fair market value of total consideration received.* (When the list price method, (1), is used, the market value of the old asset is assumed to be the list price of the new asset plus the amount of cash received by the party trading in.)

The results of applying *GAAP* to the example can be summarized as follows:

More Reliable Information As to Fair Market Value	Old Asset Compared with New Asset	
	Similar	**Not Similar**
New Asset List Price	A = $7,500 B = 0	A = $10,000 B = 2,500 gain
Old Asset Market Price	A = $7,000 B = 500 loss	A = $ 7,000 B = 500 loss

trademark. A distinctive word or symbol affixed to a product, its package or dispenser, which uniquely identifies the firm's products and services. See *trademark right.*

trademark right. The right to exclude competitors in sales or advertising from using words or symbols that may be confusingly similar to the firm's *trademarks.* Trademark rights last as long as the firm continues to use the trademarks in question. In the United States, trademark rights arise from use and not from government registration. They therefore have a legal life independent of the life of a registration. Registrations last 20 years and are renewable as long as the trademark is being used. Thus, as an asset, purchased trademark rights might, like land, not be subject to amortization if management believes that the life of the trademark is indefinite. In practice, accountants amortize a trademark right over some estimate of its life, not to exceed 40 years. Under *SFAS No. 2,* internally developed trademark rights must be *expensed.*

trading on the equity. Said of a firm engaging in *debt financing*; frequently said of a firm doing so to a degree considered abnormal for a firm of its kind. *Leverage.*

transaction. A *transfer* (of more than promises—see *executory contract*) between the accounting *entity* and another party, or parties.

transfer. *SFAC No. 6* distinguishes "reciprocal" and "nonreciprocal" transfers. In a reciprocal transfer, or "exchange," the entity both receives and sacrifices. In a nonreciprocal transfer the entity sacrifices but does not receive (examples include gifts, distributions to owners) or receives but does not sacrifice (investment by owner in entity). *SFAC No. 6* suggests that the term "internal transfer" is self-contradictory and that the term "internal event" be used instead.

transfer agent. Usually a bank or trust company designated by a corporation to make legal transfers of *stock (bonds)* and, perhaps, to pay *dividends (coupons).*

transfer price. A substitute for a *market,* or *arm's length, price* used in *profit* or *responsibility center, accounting* when one segment of the business "sells" to another segment. Incentives of profit center managers will not coincide with the best interests of the entire business unless transfer prices are properly set.

transfer pricing problem. The problem of setting *transfer prices* so that both buyer and seller have *goal congruence* with respect to the parent organization's goals.

translation gain (or loss). *Foreign exchange gain (or loss).*

transportation-in. *Freight-in.*

transposition error. An error in record keeping resulting from reversing the order of digits in a number, such as recording "32" for "23." If an error of this sort has been made in a number added in a total, then the incorrect total will always differ from the correct total by a number divisible by nine. Thus if *trial balance* sums differ by a number divisible by nine, one might search for a transposition error.

treasurer. The name sometimes given to the chief financial officer of a business.

treasury bond. A bond issued by a corporation and then reacquired; such bonds are treated as retired when reacquired and an *extraordinary gain or loss* on reacquisition is recognized. Also, a *bond* issued by the U.S. Treasury Department.

treasury shares. *Capital stock* issued and then reacquired by the corporation. Such reacquisitions result in a reduction of *shareholders' equity,* and are usually shown on the balance sheet as *contra* to shareholders' equity. Neither *gain* nor *loss* is recognized on transactions involving treasury stock. Any difference between the amounts paid and received for treasury stock transactions is debited (if positive) or credited (if negative) to *additional paid-in capital.* See *cost method* and *par value method.*

treasury stock. *Treasury shares.*

trial balance. A listing of *account balances*; all accounts with *debit* balances are totaled separately from accounts with *credit* balances. The two totals should be equal. Trial balances are taken as a partial check of the arithmetic accuracy of the entries previously made. See *adjusted, pre-closing, post-closing, unadjusted trial balance, plug.*

troubled debt restructuring. As defined in *SFAS No. 15,* a concession (changing of the terms of a *debt*) granted by a *creditor* for economic or legal reasons related to the *debtor's* financial difficulty that the creditor would not otherwise consider.

turnover. The number of times that *assets,* such as *inventory* or *accounts receivable,* are replaced on average during the period. Accounts receivable turnover, for example, is total sales on account for a period divided by average accounts receivable balance for the period. See *ratio.*

turnover of plant and equipment. See *ratio.*

t-value. In *regression analysis*, the ratio of an estimated regression coefficient divided by its *standard error*.

two T-account method. A method for computing either (1) *foreign exchange gains and losses* or (2) *monetary gains* or *losses* for *constant dollar accounting statements*. The left hand *T-account* shows actual net balances of *monetary items* and the right hand T-account shows implied *(common) dollar* amounts.

2/10, n(et)/30. See *terms of sale*.

U

unadjusted trial balance. *Trial balance* before *adjusting* and *closing entries* are made at the end of the period.

unappropriated retained earnings. *Retained earnings* not appropriated and therefore against which *dividends* can be charged in the absence of retained earnings restrictions. See *restricted retained earnings*.

unavoidable cost. A *cost* that is not an *avoidable cost*.

uncertainty. See *risk* for definition and contrast.

uncollectible account. An *account receivable* that will not be paid by the *debtor*. If the preferable *allowance method* is used, the entry on judging a specific account to be uncollectible is to *debit* the allowance for uncollectible accounts and to *credit* the specific account receivable. See *bad debt expense* and *sales contra, estimated uncollectibles*.

unconsolidated subsidiary. A *subsidiary* not consolidated and, hence, accounted for on the *equity method*.

uncontrollable cost. The opposite of *controllable cost*.

underapplied (underabsorbed) overhead. An excess of actual *overhead costs* for a period over costs applied, or charged, to products produced during the period. A *debit balance* remaining in an overhead account after overhead is assigned to product.

underlying document. The record, memorandum, *voucher*, or other signal that is the authority for making an *entry* into a *journal*.

underwriter. One who agrees to purchase an entire *security issue* for a specified price, usually for resale to others.

undistributed earnings. *Retained earnings*; typically, this term refers to that amount retained for a given year.

unearned income (revenue). *Advances from customers*; strictly speaking, a contradiction in terms.

unemployment tax. See *FUTA*.

unencumbered appropriation. In governmental accounting, portion of an *appropriation* not yet spent or *encumbered*.

unexpired cost. An *asset*.

unfavorable variance. In *standard cost* accounting, an excess of actual cost over standard cost assigned to product.

unfunded. Not *funded*. An obligation or *liability*, usually for *pension costs*, exists but no *funds* have been set aside to discharge the obligation or liability.

Uniform Partnership Act. A model law, enacted by many states, to govern the relations between partners where the *partnership* agreement fails to specify the agreed-upon treatment.

unissued capital stock. *Stock* authorized but not yet issued.

units-of-production method. The *production method of depreciation*.

unlimited liability. The legal obligation of *general partners* or the sole proprietor for all debts of the *partnership* or *sole proprietorship*.

unqualified opinion. See *auditor's report*.

unrealized appreciation. An *unrealized holding gain*; frequently used in the context of *marketable securities*.

unrealized gross margin (profit). A *contra* account to *installment accounts receivable* used with the *installment method* of revenue recognition. Shows the amount of profit that will eventually be realized when the receivable is collected. Some accountants show this account as a *liability*.

unrealized holding gain. See *inventory profit* for definition and an example.

unrealized loss on marketable securities. An *income statement account* title for the amount of *loss* during the current period on the portfolio of *marketable securities* held as *current assets*. *SFAS No. 12* requires that losses caused by declines in price below market be *recognized* in the income statement, even though they have not been *realized*.

unrecovered cost. *Book value* of an *asset*.

usage variance. *Efficiency variance*.

use of funds. Any transaction that reduces funds (however funds is defined).

useful life. *Service life*.

V

valuation account. A *contra account* or *adjunct account*. When *marketable securities* are reported at *lower of cost or market*, any declines in market value below cost will be credited to a valuation account. In this way, the acquisition cost and the amount of price declines below cost can both be shown. *SFAC No. 6* says a valuation account is "a separate item that reduces and increases the carrying amount" of an asset (or liability). The accounts are part of the related assets (or liabilities) and are neither assets (nor liabilities) in their own right.

value. Monetary worth; the term is usually so subjective that it ought not to be used without a modifying adjective unless most people would agree on the amount; not to be confused with cost. See *fair market value, entry value, exit value.*

value added. *Cost* of a product or *work in process*, minus the cost of the material purchased for the product or work in process.

value variance. *Price variance.*

variable annuity. An *annuity* whose periodic payments depend on some uncertain outcome, such as stock market prices.

variable budget. *Flexible budget.*

variable costing. This method of allocating costs assigns only *variable manufacturing costs* to product and treats *fixed manufacturing costs* as *period expenses.* Contrast with *full absorption costing.*

variable costs. *Costs* that change as activity levels change. Strictly speaking, variable costs are zero when the activity level is zero. See *semivariable costs.* In accounting this term most often means the sum of *direct costs* and variable *overhead.*

variable overhead variance. Difference between actual and *standard variable overhead costs.*

variance. Difference between actual and *standard costs* or between *budgeted* and actual *expenditures* or, sometimes, *expenses.* The word has completely different meanings in accounting and statistics, where it is a measure of dispersion of a distribution.

variance analysis (investigation). The investigation of the causes of *variances* in a *standard cost system.* This term has different meaning in statistics.

variation analysis. Analysis of the causes of changes in items of interest in financial statements such as net *income* or *gross margin.*

vendor. A seller. Sometimes spelled, "vender."

verifiable. A qualitative *objective* of financial reporting specifying that items in *financial statements* can be checked by tracing back to *underlying documents*—supporting *invoices*, canceled *checks*, and other physical pieces of evidence.

verification. The auditor's act of reviewing or checking items in *financial statements* by tracing back to *underlying documents*—supporting *invoices*, canceled *checks*, and other business documents—or sending out *confirmations* to be returned. Compare with *physical verification.*

vertical analysis. Analysis of the financial statements of a single firm or across several firms for a particular time, as opposed to *horizontal* or time-series analysis where items are compared over time for a single firm or across firms.

vested. Said of an employee's *pension plan* benefits that are not contingent on the employee is continuing to work for the employer.

visual curve fitting method. Sometimes, when only rough approximations to the amounts of *fixed* and *variable costs* are required, one need not engage in a formal *regression analysis*, but need merely plot the data and draw in a line by hand that seems to fit the data, using the parameters of that line for the rough approximations.

volume variance. *Production volume variance.* Less often, used to mean *sales volume variance.*

voucher. A document that signals recognition of a *liability* and authorizes the disbursement of cash. Sometimes used to refer to the written evidence documenting an *accounting entry*, as in the term *journal voucher.*

voucher system. A method for controlling *cash* that requires each *check* to be authorized with an approved *voucher.* No *disbursements* of currency or coins are made except from *petty cash funds.*

W

wage. Compensation of employees based on time worked or output of product for manual labor. But see *take-home pay.*

warrant. A certificate entitling the owner to buy a specified number of shares at a specified time(s) for a specified price. Differs from a *stock option* only in that options are granted to employees and warrants are issued to the public. See *right.*

warranty. A promise by a seller to correct deficiencies in products sold. When warranties are given, proper accounting practice recognizes an estimate of warranty *expense* and an *estimated liability* at the time of sale. See *guarantee* for contrast in proper usage.

wash sale. The sale and purchase of the same or similar *asset* within a short time period. For *income tax* purposes, *losses* on a sale of stock may not be recognized if equivalent stock is purchased within 30 days before or 30 days after the date of sale.

waste. Residue of material from manufacturing operations with no sale value. Frequently, it has negative value because additional costs must be incurred for disposal.

wasting asset. A *natural resource* having a limited *useful life* and, hence, subject to *amortization*, called *depletion*. Examples are timberland, oil and gas wells, and ore deposits.

watered stock. Shares issued for *assets* with *fair market value* less than *par* or *stated value*. The assets are put onto the books at the overstated values. In the law, for shares to be considered watered, the *board of directors* must have acted in bad faith or fraudulently in issuing the shares under these circumstances. The term originated from a former practice of cattlemen who fed cattle ("stock") large quantities of salt to make them thirsty. The cattle then drank a lot of water before being taken to market. This was done to make the cattle appear heavier and more valuable than otherwise.

weighted average. An average computed by counting each occurrence of each value, not merely a single occurrence of each value. For example, if one unit is purchased for $1 and two units are purchased for $2 each, then the simple average of the purchase prices is $1.50 but the weighted average price per unit is $5/3 = $1.67. Contrast with *moving average*.

weighted-average inventory method. Valuing either *withdrawals* or *ending inventory* at the *weighted + average* purchase price of all units on hand at the time of withdrawal or of computing ending inventory. The *inventory equation* is used to calculate the other quantity. If the *perpetual inventory* method is in use, often called the "moving average method."

where-got, where-gone statement. A term used by W. M. Cole for a statement much like the *statement of cash flows*.

window dressing. The attempt to make financial statements show *operating* results, or *financial position*, more favorable than would be otherwise shown.

with recourse. See *note receivable discounted*.

withdrawals. *Assets* distributed to an owner. *Partner's drawings*. See *inventory equation* for another context.

withholding. Deductions from *salaries* or *wages*, usually for *income taxes*, to be remitted by the employer, in the employee's name, to the taxing authority.

without recourse. See *note receivable discounted*.

work in process (inventory account). Partially completed product; an asset that is classified as *inventory*.

work sheet. A tabular schedule for convenient summary of *adjusting* and *closing entries*. The work sheet usually begins with an *unadjusted trial balance*. Adjusting entries are shown in the next two columns, one for *debts* and one for *credits*. The horizontal sum of each line is then carried to the right into either the *income statement or balance sheet* column, as appropriate. The *plug* to equate the income statement column totals is the income, if a debit plug is required, or loss, if a credit plug is required, for the period. That income will be closed to retained earnings on the balance sheet. The income statement credit columns are the revenues for the period and the debit columns are the expenses (and revenue *contras*) to be shown on the income statement. Work sheet is also used to refer to *schedules* for determining other items appearing on the *financial statements* that require adjustment or compilation.

working capital. *Current assets* minus *current liabilities*.

working papers. The schedules and analyses prepared by the *auditor* in carrying out investigations prior to issuing an *opinion* on *financial statements*.

worth. *Value*. See *net worth*.

worth-debt ratio. Reciprocal of the *debt-equity ratio*. See *ratio*.

write down. *Write off*, except that not all the assets' cost is charged to expense or *loss*. Generally used for nonrecurring items.

write off. *Charge* an *asset* to *expense* or *loss*; that is, *debit* expense (or loss) and *credit* asset.

write-off method. A method for treating *uncollectible accounts* that charges *bad debt expense* and credits accounts receivable of specific customers as uncollectible amounts are identified. May not be used when uncollectible amounts are significant and can be estimated. See *bad debt expense, sales contra, estimated uncollectibles* and the *allowance method* for contrast.

write up. To increase the recorded *cost* of an *asset* with no corresponding *disbursement* of *funds*; that is, *debit* asset and *credit revenue*, or perhaps, *owners' equity*. Seldom done because currently accepted accounting principles are based on actual transactions. When a portfolio of *marketable equity securities* increases in market value subsequent to a previously recognized decrease, the *book value* of the portfolio is written up—the debit is to the *contra account*.

Y

yield. *Internal rate of return* of a stream of cash flows. Cash yield is cash flow divided by book value. See also *dividend yield*.

yield to maturity. At a given time, the *internal rate of return* of a series of cash flows, usually said of a *bond*. Sometimes called the "effective rate."

yield variance. The portion of an *efficiency variance* that is not the *mix variance*.

Z

zero-base(d) budgeting. ZBB. In preparing an ordinary *budget* for the next period, a manager starts with the budget for the current period and makes adjustments as seem necessary, because of changed conditions for the next period. Because most managers like to increase the scope of the activities managed and since most prices increase most of the time, amounts in budgets prepared in the ordinary, incremental way seem to increase period after period. The authority approving the budget assumes operations will be carried out in the same way as in the past and that next period's expenditures will have to be at least as large as the current period's. Thus, this authority tends to study only the increments to the current period's budget. In ZBB, the authority questions the process for carrying out a program and the entire budget for next period. Every dollar in the budget is studied, not just the dollars incremental to the previous period's amounts. The advocates of ZBB claim that in this way: (1) programs or divisions of marginal benefit to the business or governmental unit will more likely be deleted from the program, rather than being continued with costs at least as large as the present ones and (2) alternative, more cost-effective, ways of carrying out programs are more likely to be discovered and implemented. ZBB implies questioning the existence of programs, and the fundamental nature of the way they are carried out, not merely the amounts used to fund them. Experts appear to be evenly divided as to whether the middle word should be "base" or "based."

General Electric 1986 Annual Report

Authors' Introduction

This is an excerpt from GE's Annual Report. GE's Annual Reports are consistently among the best we see. The first 26 pages and pages 28, 30, 32, 34, 35, 36, 50, 51, and 52 of the annual report, which have not been reproduced, give general information about the company, illustrations, and highlights of the year's operations. In this section we comment on various aspects of the financial statements in numbered footnotes keyed to the GE Annual Report. The page numbers of the original report are left intact, and references, both in the report and in our comments, use these numbers.

Our comments appear on a page facing (or near) the page of the annual report being commented on. Our comments begin at the bottom of this page. The circled numbers shown in the margins of the annual report do not, of course, appear in the original. All accounting terms used in our comments are explained in the Glossary.

We think there is no better way to learn financial accounting than to try to understand all that appears in GE's statements. (The GE corporate symbol—known as "the meatball" at GE—as it appears above is a trademark of General Electric Company. It is, perhaps, the single most valuable asset of the Company. In accordance with generally accepted accounting principles, this asset does not appear anywhere in the financial statements.)

Authors' Comments on General Electric Annual Report

(1) This is the first of our comments. The statement shown here is the income statement.

(2) APB *Opinion No. 30* requires separate disclosure of gains and losses from disposal of businesses that are discontinued, either because of sale or abandonment. Results of operations to be discontinued are also reported separately. To be included in "Discontinued operations" on the income statement, a firm must discontinue an entire line of business. If a firm remains in a line of business but sells or abandons part of the assets of the business, the gains or losses are not included in "Discontinued operations" but classified separately, as GE does here, with other income from continuing operations.

(3) Provision usually means "estimated expense" in this country; see the Glossary at *provision* for the contrast in this word's meanings in the U.S. and the U.K.

(4) GE does not own all the shares in all of its consolidated subsidiaries. Some of the shares belong to outsiders, called the *minority interest*. Refer to the data for 1985 and 1984, where amounts are subtracted for this item. The minority interest's share of the earnings of the subsidiary companies does not belong to GE's shareholders. Hence, in deriving income to GE's shareholders the minority interest's share in earnings is subtracted from the earnings of the consolidated group of companies. Note, however, that this reduction in income uses

Statement of Earnings ①

General Electric Company and consolidated affiliates

For the years ended December 31 (In millions)		1986	1985	1984
Revenues				
Sales of goods		$28,139	$23,963	$23,646
Sales of services		7,072	4,323	4,304
Net earnings of General Electric Financial Services, Inc. (note 14)		504	413	329
Other income (note 5)		1,010	553	652
Total revenues		36,725	29,252	28,931
Costs and expenses				
Cost of goods sold		20,757	17,672	17,332
Cost of services sold		5,430	3,171	3,069
Selling, general and administrative expense		5,963	4,594	4,770
Interest and other financial charges (note 6)		625	361	335
Unusual items (note 7)				
(Gains) from sales of assets	②	(50)	(518)	(617)
Provisions for business restructuring activities		311	447	636
Special payment to non-exempt and hourly employees		—	93	—
Revaluation of goodwill and intangibles		—	—	126
Total costs and expenses		33,036	25,820	25,651
Earnings before income taxes and minority interest		3,689	3,432	3,280
Provision for income taxes (note 8)	③	(1,200)	(1,143)	(1,030)
Minority interest in earnings of consolidated affiliates	④	3	(12)	(11)
Net earnings		$ 2,492	$ 2,277	$ 2,239
Net earnings per share (in dollars)	⑤	$ 5.46	$ 5.00	$ 4.94
Dividends declared per share (in dollars)		$ 2.37	$ 2.23	$ 2.05

The notes to financial statements on pages 38-53 are an integral part of this statement. Financial information for 1986 includes RCA results from June 1, 1986. Information for prior years has been restated for the change in accounting for oil and gas properties in 1986 to the "successful efforts" method from the "full cost" method formerly used. Prior-year presentations have been reclassified to conform with the 1986 presentation. (See note 1 to the financial statements.)

Report of Independent Certified Public Accountants ⑥

To Share Owners and Board of Directors of General Electric Company

We have examined the statement of financial position of General Electric Company and consolidated affiliates as of December 31, 1986 and 1985, and the related statements of earnings and changes in financial position for each of the years in the three-year period ended December 31, 1986. Our examinations were made in accordance with generally accepted auditing standards and, accordingly, included such tests of the accounting records and such other auditing procedures as we considered necessary in the circumstances.

In our opinion, the aforementioned financial statements appearing on pages 27, 29, 31, 35 and 38-53 present fairly the financial position of General Electric Company and consolidated affiliates at December 31, 1986 and 1985, and the results of their operations and the changes in their financial position for each of the years in the three-year period ended December 31, 1986, in conformity with generally accepted accounting principles applied on a consistent basis.

Peat, Marwick, Mitchell & Co.

Peat, Marwick, Mitchell & Co.
345 Park Avenue, New York, N.Y. 10154

February 13, 1987

Statement of Financial Position

General Electric Company and consolidated affiliates

At December 31 (In millions)		1986	1985
Assets			
Cash (note 9)		$ 1,698	$ 1,606
Marketable securities (note 9)		221	951
Current receivables (note 10)		7,208	6,040
Inventories (note 11)		5,161	3,949
Current assets		14,288	12,546
Property, plant and equipment — net (note 12)		9,841	7,900
Funds held for business development (note 13)		397	726
Other investments (note 14)		3,914	3,150
Intangible assets (note 15)		3,581	222
Other assets (note 16)		2,570	1,618
Total assets		$34,591	$26,162
Liabilities and equity			
Short-term borrowings (note 17)		$ 1,813	$ 1,297
Accounts payable (note 18)		2,594	2,204
Progress collections and price adjustments accrued	⑦	2,273	2,257
Dividends payable		287	264
Taxes accrued		1,153	751
Other costs and expenses accrued (note 19)		3,341	2,146
Current liabilities		11,461	8,919
Long-term borrowings (note 20)		4,351	753
Other liabilities	⑨⑥	3,481	2,693
Total liabilities		19,293	12,365
Minority interest in equity of consolidated affiliates	⑧	189	126
Common stock (463,282,000 shares issued)		579	579
Other capital		733	641
Retained earnings		14,172	12,761
Less common stock held in treasury		(375)	(310)
Total share owners' equity (notes 21 and 22)	⑨	15,109	13,671
Total liabilities and equity		$34,591	$26,162
Commitments and contingent liabilities (note 23)			

The notes to financial statements on pages 38-53 are an integral part of this statement. Financial information for 1986 includes RCA results from June 1, 1986. Information for prior years has been restated for the change in accounting for oil and gas properties in 1986 to the "successful efforts" method from the "full cost" method formerly used. The 1985 presentation has been reclassified to conform with the 1986 presentation. (See note 1 to the financial statements.)

no cash or other funds, so that there is an adjustment on the Statement of Changes in Financial Position for this charge against income. See our comment 15. For 1986, the less-than-100-percent-owned consolidated subsidiaries apparently had a loss for the year—negative net income. GE's shareholders do not bear all of that loss, so the minority interest's share of the loss is added to the earnings of the consolidated group in deriving GE's shareholders' net income. This increase in consolidated net income provides no funds and the amount must be subtracted from net income in deriving funds provided by operations on the Statement of Changes in Financial Position. See our comment 15.

⑤ This is primary earnings per share, as called for by APB *Opinion No. 15*. Fully diluted earnings per share need not be separately shown if it is within 3 percent of primary earnings per share.

⑥ This is the auditors' report. This particular report is both nonqualified ("clean") and in standard format. The first paragraph of the auditors' report is the scope paragraph telling the work done and the last paragraph is the opinion. The auditors' report appears in the published annual report on page 37, but is reproduced here for convenience. See our comment 39.

⑦ GE uses the completed contract method of recognizing revenue from long term construction contracts; see GE's Summary of Significant Accounting Policies at "Sales" and our comment 34. As GE incurs costs on these contracts it makes journal entries such as:

Work in Process Inventory for Long Term Contracts.   X
    Various Assets and Liabilities   X
To record cost of construction activity.

Some of GE's long term construction contracts provide that the customer shall make progress payments to GE as the work is done. GE does not recognize revenue until the work is completed, so the journal entry made at the time cash is received is one such as:

Cash. . . . .   Y
    Advances from Customers on Long Term Contracts . . . .   Y
To record cash received and to set up the corresponding liability.

When the balance sheet is prepared, the amounts in the inventory accounts, X (debit balance), are netted against the amounts in the liability accounts, Y (credit balance). If there is a net credit balance, as here, with Y greater than X, then the difference, Y - X, is recorded as a liability. GE shows this liability under the title "Progress collections." On contracts where the amounts in the inventory account exceed the cash collections, then the difference, X - Y, appears as an asset under a title such as "Costs Incurred on Long term Contracts in Excess of Billings." ARB *No. 45* requires this netting of costs incurred against cash collections and the separate showing of the excesses. On many of GE's contracts the only cash collected before completion of construction is for engineering costs incurred in preparation to undertake construction. GE expenses these engineering costs, rather than accumulating them in Work in Process inventory accounts. Thus, there is no asset account to net against the liability. The "Progress collections" title is appropriate because it tends to represent gross "advances from customers," rather than a netting of work in process inventory against advances from customers. The "price adjustments accrued" represent amounts that GE expects to have to pay in the future but for which GE will not be specifically reimbursed by the buyer under the contract.

⑧ (Refer to our comment 4 for a description of "minority interest" on the income statement.) This account represents the equity of the minority shareholders in the consolidated affiliates. From the point of view of GE's shareholders, this equity belonging to the minority is a liability. From the point of view of the consolidated entity, the minority shareholders' interest is part of total owners' equity. Thus whether one believes that minority interest is a liability or an item of owners' equity depends upon whether one views the financial statements as being prepared for the shareholders of GE (the proprietorship theory) or for all potential readers (the entity theory). Note that GE avoids the issue by not classifying "minority interest" either with liabilities or with owners' equity.

Statement of Changes in Financial Position
Funds provided (used)

General Electric Company and consolidated affiliates

For the years ended December 31 (In millions)		1986	1985	1984
Funds provided from operations	⑩			
Net earnings	⑪	$ 2,492	$ 2,277	$ 2,239
Adjustments for items not representing current fund usage:				
Depreciation, depletion and amortization	⑫	1,460	1,249	1,103
Earnings retained by nonconsolidated financial services affiliates	⑬	(506)	(411)	(330)
Income tax timing differences	⑭	(158)	128	(206)
All other operating items	⑮	77	12	11
Funds provided from operations		3,365	3,255	2,817
Funds provided from (used for) changes in working capital	⑯			
Decrease (increase) in inventories	⑰	(317)	(279)	(512)
Decrease (increase) in current receivables	⑱	629	(531)	(260)
Increase (decrease) in current liabilities (except short-term borrowings)	⑲	(400)	62	(112)
Net funds provided from (used for) working capital		(88)	(748)	(884)
Total funds provided from operations and working capital	⑯	3,277	2,507	1,933
Funds used at acquisition date to purchase RCA	⑳			
Purchase price		(6,406)	—	—
Less RCA cash and marketable securities		296	—	—
New borrowings to acquire RCA — long-term	㉑	3,366	—	—
— short-term		2,040	—	—
Net reduction of funds at acquisition date		(704)	—	—
RCA financing transactions since acquisition date				
Proceeds from sales of assets		1,367	—	—
Repayments and other reductions in RCA long-term borrowings		(490)	—	—
Net addition to funds since acquisition date	㉒	877	—	—
Funds provided from (used in) investment and other long-term transactions	㉓			
Additions to property, plant and equipment		(2,042)	(1,953)	(2,419)
Dispositions of property, plant and equipment		275	142	1,346
Use of (additions to) funds held for business development		329	88	(359)
Additional investments in nonconsolidated financial services affiliates		(50)	—	—
All other transactions — net		152	153	436
Net investment transactions		(1,336)	(1,570)	(996)
Funds provided from (used in) financial transactions				
Disposition of GE shares from treasury		283	286	254
Purchase of GE shares for treasury		(348)	(283)	(284)
New issues and other increases in long-term borrowings	㉔	21	171	80
Repayments and other decreases in long-term borrowings	㉔	(67)	(171)	(242)
Net financial transactions		(111)	3	(192)
Funds used for dividends paid		(1,058)	(1,006)	(908)
Net increase (decrease) in funds	㉕	$ 945	$ (66)	$ (163)
Analysis of net change in funds				
Increase (decrease) in cash and marketable securities		$ (638)	$ 184	$ (132)
Decrease (increase) in short-term borrowings (excluding acquisition of RCA)		1,583	(250)	(31)
Increase (decrease) in funds	㉕	$ 945	$ (66)	$ (163)

The notes to financial statements on pages 38-53 are an integral part of this statement. Financial information for 1986 includes RCA results from June 1, 1986. Information for prior years has been restated for the change in accounting for oil and gas properties in 1986 to the "successful efforts" method from the "full cost" method formerly used. Prior-year presentations have been reclassified and restated to conform with the 1986 presentation. (See note 1 to the financial statements.)

⑨ GE uses the cost method of accounting for treasury stock and shows the cost of its own shares acquired on the market as contra to all of owners' equity. Refer to our comment 98.

⑩ GE defines funds as cash + marketable securities − short-term borrowings. The definition can be discerned by looking at the last three lines of the statement. Many companies define funds as working capital = current assets − current liabilities. The FASB is likely soon to require all firms to use a definition of funds equal to cash + marketable securities.

⑪ This statement, as is customary, starts with net income as shown in the income statement on page 27. The next five lines show subtractions for revenues and other credits to income that did not produce funds and additions for expenses and other charges against income that did not use funds. Total funds produced by operations appears after these adjustments to income. An acceptable alternative format, but one that is seldom used, shows only those revenues that produce funds and subtracts only those expenses that use funds in deriving funds produced by operations.

⑫ Depreciation expense reduces net income without using any funds. Hence, its amount is added to net income in deriving funds provided by operations. Funds were used some time in the past when the depreciable assets were acquired; see "Additions to property, plant, and equipment," at our comment 23, below.

⑬ All earnings of GE Financial Services, Inc. (GEFS), which were $504 million in 1986, are included in income under the equity method. GEFS declared no dividends in 1986; see GEFS's "Current and retained earnings" statement in GE's note 14. The $504 million income, therefore, provided no funds to GE (the income is reflected in a larger investment balance on GE's balance sheet; see our comment 87) and must be subtracted from net income to derive GE's funds from operations. The $504 million income differs slightly from the $506 million subtraction here because of nonconsolidated investments in financial service affiliates other than GEFS.

⑭ In 1986 and 1984, income tax expense for the year exceeded the amount of income taxes payable. See the discussion at GE's note 8 and our comments 68-73. Because less funds were used for income taxes than were reported as income tax expense, there has to be an addition for the amount of expense not using funds in deriving funds from operations. The results for 1985 show that taxes payable exceeded tax expense. The amounts shown here for 1986 appear to be the sum of

(a)	$ 95 million	(effect of U.S. timing differences; see our comment 68)
(b)	24 million	(effect of foreign timing differences; see our comment 64)
(c)	38 million	(excess of investment credit included in income of $87 million over actual investment credit earned for year of $49 million; see our comment 74)
	$157 million	(rounding error of $1 million).

This same calculation for 1985 and 1984 provides approximately the same results—the addback for income taxes is approximately the sum of U.S and Foreign timing differences plus the investment credit included in income less the investment credit actually earned as a reduction in income taxes payable for the year.

⑮ For 1985 and 1984, we can be relatively confident that this amount represents the minority's interest in earnings (of $12 million in 1985 and $11 million in 1984); see our comment 4. The charge on the income statement reduces the income reported to GE's shareholders, but does not reduce the amount of funds provided by operations of the consolidated entity. Thus, there must be an addback to net income to net income for these amounts in deriving funds provided by operations. For 1986, the minority interest involved a loss, so the amount of minority interest increases net income and requires a subtraction in deriving funds provided by operations. There is apparently some $80 (= $77 + $3) of other items being added back, but we cannot deduce what they are.

⑯ One modern view of the Statement of Changes in Financial Position is that sources and uses of funds result from three causes: operating activities, financing activities, and investment activities. When this view is adopted and funds are not defined as working capital (such as GE's definition of funds as cash plus marketable securities less short term borrowings), uses of funds to increase the other working capital items (or sources of funds from decreases in the other working capital items) must be classified either as operating activities or investing activities. GE adopts a variant of this view and reports on the sources and uses of funds for other items of working capital between the operating activities and the investing activities. Observe GE's use of a

Selected Financial Data

General Electric Company and consolidated affiliates

(Dollar amounts in millions; per-share amounts in dollars)	1986	1985	1984	1983	1982
Revenues	$ 36,725	$ 29,252	$ 28,931	$ 27,677	$ 27,189
Earnings before income taxes and minority interest	3,689	3,432	3,280	2,993	2,702
Net earnings	2,492	2,277	2,239	2,002	1,790
Net earnings per share	$ 5.46	$ 5.00	$ 4.94	$ 4.40	$ 3.94
Dividends declared per share	$ 2.37	$ 2.23	$ 2.05	$ 1.875	$ 1.675
Earned on average share owners' equity	17.3%	17.5%	19.0%	18.9%	18.7%
Dividends declared	$ 1,081	$ 1,020	$ 930	$ 852	$ 760
Shares outstanding — average (in thousands)	456,297	455,381	453,680	454,768	454,078
Share owner accounts — average	492,000	506,000	520,000	501,000	502,000
Short-term borrowings	$ 1,813	$ 1,297	$ 1,047	$ 1,016	$ 1,037
Long-term borrowings	4,351	753	753	915	1,015
Minority interest in equity of consolidated affiliates	189	126	128	167	165
Share owners' equity	15,109	13,671	12,398	11,137	10,086
Total capital invested	$ 21,462	$ 15,847	$ 14,326	$ 13,235	$ 12,303
Return on average total capital invested	13.9%	16.2%	17.6%	17.4%	16.9%
Total assets	$ 34,591	$ 26,162	$ 24,555	$ 23,047	$ 21,409
Property, plant and equipment additions other than additions by acquisition from RCA	$ 2,042	$ 1,953	$ 2,419	$ 1,671	$ 1,555
Worldwide employment — year end	359,000	292,000	316,000	335,000	342,000
Year-end orders backlog	$ 23,943	$ 23,117	$ 22,577	$ 20,589	$ 19,723

Financial information for 1986 includes RCA results from June 1, 1986, unless stated otherwise. Information for prior years has been restated for the change in accounting for oil and gas properties in 1986 to the "successful efforts" method from the "full cost" method formerly used. Prior-year presentations have been reclassified to conform with the 1986 presentation. (See note 1 to financial statements.) Share data have been adjusted for the 2-for-1 split in April 1983.

Selected Financial Data provides both a handy reference for some data frequently requested about GE and a record that may be useful in reviewing trends. Of course, as with information elsewhere in this Report, 1986 data generally include RCA, so care should be taken in understanding differences generated by the acquisition. The following comments provide additional perspective on some of these selected data.

• **GE's net earnings have increased** at an average annual rate of 9% over the last five years. The minor effect of restating for the change in accounting for oil and gas properties discussed in note 1 to the financial statements has virtually no impact on the growth rate. Also, the inclusion of RCA for only seven months of 1986 had no appreciable impact on the long-term growth rate to date.

• **The backlog of unfilled orders** at the end of 1986 was $23.9 billion. Orders constituting the Company's backlog may be canceled or deferred by customers (subject in certain cases to cancellation penalties).

The significance of backlogs in understanding the Company's businesses has changed. Total revenues in 1986 were 32% more than five years earlier (1981), but the orders backlog at year-end 1986 was only 14% higher. The principal reason for the smaller increase in backlogs is that businesses where order-to-shipment cycles are short, and large backlogs are not standard, have been the source of much of GE's recent growth. This includes businesses such as major appliance, plastics and numerous services operations.

GE stock price range

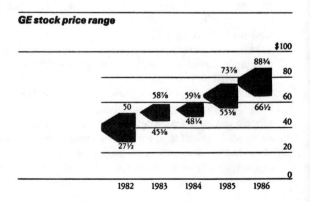

boldface caption for the sum of operating activities and investments (or disinvestments) in working capital. GE appears to place a greater emphasis on this total than on the subtotal for funds provided from operations, excluding changes in working capital.

(17) Increases in inventories use funds, just as increases in property and plant use funds. Conversely, decreases in inventories provide funds.

(18) Increases in accounts receivables use funds, just as increases in property and plant use funds. Conversely, decreases in accounts receivable provide funds.

(19) Increases in accounts payable provide funds, just as increases in long-term debt provide funds. Conversely, decreases in accounts payable use funds.

(20) GE points out (on page 30 of its report, not reproduced here) that it modified the form of this statement "to portray certain significant aspects of the financing the purchase of RCA. A separate section . . . summarizes transactions at the closing date. An additional section . . . summarizes major financial transactions since acquisition. . . . Purchase of RCA was the major funds transaction in 1986. . . . GE paid $6.4 billion for . . . all of its [RCA's] assets and liabilities [which] included funds (cash and marketable securities)" of $296 million.

(21) From the disclosures here, we can see that GE financed its acquisition primarily with new borrowings, but used funds of $1 billion, which net of the $296 million of cash and marketable securities acquired, required only $704 (= $1,000 − $296) million of GE's cash and marketable securities.

(22) GE then sold off assets acquired from RCA for $1,367 million and used those proceeds to repay some of RCA's long-term debt and (more than) replenish its own cash and marketable securities.

(23) The primary use of funds for most companies most of the time is the acquisition of new property, plant, and equipment to replace the old as it wears out and to grow. The amounts here will appear on the income statement in future periods as depreciation charges. Funds are reduced when the assets are acquired. Income is reduced in later periods when the assets are used.

(24) As is preferable, GE shows separately funds provided by new borrowings and funds used to reduce old borrowings. Some companies show only the net effect either as a source or as an application of funds; they provide no information about the amount of actual borrowings and repayments during the period.

(25) Notice the self-balancing nature of this statement. The actual increase in funds (= cash + marketable securities − short-term borrowings) of $945 million in 1986 is exactly explained in the top part of the statement. Some companies do not place the "Analysis" section at the bottom of the statement, thus obscuring the elegance of the statement; these companies show the "Analysis" in a footnote.

Notes to Financial Statements

1 Summary of significant accounting policies ㉖

Financial statement presentation. In 1986, the Company changed the format of certain of its financial statements. The Statement of Earnings has been revised to reflect (1) the growing importance of revenues and related costs and expenses from transactions other than sales of tangible products, and (2) a recent U.S. Securities and Exchange Commission release with respect to cost classifications. Also, the Statement of Changes in ㉗ Financial Position has been modified to portray certain significant aspects of purchasing RCA. Prior-year amounts shown in the statements and related notes have also been reclassified as appropriate to conform with the 1986 presentation. Additionally, prior-year amounts ㉘ have been restated for the change in accounting for costs associated with oil and gas production, as discussed separately in this note, and industry segment data have been revised as presented in the Summary of Industry Segments, which is explained more fully in note 24 to the financial statements.

㉙ **Consolidation.** The financial statements represent the adding together of General Electric Company and all companies, except financial services companies, which GE controls through a majority interest or otherwise (affiliated companies). The effect of transactions among related companies is eliminated.   ㉚

The principal financial services affiliate is General Electric Financial Services, Inc. (GEFS), a wholly owned company which in turn owns all of the stock of General Electric Credit Corporation and Employers Reinsurance Corporation and 80% of the stock of Kidder, Peabody Group Inc. These financial services companies are so dif- ㉛ ferent from the other GE companies that GE's financial statements are more understandable if financial services affiliates' statements are shown separately. Therefore, separate condensed statements of GEFS are shown in note 14 and the nonconsolidated financial services affiliates are in- ㉜ cluded on the equity basis as "one line" in other investments in the Statement of Financial Position and in the Statement of Earnings.

Companies in which GE owns between 20% and 50% ㉝ (associated companies) are also included on a "one line" basis.

Sales. A sale is recorded principally when title passes to customers or when services are performed in accordance with contracts.   ㉞

Investment tax credit (ITC). The ITC was repealed, with ㉟ some transitional exceptions, effective January 1, 1986. However, for financial reporting purposes, GE has deferred recognition of the ITC each year and continues to amortize ITC as a reduction of the provision for income taxes over the lives of the facilities to which the credit applies.

Pensions and other retirement benefits. In 1986, the Company adopted new pension accounting procedures prescribed by the Financial Accounting Standards Board. Accounting policies for pensions, including the effect of adopting the new procedures, as well as policies for other retirement benefits, are discussed in note 4.

Inventories. The values of most inventories are deter- ㊱ mined on a last-in first-out, or LIFO, basis and do not ㊲ exceed realizable values.

Depreciation, depletion and amortization. The cost of most manufacturing plant and equipment, other than that acquired in the purchase of RCA Corporation (RCA) in 1986, is depreciated using an accelerated method based primarily on a sum-of-the-years digits formula. Plant and equipment of RCA operations continues to be depreciated on a straight-line basis. If manufacturing plant and equipment is subject to abnormal economic conditions or obsolescence, additional depreciation is provided. Mining properties, which were sold in 1984 and 1985, were depreciated, depleted or amortized mainly by the unit-of-production method. Mining exploration costs were charged directly to expense until development of a specific mineral deposit was likely to be economically feasible. After such determination, all related development costs were capitalized and subsequently amortized over the productive life of the property, commencing with the start-up of production.

Restatement of prior years' financial statements for ㊳ **the change in method of accounting for oil and gas properties.** In 1986, the Company changed its method of accounting for oil and gas properties from the "full cost" method to the "successful efforts" method. Management considers this change prudent in view of the weakness of oil and gas prices and the uncertain outlook for prices in the industry. Fewer costs are capitalized under the "successful efforts" method than under the "full cost" method, thus reducing the risk of non-recovery of asset values.

This change in method must be applied retroactively. Accordingly, previously reported net earnings have been restated downward by $59 million (13 cents per share) for ㊴ 1985 and $41 million (9 cents per share) for 1984. The balance of retained earnings at January 1, 1984, has been restated downward by $133 million (29 cents per share) for the cumulative effect on operations of years before 1984.

㉖ APB *Opinion No. 22* requires that all annual reports include a summary of significant accounting policies used so that the reader can know which accounting alternatives have been chosen by the company.

㉗ See our comments 20, 21, and 22.

㉘ APB *Opinion No. 20* requires this retroactive restatement of earnings for a change to or from the full-cost method of accounting in the extractive industries. APB *Opinion No. 20* does not require such a retroactive restatement for most changes in accounting principles. Some of the other exceptions, which require retroactive restatements, are changes from LIFO to another cost flow assumption, a change in the method of accounting for long-term construction contracts, and changes in accounting for intercorporate investments caused by certain changes in ownership percentages. See our comment 39.

㉙ A parent, such as GE, usually consolidates a subsidiary when all three of the following criteria are met:
  (i) The parent owns more than 50 percent of the voting shares of the subsidiary.
  (ii) There are no important restrictions on the ability of the parent to exercise control of the subsidiary.
  (iii) The asset and equity structure of the subsidiary is not significantly different from that of the parent.
  The FASB is likely soon to eliminate the third criterion above, requiring consolidation when the first two are met. When this requirement becomes effective, GE will have to consolidate the majority-owned financial service companies, as well. See our comment 90.

㉚ Consolidated financial statements present information about a group of affiliated companies as if the group were one economic entity. Consequently, gains or losses on sales of assets between companies in the consolidated group must be eliminated from reported financial statements. The recognition of such gains or losses is postponed until the assets are sold by one company of the consolidated group to a buyer outside of the consolidated group.

㉛ GE tells us here that it consolidates all "majority owned" (greater than 50 percent) and "controlled" companies except the finance companies which are not similar to the others in the consolidated group. Instead, the finance affiliates are accounted for under the equity method. As can be seen from GE Financial Services's balance sheet in note 14, much (42 percent at year-end 1986) of the Credit Corporation's assets are receivables and most (87 percent) of its equities are debt, rather than owner's equity. In this sense, the operations of the finance affiliates "are not similar to those of the consolidated group." As our comment 90 points out, the nonconsolidation of the finance company makes GE's balance sheet differ substantially from its appearance if the finance affiliates were consolidated. (This difference is part of the reason the FASB is expected to change the rules for consolidation, mentioned in our comment 29.) Although there is no effect on final net income, the components of income are affected.

㉜ GE uses the equity method for the nonconsolidated finance affiliates. Under the equity method, GE's net earnings include its share of the earnings, not just the dividends, of these companies. See our comment 13.

㉝ The "one line basis" is the equity method.

㉞ GE uses the completed contract method of recognizing revenue on long-term construction projects. We know this, not because the language here is perfectly clear, but because we have asked GE about these words. See our comment 7.

㉟ See our comment 74 for a discussion of the investment credit and the effect of GE's using the conservative deferral method.

㊱ Most foreign governments do not allow LIFO for tax purposes.

㊲ GE tells us it will not show an item of inventory on the balance sheet at an amount greater than net realizable value; we can deduce that it must be using a lower-of-cost-or-market valuation basis.

㊳ GE has used "full cost" accounting for its oil and gas operations, but has switched to the successful efforts method. See the Glossary at *reserve recognition accounting* for discussion of the options. The U.S. Congress passed a law that required the SEC (and FASB) to set uniform accounting in the petroleum industry by the end of 1977. FASB *Statement No. 19* was issued in 1977 to comply. The statement required successful efforts accounting and forbade full cost accounting. In 1978, the SEC said it would allow either successful efforts or full cost accounting until it could write rules for "reserve recognition accounting." In 1981, the SEC indicated that it was delaying indefinitely use of reserve recognition accounting in the principal financial statements; either successful efforts or full cost can be used.

㊴ GE's reported income is lower as a result of its switch from full costing to successful efforts. The amounts appear here. See our comment 28. The amounts of the change were apparently not material enough to warrant a qualified opinion by the independent accountants.

2 RCA acquisition

On June 9, 1986, GE acquired RCA Corporation and its subsidiaries (RCA) in a transaction for which the total consideration to former RCA shareholders was $6.406 billion in cash. RCA businesses include the manufacture and sale of a wide range of electronic products and related research and services for consumer, commercial, military and space applications; the National Broadcasting Company's (NBC) radio and television stations and network broadcasting services; and domestic and international message and data communications services.

The acquisition was accounted for as a purchase, and the operating results of RCA have been consolidated with those of GE since June 1, 1986. In preparing 1986 financial information, the purchase price ($6.426 billion, including an estimated $20 million of related costs) has been allocated to the assets and liabilities of RCA based on estimates of fair market values. The excess of purchase price over the estimate of fair values of net assets acquired (goodwill) was $2.7 billion, which is being amortized on a straight-line basis over 40 years. The final purchase price allocation may differ from estimates as a result of changes due to appraisals and evaluations of RCA's assets and liabilities. Completion of these appraisals and evaluations is not expected until sometime in 1987.

Unaudited pro forma consolidated results of operations for the years 1986 and 1985, assuming RCA had been acquired at the beginning of each period, are shown below.

Pro forma consolidated operations

(Dollar amounts in millions; per-share amounts in dollars)	1986	1985
Sales	$38,997	$37,258
Net earnings	2,471	2,143
Net earnings per share	5.42	4.71

These pro forma results are not necessarily indicative of the consolidated results which would have been reported if the RCA acquisition had actually occurred at the beginning of each respective period presented, or which may be reported in the future.

Sources of funds to pay RCA shareholders at the closing date included: net proceeds from 11 public debt offerings in domestic and foreign markets aggregating $3.366 billion at varying rates (weighted average borrowing cost to the Company of 7.4%) and maturities (ranging from 1989 to 2016); short-term borrowings aggregating $2.040 billion; and cash and cash equivalents of GE in the amount of $1.0 billion.

The pro forma consolidated results of operations shown above are based on assumptions concerning a financing structure in effect after repayment of most interim short-term financing with medium- and long-term borrowings. For purposes of calculating pro forma interest expense as it might have been for the year 1986 if the merger had occurred January 1, 1986 (as shown above), the weighted average interest rate used was 8.94% and was representative of rates GE would have experienced on the basis of the assumed final mix of short-, medium- and long-term debt in place at January 1, 1986. Similarly, assuming the same financing structure and consummation of the merger at January 1, 1985, the weighted average interest rate used for the year 1985 shown above was 11.15%. A change of one percentage point in the interest rate assumption would change annual interest expense (or income) by approximately $64 million before taxes or $35 million after taxes (8 cents per share).

In accordance with agreements with agencies of the United States government, GE is required to sell its military vidicon business (which sale was completed in 1986) and five radio stations owned by NBC. Also, in December 1986, GE sold RCA businesses involving audio tapes and records, carpets and an insurance subsidiary, which are not consistent with GE's long-range strategic plans. These required or completed dispositions have no significant effect on the pro forma sales and net earnings presented above.

It is possible that further evaluation will result in other dispositions of businesses or assets, but no such dispositions are reflected in the pro forma information inasmuch as management presently has no plans that it expects would result in any material non-recurring charges or credits to earnings arising directly from acquisition of RCA.

(40) As opposed to a pooling of interests, under which the assets acquired would be shown at lower, old book values, rather than at current market values at the time of acquisition. As a result of purchase accounting, net income in the future will be lower than it would have been under pooling. The acquiring firm does not have a choice of accounting methods, once it sets the form of the acquisition. But some acquisition formats require pooling of interests accounting.

(41) Goodwill is being amortized over 40 years, the longest period allowed under APB *Opinion No. 17.*

(42) See our comments 20, 21, and 22. GE provides helpful detail about the form of the financings summarized in the Statement of Changes in Financial Position.

(43) This is a good example of *sensitivity analysis;* see the Glossary.

3 Supplemental cost details (excluding unusual items)

Supplemental cost details are shown in the table below.

Supplemental cost details (In millions)	1986	1985	1984
Employee compensation, including benefits	$11,775	$10,468	$10,939
Depreciation, depletion and amortization	1,460	1,249	1,103
Company-funded research and development ㊹	1,300	1,069	1,038
Maintenance and repairs	803	692	744
Social Security taxes	725	626	616
Advertising	481	367	356
Taxes, except Social Security and those on income	288	247	264

4 Pensions and other retiree benefits

GE and its affiliates sponsor a number of pension and other retiree benefit plans. This note summarizes important financial aspects of GE's obligations for these plans. Measurements of obligations and costs are based on actuarial calculations involving various assumptions as to future events.

● **Principal pension plans:**

The General Electric Pension Plan (GE Plan) covers substantially all employees in the United States except RCA employees. Generally, benefits are based on the greater of a formula recognizing career earnings or a formula recogniz-
㊺ ing length of service and final average earnings. GE Plan benefits are funded through the General Electric Pension Trust (GE Trust). The information shown herein for the GE Plan and GE Trust includes amounts related to two pension plans covering certain employees at government-owned, GE-operated facilities. These plans were established in 1986 subject to government and other approvals and contain the same benefit formulas as the GE Plan. At the end of 1986, approximately 213,300 employees were covered by the GE Plan, approximately 67,000 former employees with vested rights were entitled to future benefits and approximately 119,900 retirees or beneficiaries were receiving benefits.

The RCA Retirement Plan (RCA Plan) covers substantially all RCA employees in the United States. Generally, benefits are based on the greater of a formula recognizing career earnings or a formula recognizing length of service and final average earnings. RCA Plan benefits are funded through the RCA Retirement Plan Master Trust (RCA Trust). At the end of 1986, approximately 44,700 employees were covered by the RCA Plan, approximately 28,100 former employees with vested rights were entitled to future benefits and approximately 15,700 retirees or beneficiaries were receiving benefits.

The General Electric Supplementary Pension Plan is an unfunded plan providing supplementary retirement benefits primarily to higher-level, longer-service GE management and professional employees in the United States. At the end of 1986, approximately 3,800 employees were eligible for this plan and approximately 3,600 retirees or beneficiaries were receiving benefits.

Other pension plans are sponsored by domestic and foreign affiliates, but these are not considered to be significant individually or in the aggregate to GE's financial position.

GE adopted Statement of Financial Accounting Standards No. 87 (SFAS 87) for pension accounting effective January 1, 1986. SFAS 87 requires use of the projected unit credit cost method to determine the projected benefit ㊻ obligation and plan cost. The projected benefit obligation is the actuarial present value of the portion of projected future benefits that is attributed to employee service to date. The benefit cost for service during the year is the portion of the projected benefit obligation that is attributed to employee service during the year. This cost method recognizes the effect of future compensation and service in projecting the future benefits, and it had been used for the GE Plan and RCA Plan before adoption of SFAS 87.

In addition, SFAS 87 requires calculation of a "transition gain" that is the excess at January 1, 1986, of the current fair market value of plan assets over the plan's ㊼ projected benefit obligation. This transition gain is being amortized over 15 years, except that the net transition gain for the RCA Plan has been recognized as an asset in accounting for the RCA acquisition.

Changes in pension benefits which are allocable to previous service of employees will be amortized over the average future-service period of employees. Gains and losses that occur because actual experience differs from that assumed will be amortized in the same manner.

Actuarial assumptions for the principal pension plans include 8.5% for both the assumed discount rate used to ㊽ determine the present value of future benefits and the expected long-term rate of return on plan assets (the GE Plan used 8% in 1985 and 7.5% in 1984, excluding the effect of a dedicated portfolio in those years). The 1986 assumed rate of average future increases in pension benefit compensation was 6.5% (the GE Plan used 7% in 1985 and 1984).

(44) *SFAS No. 2* requires the expensing of research and development costs, and the disclosure, such as GE's here, of the costs incurred during the year for R & D. *SFAS No. 2* allows the capitalizing of R & D costs that are incurred under contract and that are reimbursable. GE is making clear that these costs ($1,300 million in 1986) do not qualify for capitalization by stating that they are Company funded.

(45) That is, these are *defined benefit* plans, in contrast to *defined contribution plans;* see the Glossary.

(46) As opposed to an accumulated benefit method, where calculations are based on salaries earned to date, rather than on projections of future salaries. See the Glossary at *projected benefit obligation.*

(47) See GE's first schedule on page 41 and our comment 54.

(48) Increasing the discount rate decreases the present value of a future obligation. This increase in the discount rate lowered reported pension expense, as discussed in GE's next paragraph.

(49) GE had been using an even more conservative actuarial cost method than that required by *SFAS No. 87.* As a result of switching to the newly-required method, GE's reported income increases.

(50) This cost, sometimes called current service benefits, arises solely because employees have worked for a year while covered by the pension plan.

(51) At any time, a pension plan has an obligation to employees and ex-employees for work performed before that time. As time passes, the obligation grows in amount because of interest accumulation. This amount is the interest on the obligation to the beneficiaries at the start of the year.

(52) Assets of the plan are invested; these are the earnings for the year, which are less than the amounts projected to have been earned; see our next comment.

(53) Because the projected return on the assets (of 7 percent; see GE's preceding paragraph) was less than the actual return, there is extra income (or less expense) to be recognized. GE recognizes that extra income over future periods, in accordance with *SFAS No. 87.* Thus, not all of the pension plan's income is recognized in the current year.

(54) This amortization includes the benefit (expense reduction) to GE arising from the fact that at its adoption of *SFAS No. 87,* GE's pension plan had market value of assets larger than the present value of the benefits projected to be payable.

(55) Market-related value differs from market value in that the latter is the fair market value on a given date of an asset. Market-related value does not recognize all of the gain or loss in value as the gain or loss occurs, but spreads it over five years. We think market value of publicly-traded stocks and bonds is more relevant for decision making than is market-related value. GE disagrees.

(56) GE has larger pension expense than its allowable income tax deduction for pensions. This leads to a deferred tax debit, reducing income tax expense relative to income taxes payable. See our comment 72.

(57) The amount of this liability appears on GE's balance sheet, probably included in the amount called "Other liabilities."

(58) GE shows here the annual cost of its other post-employment benefits. The present value of the benefits already earned by current and ex-employees is not required to be disclosed, nor counted as an accounting liability. The amounts can be significant and a controversial topic over the next few years will be the required accounting, if any, for these other post-employment benefits.

(59) "Customer financing" is interest on receivables held by GE arising from some of its sales.

(60) *SFAS No. 34* requires separate disclosure of amounts of interest capitalized into plant under construction.

(61) This first schedule shows the details of income tax expense, called a "provision." The bottom line of the first schedule is the total expense reported on the statement of earnings. It is the sum of U.S. federal, foreign, and other income tax expenses. The U.S. federal and foreign income tax expense amounts are derived in essentially two steps: first is shown the amount of taxes payable; then there is an adjustment for timing differences; GE also shows the effect of the investment credit, which is discussed in our comment 74.

(62) In 1986 and 1984, U.S. federal income taxes payable exceeded income tax expense because of timing differences. In 1985, U.S. federal income tax expense exceeded income taxes payable because of timing differences. See the Glossary for an explanation of *timing differences.* The details of the U.S. federal timing differences appear in the schedule in the right-hand column on page 43.

(63) GE uses the deferral method of accounting for the investment credit; see our comment 74.

Employer costs for principal pension plans were $143 million in 1986, $479 million in 1985 and $582 million in 1984. GE Plan costs were lower in 1986 because of the adoption of SFAS 87 and changes in the assumed discount and benefit compensation increase rates. The impact of these lower costs, after recognizing income tax effects and government cost reimbursement, was equal to $81 million (18 cents per share) from the adoption of SFAS 87 and $79 million (17 cents per share) from the rate changes. Causes of the cost reduction from 1984 to 1985 included a change in the assumed discount rate, the full-year impact of a dedicated portfolio and amortization of continued favorable GE Trust income experience.

Details of 1986 cost for the principal pension plans are shown in the next table.

Cost for principal pension plans

For the year (In millions)		1986
Benefit cost for service during the year	⑤⓪	$ 349
Interest cost on projected benefit obligation	⑤①	1,074
Actual return on plan assets	⑤②	(2,739)
Amount deferred to future periods		1,672
Recognized return on plan assets	⑤③	(1,067)
Net amortization	⑤④	(213)
Net pension cost		$ 143

Recognized return on plan assets is determined by applying the expected long-term rate of return to the market-related value of assets. The market-related value of assets is based on amortized cost plus recognition over five years of market appreciation and depreciation in the portfolio.

The funding policy for the GE Plan and RCA Plan is to contribute amounts sufficient to meet minimum funding requirements set forth in U.S. employee benefit and tax laws plus such additional amounts as GE may determine to be appropriate from time to time. Covered employees also make contributions toward funding of the plans.

A measure of the funding status for an ongoing plan compares the market-related value of assets with the projected benefit obligation. GE believes the market-related value of assets is more realistic than current fair market value because the market-related value reduces the impact of short-term market fluctuations. A summary for the GE Plan follows.

GE Plan — funding status

December 31 (In millions)	1986	1985	1984
Market-related value of assets	$13,311	$10,924	$ 9,704
Projected benefit obligation	11,965	11,598	11,116

Market-related values were increased by $659 million at January 1, 1986, to comply with SFAS 87. Changes in interest rate assumptions reduced projected benefit obligations by $210 million and $699 million in 1986 and 1985, respectively.

For the RCA Plan, the projected benefit obligation was $2,586 million and the market-related value of assets was $2,330 million at the end of 1986.

A schedule reconciling the projected benefit obligation for principal pension plans with GE's recorded pension liability is shown below.

Reconciliation of projected benefit obligation with pension liability for principal pension plans

December 31 (In millions)	1986
Projected benefit obligation	$ 14,846
Less current fair market value of Trust assets	(19,547)
Unrecognized SFAS 87 transition gain	2,154
RCA Plan valuation adjustment for future tax effects and government cost reimbursement	162
Other unrecognized net experience gains	2,538
Recorded prepaid pension assets	218
Recorded pension liability	$ 371 ⑤⑦

The portion of the December 31, 1986, projected benefit obligation representing the accumulated benefit obligation was $12,258 million and the vested benefit obligation was $11,958 million. These amounts are based only on compensation and service to date. Other unrecognized net experience gains resulted principally from favorable investment performance and the changes in assumed discount and benefit compensation increase rates.

GE Trust and RCA Trust assets, which are not consolidated with those of GE, consist mainly of common stock and fixed income investments. GE common stock held by these Trusts totaled $105 million at the end of 1986. A summary of changes in net assets of the GE Trust follows.

GE Trust — change in net assets at current fair market value

For the year (In millions)	1986	1985	1984
Net assets at January 1	$14,362	$11,350	$ 9,886
Employer contributions	94	434	503
Employee contributions	94	107	101
Investment income including market appreciation	2,700	2,968	1,281
Benefits paid	(579)	(497)	(421)
Net assets at December 31	$16,671	$14,362	$11,350

The current fair market value of RCA Trust net assets was $2,876 million at December 31, 1986.

- **Principal retiree health care and life insurance plans:**

GE and its affiliates have a number of plans providing retiree health care and life insurance benefits. GE's aggregate cost for the principal GE and RCA plans was $84 million in 1986, $74 million in 1985 and $138 million in 1984. The increase in 1986 costs is attributable to inclusion of RCA plans, offset partially by an increase in the assumed discount rate used to determine the present value of future benefits. A reduction in life insurance reserve requirements attributable to an updating of mortality assumptions was the primary cause of the 1985 decrease.

Generally, GE and RCA employees who retire or terminate after qualifying for optional early retirement under the GE Plan or RCA Plan are eligible to participate in the corresponding retiree health care and life insurance plans. Health care benefits for eligible retirees under age 65 and

41

(64) The SEC requires disclosure of the disaggregation of pretax income into domestic and foreign sources. (See the last paragraph at the end of GE's note 8.) The analyst can thereby compute an effective domestic tax rate for 1986 of 30.2 percent (= $929/$3,021) and an effective foreign tax rate of 28.6 percent (= $174/$608). These foreign timing differences are part of the addback for deferred taxes shown on the Statements of Changes in Financial Position. See our comment 14.

(65) The Internal Revenue Service and the Courts have not yet closed the audit of GE's tax returns for any year since 1972 except 1974.

(66) APB *Opinion No. 11* says that income of affiliates that is expected to be indefinitely reinvested in the affiliate need not be subject to income tax provisions by the parent. If the parent expects to receive dividends from the affiliate in the foreseeable future, then the parent must make an income tax provision. One of the most controversial rules the FASB has ever proposed is to require that income taxes be provided for all such income of all affiliates, whether expected to be indefinitely reinvested or not. As this book goes to press, the FASB has not indicated whether it will change the reporting rules.

(67) GE consolidates GEFS for tax purposes, but uses the equity method for financial reporting. This can make understanding the income tax position of the combined entity hard to follow. GE alerts us to these facts and, at the bottom of the left-hand column of page 45 in the annual report, invites the reader to send for the separate financial statements of GEFS, in which many of the tax details can be seen.

(68) This schedule shows the components of the timing differences on U.S. federal income taxes.

(69) Depreciation on the tax return exceeded the amount included in cost of goods sold and other expenses on the financial statements. For most companies, tax depreciation exceeds book depreciation because an accelerated method is used for taxes and the straight line method is used for financial reporting. GE, however, uses an accelerated method (based on the sum of the years' digits) in its financial statements; see the Summary of Significant Accounting Policies. The excess of tax deductions for depreciation over book depreciation expense for GE arises from GE's using shorter depreciable lives for tax than for book calculations. See the Glossary at *asset depreciation range*. We can compute the excess of tax depreciation deductions over the book depreciation expense reported in the financial statements by using the $87 million timing difference shown here for 1986. If income tax expense exceeds income taxes payable by $87 million because of depreciation timing differences and if the marginal income tax rate is 46 percent of pretax income, then depreciation on the tax return must have exceeded depreciation on the financial statements by $189 million, which we can deduce by solving for x where

$$.46x = \$87 \text{ million or}$$
$$x = \$87 \text{ million}/.46, \text{ or}$$
$$x = \$189 \text{ million}.$$

(70) GE makes sales on credit, with cash payments from the customer to GE spread over time. Such sales are called "installment sales." APB *Opinion No. 10* requires that revenue (and associated cost of goods sold) from most such sales be recognized in the financial statements for the period of sale. For tax purposes, GE recognizes revenue later, when the cash payments are collected. Thus a timing difference arises. The amount shown here for GE is relatively small because GE tends not to have large percentages of its sales on the installment method. In 1985 and 1984, gross margins from installment sales on the income statement exceeded taxable cash collections from customers. In 1986, taxable cash collections from customers exceeded financial statement gross margins, reversing some of the previously-established timing differences.

(71) Estimated warranty expense recognized by the "allowance method" does not qualify as a tax deduction. GE uses the "allowance method" of recognizing warranty expense for financial reporting. As products carrying warranties are sold, GE makes the following entry recognizing the estimated liability for future repairs and replacements:

Estimated Warranty Expense (Provision) X
    Estimated Warranty Liability... X
Entry made in the period of sale for expected warranty costs.

---

eligible dependents are included in costs as covered expenses are actually incurred. For eligible retirees and spouses over age 65, health care benefits are funded or accrued and included in costs in the year the retiree becomes eligible for benefits. The present value of life insurance benefits for eligible retirees is funded and included in costs in the year of retirement.

Most retirees outside the United States are covered by government programs and GE's cost for such retiree health care and life insurance is not significant.

5 Other income

(In millions)	1986	1985	1984
Marketable securities and bank deposits	$ 316	$258	$323
Royalty and technical agreements	232	78	83
Customer financing ⑤⑨	78	66	75
Associated companies	42	37	33
Other investments: Interest	62	23	19
Dividends	11	11	11
Other sundry items	269	80	108
	$1,010	$553	$652

Income from royalty and technical agreements increased substantially in 1986 from the acquisition of RCA. Other sundry items included gains of $178 million, $38 million and $39 million in 1986, 1985 and 1984, respectively, from sales of portions of the Company's long-held passive investment in equity securities of Toshiba Corporation.

6 Interest and other financial charges ⑥⓪

Interest capitalized on major property, plant and equipment and real estate development projects was $38 million in 1986, $32 million in 1985 and $20 million in 1984.

7 Unusual items

Unusual items include pretax gains from certain asset sales and pretax expense provisions for costs of several different types of transactions. Gains from sales of assets which management has determined are not complementary to the Company's future business focus (other than sales of certain assets acquired from RCA) were $50 million in 1986, $518 million in 1985 and $617 million in 1984. Total unusual expenses aggregated $311 million in 1986, $540 million in 1985 and $762 million in 1984. Details of these unusual gains and expenses follow.

• *Unusual gains in 1986 arose from* the sale of a small foreign affiliate ($12 million) and adjustments to previous unusual disposition provisions ($38 million).

• *Unusual gains in 1985 arose from:*

(1) Sale of the 15.5% interest in Australian coal properties which had been retained at the time of the disposition in 1984 of most of Utah International Inc. (Utah). The 15.5% interest was sold to three buyers for cash amounting to $387 million and occurred in the second and third quarters. The gain from these three transactions was $247 million before taxes. The contribution to GE's operating results from these interests during the portion of 1985 prior to their disposition was not significant.

(2) Disposition of the remaining 37% of GE's interest in the cablevision company into which GE's former cablevision operations had been merged in 1984. The 1985 transaction was completed in December for a pretax gain of $132 million. Payment included $43 million in cash and a non-interest-bearing note due one year from closing. Earnings from this investment prior to disposition were an insignificant portion of GE's total 1985 results.

(3) Other transactions resulting from adjustments to previous unusual disposition provisions. These aggregated $139 million before taxes in 1985.

• *Unusual gains in 1984 included:*

(1) Sale of most of Utah to The Broken Hill Proprietary Company Limited in a transaction valued at $2.4 billion, representing the cash proceeds from the sale as well as the value of the 15.5% interest in several Australian coal properties which the Company acquired and retained and subsequently sold in 1985. (GE also retained Ladd Petroleum Corporation, formerly a wholly owned Utah affiliate.) GE's share of the total assets of new and retained properties at December 31, 1984, is shown as "all other" in note 24. GE's revenues and net earnings for 1984 included $373 million and $70 million, respectively, from Utah for the first quarter, while "all other" results for the remainder of 1984 are only for the properties owned subsequent to the sale. The 1984 gain from the Utah transaction was $500 million before taxes and after providing for future contractual obligations.

(2) Sale of GE's small household appliance operations, both domestically and abroad, to The Black and Decker Manufacturing Company (B&D) in April. Small appliance operations accounted for less than 2% of GE's consolidated sales. This transaction did not include any of GE's other consumer products lines. GE received cash, three million shares of B&D stock (one-half of which was subsequently sold in January 1986) and approximately $50 million in a three-year note. GE has agreed not to sell the remaining B&D stock, except in certain circumstances, nor to purchase additional B&D stock until 1987. The note was interest-free for the first year and bears interest of 9% annually thereafter. The gain from this disposition was $28 million before taxes and after providing for future contractual obligations.

Later, when repairs are made, and warranty costs are incurred, the entry is:

Estimated Warranty Liability . . . .   Y
   Assets Used and Liabilities Incurred . . . .   Y
To recognize cost of actual repairs and replacements.

The repair and, therefore, the second entry often occur in a year subsequent to the year of sale. The cost of providing the warranty services does not become a tax deduction until the repair is actually made. Thus timing differences are created: an expense is subtracted on the financial statements in one year but is deducted on the tax return in a later year. In 1985 and 1984, the amounts spent for warranty repairs, Y above, exceeded the estimated warranty expense, X above. The amount for 1985 is approximately $50 (= $23/.46) million. We can make the following statement about 1986: The provision for warranties (the estimated expense) results in income taxes payable being larger than income tax expense. Therefore, it must be true that the estimated expense of rendering warranty services in future years for sales made in 1986 is greater than the actual costs of the warranty repairs made in 1986, most of which relate to sales of earlier years.

⑫ See the GE report at our comment 56. GE has a larger financial income expense for pensions than its income tax deduction. This results in a negative timing difference, or income taxes payable larger than income tax expense related to pensions.

⑬ Primarily because of the accounting for warranties (explained in our comment 71), GE's cumulative income tax payments over all the time span that has elapsed since it began accounting for deferred income taxes have exceeded cumulative income tax expense reported in the financial statements. This cumulative excess decreased in 1985 and increased in 1986. This has resulted in a "deferred tax debit" (whereas most companies have the reverse situation and a "deferred tax credit") of $180 million, which GE reports among its "Other assets"; see GE's note 16. Starting in 1987, GE (and all other companies) will have negative timing differences relating to uncollectible accounts. The tax deduction will be for accounts actually written off during the year (using the direct write-off method), while the financial statement charge for bad debt expense will be estimated using the allowance method. The timing differences will be like those for warranties—deferred tax debits in the year of sale, with deferred tax credits in later years when the actual accounts are written off. The effect of the change in the tax law will be to accelerate income tax payments in the future relative to the past treatment and to increase the size of GE's deferred tax asset (or decreasing the size of other companies' deferred tax liability).

⑭ GE uses the deferral method of accounting for the investment credit, rather than the less conservative flow-through method. (Most U.S. corporations use the flow through method.) GE realized $49 million of investment credits during 1986. A portion (which cannot be computed from the published data) of this $49 million reduced reported tax expense in 1986; the remainder is part of the $376 million deferred investment credit mentioned in the second sentence at the top of GE's page 44. In principle, this $376 million appears on the balance sheet, but GE does not separately identify it. The amount is probably included under the caption "Other liabilities." A portion of previous years' investment credits, which had been deferred, also served to reduce 1986 reported tax expense. The total of these two reductions of reported tax expense in 1986 was $87 million. If GE had used the flow-through method, income tax expense would have been increased by an additional $38 (= $87 − $49) million and 1986 net income would have been $38 million smaller. Under the flow-through method, retained earnings at the end of 1986 would have been $376 million larger.

    GE earns investment credits in the year it acquires new qualifying assets. Because it uses the conservative deferral method for investment credits, it recognizes the effect on income over the lives of the assets acquired. More funds are provided by the investment credit than are recognized in income in the year of acquisition. In later years when the previously-deferred investment credits are amortized to income, more funds are used for income taxes payable than the amount reported for income tax expense. As a result of this phenomenon, funds provided by operations on the 1986 Statement of Changes in Financial Position are smaller than they would be if GE had used the flow-through method of financial accounting. See our comment 14, item (c).

(3) Merger of General Electric Cablevision Corporation in the fourth quarter of 1984 into a subsidiary of United Artists Cablesystems Corporation (Cablesystems). In this transaction, GE received cash and 37% of the stock of Cablesystems. Cablevision operations were minor in relation to GE's total results. The gain on this transaction was $89 million before taxes and after providing for future contractual obligations.

• *Unusual costs include the following:*

Expense provisions to cover corporate restructurings — $311 million in 1986, $447 million in 1985 and $636 million in 1984. These represent the provisions for expenses of refocusing a wide variety of business and marketing activities and reducing foreign and domestic risk exposures. These provisions include costs of rationalizing and improving a large number of production facilities, rearranging production activities among a number of existing plants, and reorganizing, phasing out or otherwise concluding other activities no longer considered essential to the conduct of the Company's business.

Special cash payment to certain employees in 1985 — $93 million. The payment was equal to 3% of normal straight-time annual earnings in July 1985 to hourly union employees, in accordance with new union contracts, and also to certain other hourly and non-exempt salaried employees. The total payment aggregated $103 million and was reflected as an unusual expense for the quarter or was capitalized in inventory, depending on employees' work assignments, with inventoried amounts recorded as expense when the inventories are sold.

Revaluations of goodwill and intangibles. In 1984, goodwill and intangibles were revalued downward by $126 million to recognize the rapid changes occurring in certain technology businesses.

8 Provision for income taxes (61)

(In millions)		1986	1985	1984
U.S. federal income taxes:				
Estimated amount payable		$1,062	$ 842	$1,051
Effect of timing differences	(62)	(95)	90	(161)
Investment credit deferred (amortized) — net	(63)	(38)	35	41
		929	967	931
Foreign income taxes:	(64)			
Estimated amount payable		198	135	143
Effect of timing differences		(24)	(4)	(88)
		174	131	55
Other (principally state and local income taxes)		97	45	44
		$1,200	$1,143	$1,030

All GE consolidated U.S. federal income tax returns have been closed through 1972. (65)

• Provision has been made for U.S. federal income taxes to be paid on that portion of the undistributed earnings of affiliates and associated companies expected to be remitted to the parent company. Undistributed earnings intended to be reinvested indefinitely in affiliates and associated companies totaled $1,063 million at the end of 1986, (66) $946 million at the end of 1985 and $883 million at the end of 1984.

• General Electric Financial Services, Inc. (GEFS) is a (67) nonconsolidated affiliate for financial reporting but is included in GE's consolidated U.S. federal income tax return. Taxes payable by the consolidated companies shown in the preceding table exclude the effect of significant tax credits and deductions of GEFS, which arise primarily from leasing activities. GE and GEFS together had net taxes payable for 1986, 1985 and 1984. Existing leases of GEFS will generate taxable income in future years, which is provided for in the deferred income taxes of GEFS (see note 14). At December 31, 1986, 1985 and 1984, tax credit carryforwards totaling $275 million, $358 million and $92 million, respectively, were recorded by GEFS as a partial offset to deferred taxes. For financial reporting purposes, investment tax credit carryforward amounts are amortized to earned income over lease periods (as are investment tax credits currently usable). For tax purposes, they will be offset against taxes payable in the future.

Some items are reported in financial statements in different years than they are included in tax returns. Deferred taxes are provided on these timing differences as summarized below.

Effect of timing differences on U.S. federal income taxes (68)

Increase (decrease) in provision for income taxes (In millions)		1986	1985	1984
Tax over book depreciation	(69)	$ 87	$ 124	$ 168
Margin on installment sales	(70)	(33)	48	28
Provision for warranties	(71)	(27)	23	24
Provision for pensions	(72)	(52)	(171)	(47)
Other — net		(70)	66	(334)
	(73)	$(95)	$ 90	$(161)

Other — net reflects a number of individual timing differences, including those related to various portions of transactions involving business dispositions, restructuring expense provisions and, in 1984, reductions of intangibles.

• The U.S. investment tax credit (ITC) was repealed, with some transitional exceptions, effective January 1, 1986. (74) ITC in 1986, 1985 and 1984 aggregated $49 million,

(75) Most readers of financial statements are aware that the U.S. federal tax rate on most corporate income was 46 percent of pretax income in 1986. The SEC requires that companies report in its notes why the reported income tax expense rate differs from the statutory rate, 46 percent in 1986.

(76) See the Glossary at *DISC* and *FSC;* some of the income of such an entities is not currently taxed or is taxed at rates different from usual rates.

(77) The $504 million of income in 1986 from GEFS reported in GE's income statement using the equity method is after taxes. Yet it appears in GE's income statement before the income tax calculation. GE need pay no further taxes on the income from GEFS; this accounts for part of the difference between GE's effective tax rate on "pretax income," 32.5 percent in 1986, and the statutory rate, 46 percent.

(78) The investment credit reduces taxes otherwise payable and this accounts for another part of the difference between the effective rate and the statutory rate.

(79) Capital gains are taxed at a rate lower than the statutory 46 percent rate. Thus the effective tax rate is lowered to the extent that pretax income contains capital gains taxed at the lower rate.

(80) The 32.5 percent figure for 1986 results from dividing income tax expense of $1,200 million by the pretax income of the enterprise. Pretax income of the enterprise is $3,689 million, the sum of $1,200 (income tax expense) + $2,492 (net earnings) − $3 (minority interest in losses of consolidated affiliates). Refer to our comment 4 for a discussion of minority interest in earnings. The minority's share of the income taxes of the less-than-100%-owned consolidated affiliates is included in the $975 in the numerator. Thus, the entire pretax income (or loss) of the affiliate must be included in the denominator so that both the numerator and the denominator refer to the same business entity, at least with respect to the partially-owned affiliates. The minority interest in losses for 1986, $3 million, is such a small number that omitting this refinement will give the same arithmetic result, 32.5 percent, for 1986. But to derive the 33.3 percent for 1985, one must make this adjustment in order to derive the figure that GE publishes.

(81) See *compensating balance* in the Glossary. Compensating balances increase the stated cost of borrowing; accordingly, the SEC requires disclosure of such amounts, if they are significant. GE states that its compensating balances are not significant.

(82) *SFAS No. 12* requires disclosure of aggregate cost and aggregate market value of marketable securities held as current assets.

(83) GE uses a LIFO cost flow assumption for inventories, but manages its inventories, as most sensible businesses would, on FIFO, using the older materials and finished goods before the newer. It keeps its records internally on a FIFO basis (the amount is $6,913 million at year-end 1986) and makes an adjustment at year-end to convert the internal records to LIFO. The adjustment involves a debit to Cost of Goods Sold (or Work in Process Inventory) and a credit to Ending Inventory for the $1,752 million shown opposite our callout for comment 84. The numbers given for "Less revaluation to LIFO" allow the computation of pretax income had GE used FIFO, rather than LIFO. See our next comment. Some business analysts call this amount the "LIFO reserve," but we prefer GE's more descriptive caption.

(84) GE provides information that allows us to calculate what the operating income would have been if a FIFO cost flow assumption had been used. The IRS does not allow companies using LIFO for tax purposes to disclose in the financial statements what income would have been under FIFO. But the SEC requires the disclosure of beginning and ending inventories as they would have been under FIFO, if these amounts are significantly different from the LIFO amounts. The SEC's required disclosure of FIFO beginning and ending inventories allows the reader to compute the income difference. As of December 31, 1986, cumulative pretax income is $1,752 million less than it would have been under FIFO. As of January 1, 1986, cumulative pretax income is $1,856 million less than it would have been under FIFO. This difference decreased by $104 (= $1,856 − $1,752) million during the year 1986. Hence 1986 pretax income would have been $104 million smaller if FIFO had been used. This calculation may be seen more clearly in the exhibit at the top of page 105. Generally, FIFO leads to larger income than does LIFO. Because of the dips into old LIFO layers, however, LIFO cost of goods sold is even smaller than would have been FIFO cost of goods sold. See the next comment.

$111 million and $110 million, respectively. In 1986, $87 million was included in net earnings, compared with $76 million in 1985 and $69 million in 1984. At the end of 1986, the amount deferred which will be included in net earnings in future years was $376 million.

Reconciliation from statutory to effective (75)
income tax rates

	1986	1985	1984
U.S. federal statutory rate	46.0%	46.0%	46.0%
Reduction in taxes resulting from:			
(76) Varying tax rates of consolidated affiliates (including DISC and FSC)	(2.2)	(3.6)	(3.9)
(77) Inclusion of GEFS earnings in before-tax income on an after-tax basis	(6.3)	(5.5)	(4.5)
(78) Investment credit	(2.3)	(2.2)	(2.1)
Unusual items (varying tax rates)	(0.4)	(0.6)	(2.4)
(79) Income tax at capital gains rate	(1.4)	(0.2)	(0.3)
Other — net	(0.9)	(0.6)	(1.4)
Effective tax rate (80)	32.5%	33.3%	31.4%

● Based on the location of the component furnishing goods or services, domestic income before taxes was (64) $3,081 million in 1986 ($3,232 million in 1985 and $2,956 million in 1984). The corresponding amounts for foreign-based operations were $608 million, $200 million and $324 million in each of the last three years, respectively. Provision for income taxes is determined on the basis of the jurisdiction imposing the tax liability. Therefore, U.S. and foreign taxes shown previously do not compare directly with these segregations.

9 Cash and marketable securities

(81) Deposits restricted as to usage and withdrawal or used as partial compensation for short-term borrowing arrangements were not material.

Carrying value of marketable securities was substantially the same as market value at year-end 1986 and (82) 1985. Equity securities in the portfolio were carried at a cost of $48 million and $206 million at December 31, 1986 and 1985, respectively.

10 Current receivables

December 31 (In millions)	1986	1985
Receivable from:		
Customers	$5,748	$4,571
Associated companies	178	114
Nonconsolidated affiliates	13	15
Others	1,425	1,434
	7,364	6,134
Less allowance for losses	(156)	(94)
	$7,208	$6,040

11 Inventories

December 31 (In millions)		1986	1985
Raw materials and work in process		$ 4,305	$3,618
Finished goods		2,379	1,926
Unbilled shipments		229	261
	(83)	6,913	5,805
Less revaluation to LIFO	(84)	(1,752)	(1,856)
LIFO value of inventories		$ 5,161	$3,949

About 80% of total inventories is valued using the LIFO method of inventory accounting.

● LIFO revaluations decreased by $104 million, $171 million and $125 million during 1986, 1985 and 1984, respectively. Included in these decreases were $51 million, $128 million and $125 million (1986, 1985 and 1984, (85) respectively) due to lower inventory levels, mainly in power systems. Also, in 1986 and 1985, there were net current-year price decreases. In 1984, $32 million of the total decrease was due to business dispositions partly offset by higher current-year prices.

12 Property, plant and equipment

(In millions)		1986	1985
Major classes at December 31:			
Manufacturing plant and equipment			
Land and improvements		$ 271	$ 178
Buildings, structures and related equipment		4,087	3,449
Machinery and equipment		12,061	10,218
Leasehold costs and manufacturing plant under construction		1,140	906
Oil and gas properties		815	955
		$18,374	$15,706
Cost at January 1		$15,706	$14,458
Additions — acquired with RCA		1,638	—
— other		2,042	1,953
Dispositions		(1,011)	(678)
Other changes		(1)	(27)
Cost at December 31		$18,374	$15,706
Accumulated depreciation, depletion and amortization			
Balance at January 1		$ 7,806	$ 7,089
Current-year provision	(86)	1,460	1,249
Dispositions		(736)	(536)
Other changes		3	4
Balance at December 31	(86)	$ 8,533	$ 7,806
Property, plant and equipment less depreciation, depletion and amortization at December 31		$ 9,841	$ 7,900

Inventory Data from Financial Statements and Footnotes (For Authors' comment 84. Amounts shown in **boldface** are given in General Electric Company's financial statements. Other amounts are computed as indicated.)

	LIFO Cost-Flow Assumption (Actually Used)	+	Excess of FIFO over LIFO Amount	=	FIFO Cost-Flow Assumption (Hypothetical)
	(Dollar Amounts in Millions)				
Beginning Inventory.	$ 3,949		$ 1,856		$ 5,805
Purchases	21,969[a]		0		21,969
Cost of Goods Available for Sale.	$25,918		$ 1,856		$27,774
Less Ending Inventory	5,161		1,752		6,913
Cost of Goods Sold	$20,757		$ 104		$20,861
Sale of Goods.	$28,139		$ 0		$28,139
Less Cost of Goods Sold	20,757		104		20,861
Gross Margin on Sales.	$ 7,382		($ 104)		$ 7,278

[a]Computation of Purchases not presented in GE's financial statements:

Purchases   =   Cost of Goods Sold   +   Ending Inventory   −   Beginning Inventory

$21,969   =   **$20,757**   +   **$5,161**   −   **$3,949**

⑧⑤ See the Glossary at *LIFO inventory layer*, particularly the last sentence. When the layers assumed sold cost less than current purchases would have cost, cost of goods sold is decreased and income for the period is increased. GE tells us that 1986 pretax income is $51 million larger because of the dips into old LIFO layers. The rest of the 1986 $104 million decrease in LIFO revaluation (and $104 million increase in pretax income) results from price declines.

⑧⑥ If an asset costing $1,000 is being depreciated on a straight-line basis in the amount of $100 per year and has accumulated depreciation of $400 at year-end, then the asset must be four (= $400/$100) years old. If GE used straight-line depreciation for financial reporting, then the analogous computation indicates the dollars used by GE to acquire Property, plant, and equipment were spent, on average, 5.8 (= $8,533/$1,460) years prior to the end of 1986. GE uses accelerated depreciation for some of its depreciable assets (see page 38 of the GE Annual Report); thus, accumulated depreciation builds up at a faster rate than under straight-line depreciation, and we can conclude that dollars for plant were spent on average less than 5.8 years prior to the end of 1986. GE has a relatively young plant compared to some: U.S. Steel (now called USX), for example, spent its dollars for plant, on average, more than 10 years before the end of 1986.

⑧⑦ Notice the plural, affiliate*s*. GE's primary nonconsolidated finance affiliate is GE Financial Services, Inc. (GEFS), whose financial statements appear in the next column. GE uses the equity method for GEFS. Because GE has owned 100 percent of GEFS since it was organized, GE's investment (asset) account for GEFS is the mirror image of GEFS's owners' equity accounts. Consider the possible transactions. GE makes an investment in GEFS by sending it cash: GE debits the investment account; GEFS credits a contributed capital account. GEFS earns income: GEFS credits retained earnings and GE, using the equity method, debits the investment account. GEFS declares a dividend: GEFS debits retained earnings; GE, using the equity method, credits the investment account.

At the end of 1986, GEFS's owners' equity totals $2,994 million; see its balance sheet in the next column. Thus, we can deduce that GE's investment in financial affiliates *other* than GEFS amounted to $60 (= $3,054 − $2,994) million at the end of 1986. $24 million is explained in GE's note (a) below the "Other investments" schedule.

13 Funds held for business development

Funds held for longer-term future business development are invested in a variety of securities, principally state, county and municipal bonds and corporate preferred stocks. Estimated realizable value of these investments was about the same as cost at December 31, 1986 and 1985.

14 Other investments

December 31 (In millions)		1986	1985
Nonconsolidated financial services affiliates (a) ⑧⑦		$3,054	$2,311
Associated companies (a)		414	293
Miscellaneous investments (at cost) (b):			
Government and government-guaranteed securities		177	158
Other		258	344
		435	502
Marketable equity securities (c) ⑧⑧		74	81
Less allowance for losses		(63)	(37)
		$3,914	$3,150

⑧⑦ (a) Includes advances at December 31, 1986, of $24 million (non-consolidated financial services affiliates) and $13 million (associated companies).

(b) Estimated realizable value about the same as cost at year end.

⑧⑧ (c) Carried at cost. Aggregate market value was $65 million and $209 million at year-end 1986 and 1985, respectively. Gross unrealized gains were $16 million and gross unrealized losses were

⑧⑨ $25 million at December 31, 1986.

● Investment in nonconsolidated financial services affiliates represents predominately GE's investment in General Electric Financial Services, Inc. (GEFS). GEFS includes wholly owned General Electric Credit Corporation (GECC) and Employers Reinsurance Corporation (ERC), and an 80% interest in Kidder, Peabody Group Inc. (Kidder). The investment in Kidder was acquired by GEFS in June 1986 and was accounted for as a purchase. During the normal course of business, GEFS and its affiliates have minor transactions with GE and certain of its consolidated affiliates. Virtually all products financed by GECC are manufactured by companies other than GE. GEFS is included in GE's consolidated U.S. federal income tax return. Condensed consolidated financial statements for GEFS follow, which include operations of Kidder and ERC from their dates of acquisition.

Pro forma net earnings of GEFS for the years 1986 and 1985, assuming acquisition of Kidder had been completed at the beginning of each of those years, would not have been significantly different from amounts actually reported.

More information about GEFS is in its annual report, which may be obtained from General Electric Financial Services, Inc., P.O. Box 8300, Stamford, Conn. 06904.

General Electric Financial Services, Inc. and consolidated affiliates

Current and retained earnings

For the year (In millions)	1986	1985	1984
Earned income:			
Earned income from operations	$5,976	$3,805	$2,933
Effect on investment in leveraged leases of change in tax rate assumptions	(172)	—	—
Sale of stock by nonconsolidated affiliate	10	—	—
Total earned income	5,814	3,805	2,933
Expenses:			
Interest and discount expense	2,063	1,339	1,123
Operating and administrative expense	1,402	768	602
Losses and policyholder benefits of insurance affiliates	1,439	876	583
Provision for losses on financing receivables	558	185	109
Provision for losses on other assets	10	3	1
Depreciation and amortization	403	210	161
Total expenses	5,875	3,381	2,579
Earnings (loss) before income taxes	(61)	424	354
Provision for income taxes:			
Income tax provision (credit) from operations	(173)	11	25
Effect on income taxes of change in tax rate assumptions for leveraged leases	(392)	—	—
Total provision (credit) for income taxes	(565)	11	25
Net earnings	504	413	329
Retained earnings at beginning of period	1,139	726	397
Retained earnings at end of period	$1,643	$1,139	$ 726

Financial position ⑨⓪

December 31 (In millions)	1986	1985
Financing receivables:		
Time sales and loans, net of deferred income	$14,930	$11,854
Investment in financing leases	8,347	7,267
Total financing receivables	23,277	19,121
Allowance for losses	(603)	(492)
Financing receivables — net	22,674	18,629
Cash and short-term investments	405	509
Marketable securities at cost	3,680	2,746
Marketable securities at market	5,646	166
Securities purchased under agreements to resell ⑨①	12,961	—
Other receivables — net	4,325	938
Equipment on operating leases — net	1,726	1,113
Other assets	2,406	1,539
Total assets	$53,823	$25,640
Notes payable:		
Due within one year	$17,741	$11,563
Long-term	5,656	4,830
Securities sold under agreements to repurchase	13,070	—
Securities sold but not yet purchased at market	3,525	—
Reserves of insurance affiliates	2,880	2,048
Other liabilities	4,076	1,265
Total liabilities	46,948	19,706
Deferred income taxes	3,838	3,581
Deferred investment tax credits	43	51
Capital stock	1	1
Additional paid-in capital	1,347	1,152
Retained earnings	1,643	1,139
Other	3	10
Equity	2,994	2,302
Total liabilities, deferred tax items and equity	$53,823	$25,640

(88) *SFAS No. 12* requires that the portfolio of marketable equity securities be valued at lower of aggregate cost or market and that the total amounts of unrealized gains and losses on individual holdings in this portfolio be separately disclosed. We are frankly puzzled at GE's showing its portfolio "carried at cost," of $74 million at the end of 1986, when this is greater than market value of $65 million. GE is not using lower of cost or market for this portfolio.

(89) The aggregate market value of these securities at year-end 1986 is $65 million; their cost is $74 million. Thus, the unrealized holding loss at the end of 1986 is $9 (= $74 − $65) million. The $9 million consists of unrealized holding losses of $25 million offset by $16 million of holding gains. At year-end 1985, the unrealized holding gain was $128 (= $209 market value − $81 cost) million. Thus, the unrealized holding loss during the year 1986 was $137 (= $9 + $128) million.

(90) The FASB proposes to require that all majority-owned and controlled subsidiaries be consolidated. If GE Financial Services (GEFS) were consolidated, rather than accounted for on the equity method, all these assets, liabilities, and deferred credits would be shown on GE's balance sheet. GE's consolidated retained earnings would be no different, however, because the equity method records income of unconsolidated subsidiaries as earned. The $2,994 (= $53,823 − $46,948 − $3,838 − $43) million of net assets added to GE's balance sheet would be offset with the elimination of $2,994 million of the $3,054 Other Investments shown on the balance sheet and detailed in GE's note 14. If GE were to consolidate GEFS, the results would be as shown in the exhibit on page 109. We also show two key financial ratios, as they would be calculated from year-end account balances. The consolidation policy with respect to GEFS affects the appearance of the financial statements. For an even larger effect, refer to the financial statements of General Motors Corporation and go through the exercise of consolidating GMAC (General Motors Acceptance Corporation), which GM accounts for by the equity method.

Adjusting entry (1) adds the revenues and expenses of GEFS to the consolidated totals, while removing the equity method revenue reported by GE. Adjusting entry (2) adds the assets and liabilities of GEFS to the consolidated totals, while removing GE's net investment from the asset account for Investments.

(91) These assets were acquired in the purchase of Kidder described in the text just to the left.

(92) GE describes the goodwill acquired in the purchase of RCA on its page 39, near the callout for our comment 41.

(93) Intangibles acquired before October 1970 need not be amortized. APB *Opinion No. 17* requires that licenses and intangibles acquired after October 1970 be amortized over a period not to exceed 40 years.

15 Intangible assets

December 31 (In millions)		1986	1985
Goodwill	㉒	$2,793	$117
Other intangibles		788	105
		$3,581	$222

Accumulated amortization of goodwill was $147 million and $111 million at December 31, 1986 and 1985, respectively. Accumulated amortization of other intangibles was $308 million and $239 million at December 31, 1986 and 1985, respectively. Goodwill and other intangibles at year-end 1986 were mainly from the RCA acquisition, for which goodwill is being amortized on a straight-line basis over 40 years. Other intangibles and goodwill are being amortized over shorter periods as appropriate, ranging from five to 20 years.

16 Other assets

December 31 (In millions)	1986	1985
Long-term receivables	$ 555	$ 549
Television program costs	461	—
Recoverable engineering costs on government contracts	405	422
Deferred charges	318	122
Deferred income taxes	180	160
Real estate development projects	169	181
Customer financing	79	94
Other	403	90
	$2,570	$1,618

The National Broadcasting Company capitalizes program costs (including rights to broadcast) when paid or when a program is ready for broadcast, if earlier. These costs are amortized based upon projected revenues or expensed when a program is determined to have no value.

17 Short-term borrowings

December 31 (In millions)	1986		1985	
	Amount	Average rate at Dec. 31	Amount	Average rate at Dec. 31
General Electric Company:				
Notes with trust departments	$ 359	6.4%	$ 304	7.5%
Commercial paper	897	6.2	50	7.9
Consolidated affiliate bank borrowings	334	29.6	601	31.6
Other, including current portion of long-term borrowings	223		342	
	$1,813		$1,297	

● Other borrowings at December 31, 1986, included amounts from nonconsolidated affiliates of $146 million ($89 million at December 31, 1985). Other borrowings at December 31, 1985, also included $170 million of repurchase agreements. These agreements represented a loan by GE of U.S. Treasury Notes (classified as current marketable securities of $162 million) in connection with the borrowings.

● The average balance of short-term borrowings, excluding the current portion of long-term borrowings, was $3,200 million in 1986 (calculated by averaging month-end balances for the year), compared with an average balance of $1,391 million in 1985. The maximum balances in these calculations were $4,742 million and $1,813 million at the end of September 1986 and 1985, respectively. The average worldwide effective interest rate for the year 1986 was 8% and for 1985 was 15%. These average rates represent total short-term interest incurred divided by the average balance outstanding.

● Although the total unused credit available to the Company through banks and commercial credit markets is not readily quantifiable, confirmed credit lines of approximately $1.4 billion had been extended by about 49 banks at year-end 1986. Substantially all of these lines are also available for use by GECC and General Electric Financial Services, Inc. in addition to their own credit lines.

18 Accounts payable

December 31 (In millions)	1986	1985
Trade accounts	$1,972	$1,757
Collected for the account of others	342	180
Due to nonconsolidated affiliates	280	267
	$2,594	$2,204

GENERAL ELECTRIC AND GE FINANCIAL SERVICES, INC., 1986
(For Authors' comment 90)

Income Statement	Equity Method (as Reported)	Adjustment Debit	Adjustment Credit	Consolidated
Revenues (other than from GEFS)[a]	$36,221		$5,814 (1)	$42,035
Equity Method				
Revenues from GEFS	504	$ 504 (1)		0
Total Revenues[b].	$36,725			$42,035
Total Expenses[c].	34,233	5,310 (1)		39,543
Net Income	$ 2,492			$ 2,492
Balance Sheet				
All Assets Except				
Investments in GEFS.	$31,597	53,823 (2)		$85,420
Investment in GEFS	2,994		2,994 (2)	0
Total Assets	$34,591			$85,420
Liabilities				
(including Minority				
Interest)	$19,482		50,829[d] (2)	$70,311
Owner's Equity.	15,109			15,109
Total Equities	$34,591	$59,637	$59,637	$85,420

Rate of Return on Assets:

$$\frac{\$2,492 - \$3^e + (.54 \times \$625^f)}{\$34,591} \qquad \frac{\$2,492 = \$3^e + .54 \times (\$625^f + \$2,063^g)}{\$85,420}$$

$$= \frac{\$ 2,827}{\$34,591} = 8.2\% \qquad = \frac{\$ 3,941}{\$85,420} = 4.6\%$$

Debt-Equity Ratio:

$$\frac{\$19,482}{\$34,591} = 56\% \qquad \frac{\$70,311}{\$85,420} = 82\%$$

a. $28,139 + $7,072 + $1,010.
b. See GE's income statement.
c. $33,036 (total costs and expenses) + $1,200 (income taxes) − $3 (minority interest).
d. GEFS's liabilities ($46,948) + deferred income taxes ($3,838) + deferred investment credits ($43).
e. Minority interest in net income from income statement.
f. GE's interest expense. Multiply by .54 to state on aftertax basis.
g. GEFS's interest expense. Multiply .54 to state on aftertax basis.

19 Other costs and expenses accrued

The balances at year-end 1986 and 1985 included compensation and benefit costs accrued of $1,067 million and $756 million, respectively.

20 Long-term borrowings

Outstanding December 31 (In millions)	1986	1985
7⅛% Notes Due 1989	$ 500	$ —
6⅞% Notes Due 1989	500	—
12¼% Australian Dollar Notes Due 1989 (a)	108	—
16¼% Notes Due 1987-1989 (b)	85	—
11½% Notes Due 1990 (b)	75	—
5¾% Notes Due 1972-1991	25	32
6⅞% Notes Due 1991	500	—
7⅛% Euro-dollar Notes Due 1991	300	—
5.30% Sinking Fund Debentures Due 1973-1992	34	34
12¾% Notes Due 1992 (b)	100	—
5¾% Euro-yen Notes Due 1993 (c)	194	—
4⅛% Euro-dollar Discount Notes Due 1993	200	—
7% Euro-dollar Extendible Notes Due 1998 (d) (g)	200	—
8½% Debentures Due 1985-2004	217	217
8% Euro-dollar Extendible Notes Due 2006 (e) (g)	300	—
7⅜% Euro-dollar Extendible Notes Due 2006 (f) (g)	300	—
8⅝% Sinking Fund Debentures Due 2016	300	—
Industrial development bonds	248	251
All other	165	219
	$4,351	$753

(a) The Company has entered into certain contracts which result in a fixed U.S. dollar interest cost of 7.67%.

(b) Debt originally incurred by RCA but for which GE is now the obligor.

(c) Notes are yen 35 billion at a fixed exchange rate of yen 180.41 = $U.S. 1.00.

(d) Interest rate subject to annual adjustment at the Company's option beginning in 1989.

(e) Interest rate subject to annual adjustment at the Company's option beginning in 1993.

(f) Interest rate subject to annual adjustment at the Company's option beginning in 1991.

(94) (g) At annual rate adjustment dates, notes are redeemable in whole or in part at the option of the Company or repayable at the option of the holders.

• All other long-term borrowings include original issue premium and discounts, an adjustment to bring RCA borrowings at acquisition date to fair market value and a variety of borrowings by affiliates and parent components with various interest rates and maturities. Amounts due to nonconsolidated affiliates were $6 million at the end of 1986 and 1985.

(95) • Long-term borrowing maturities during the next five years, including the portion classified as current, are $66 million in 1987, $30 million in 1988, $1,305 million in 1989, $137 million in 1990 and $821 million in 1991. These amounts are after deducting debentures which have been reacquired for sinking-fund needs. (96)

21 Share owners' equity

Preferred stock up to 2,000,000 shares ($1.00 par value) is authorized, but no such shares have been issued. Common stock (par value $1.25) shares authorized total 550,000,000.

Shares of common stock

December 31 (In thousands)	1986	1985	1984
Issued January 1	463,282	462,928	462,928
Shares for pooling of interests	—	354	—
Issued December 31	463,282	463,282	462,928
In treasury	(7,387)	(7,306)	(8,052)
Outstanding	455,895	455,976	454,876

Share owners' equity (97)

(In millions)	1986	1985	1984
Common stock issued			
Balance January 1 and December 31	$ 579	$ 579	$ 579
Other capital			
Balance January 1	$ 641	$ 640	$ 657
Foreign currency translation adjustments	75	(18)	(10)
Unrealized gains (losses) on securities held by insurance affiliates	(6)	15	(5)
Gain (loss) on treasury stock (98) dispositions	23	4	(2)
Balance December 31	$ 733	$ 641	$ 640
Retained earnings			
Balance January 1	$ 12,761	$11,493	$10,317
Adjustments	—	11	(133)
Net earnings	2,492	2,277	2,239
Dividends declared	(1,081)	(1,020)	(930)
Balance December 31	$14,172	$12,761	$11,493
Common stock held in treasury			
Balance January 1	$ 310	$ 313	$ 283
Purchases	348	283	284
Dispositions:			
Employee savings plans	(109)	(113)	(133)
Stock options and appreciation rights	(71)	(64)	(39)
Employee stock ownership plan	(41)	(43)	(37)
Dividend reinvestment and share purchase plan	(33)	(29)	(26)
Contribution to GE Pension Trust	(26)	(22)	—
Conversion of GEOCC long-term debt	(7)	(25)	(11)
Incentive compensation plans	4	10	20
Exchange for GE long-term debt	—	—	(20)
Business acquisitions	—	—	(8)
Balance December 31	$ 375	$ 310	$ 313

The current Proxy Statement includes a proposal recommended by the Board of Directors on February 13, 1987, which, if approved by share owners, would (a) increase the number of authorized shares of common stock from 550,000,000 shares each with a par value of $1.25 to 1,100,000,000 shares each with a par value of $.63; (b) split each presently issued common share, including

(94) Long-term borrowings that are redeemable at the option of the borrower and callable at the option of the lender will almost surely be paid off at the option date unless the interest rate is adjusted to suit whichever party to the loan has benefited from the change in interest rates during the year just ended. Thus, it is likely that either the interest rate will be changed or the debt will be paid off at each annual option date. Thus, the economic substance of such lending is, we think, short-term debt, not long-term debt, because the lender can require the debt be paid, even on a whim. Those who set GAAP do not agree, however.

(95) GE's note 17 gives the details of its short-term borrowings. GE's note 20 gives the details of its long-term borrowings. This paragraph helps the analyst to understand GE's intermediate-term borrowings. From these data, the analyst can estimate cash requirements for debt retirements over the next several years.

(96) GE does not provide details of its "Other liabilities" line on the balance sheet. We can speculate about one of the items included there. Refer to the second paragraph in the right-hand column on page 40. GE states that the costs of this pension plan are not funded. For its primary pension plan referred to in the context of the GE Pension Trust, GE funds pension liabilities as they are recognized. Thus the ordinary pension-related entries are, first, to debit Pension Expense and to credit Pension Liability:

Pension Expense..	X	
Pension Liability...		X

---

and then to fund the liability with a debit to Pension Liability and a credit to Cash:

Pension Liability...	Y	
Cash..		Y

The actual funding need not be equal to the amount of pension expense recognized in the entry just preceding.

For this supplementary pension plan, the first entry is being made, but the liability is not being funded. Therefore an explicit pension liability is included in GE's balance sheet on page 29. The amount of the liability is $371 million, as shown in the first schedule in the right-hand column of page 41 at the callout for our comment 57. The amount is likely to be included among the "Other liabilities."

(97) APB *Opinion No. 12* (1966) requires the disclosure of all changes in owners' equity accounts.

(98) Neither gain nor loss can be recognized on transactions by a company in its own shares (called *treasury shares*). GE's accounting is correct, but the use of the terms *gain* and *loss* may be misleading. When GE reissues previously acquired treasury shares, the adjustment to achieve equal debits and credits is not to a gain or loss account (to appear on the income statement), but to the account "Other capital." If treasury shares are acquired for an outlay of $1,000 and then are reissued for $1,200, then the entries would be:

Common Stock Held in Treasury	1,000	
Cash...		1,000
To record acquisition of treasury shares.		
Cash..	1,200	
Common Stock Held in Treasury..................................		1,000
Other Capital		200
To record reissue of treasury shares for an amount greater than outlay to acquire them.		

If proceeds of reissue are $800, not $1,200, then in the second entry the $200 is debited, not credited, to the "Other capital" account.

shares held in treasury, into two shares of common stock each with a par value of $.63; and (c) increase the number of authorized shares of preferred stock from 2,000,000 shares with a par value to $1.00 per share to 50,000,000 shares with a par value of $1.00 per share.

The beginning balance of retained earnings for 1984 as previously reported has been revised downward by (99) $133 million to reflect the cumulative effect on years before 1984 of the Company's change during 1986 from the "full cost" method to the "successful efforts" method of accounting for oil and gas properties. Net earnings for 1984 and 1985 have been restated to reflect this change.

In December 1985, GE issued 354,000 new shares of stock having a value of $24 million for an acquisition accounted for as a pooling of interests. The beginning 1985 balance of retained earnings was increased by $11 million for this transaction but prior years have not been restated because the acquisition was insignificant to GE's operations and financial condition.

Business activities of most foreign affiliates are mainly based on the U.S. dollar, and the effect, which is not material, of translating their financial statements is included in current-year earnings. However, the functional currency for a few affiliates is other than the U.S. dollar, and the effects of translating their financial statements are included as a reduction in other capital.

22 Other stock-related information (100)

Stock option plans, appreciation rights and performance units are described in the Company's current Proxy Statement. Requirements for stock option shares may be met within certain restrictions either from unissued or treasury shares. During 1986, options were granted to 1,043 employees. As of December 31, 1986, approximately 505 individuals were eligible to receive options and 1,528 persons held options exercisable then or in the future.

Stock option information

| | | Average per share | |
(Shares in thousands)	Shares subject to option	Option price	Market price
Balance at January 1, 1986	9,179	$49.34	$72.75
Options granted	3,013	79.78	79.78
Options exercised	(803)	35.13	75.60
Options surrendered on exercise of appreciation rights	(453)	37.36	74.29
Options terminated	(177)	62.96	—
Balance at December 31, 1986 (101)	10,759	59.23	86.00

Outstanding options and rights expire, and the award period for outstanding performance units ends, on various dates from January 1, 1987, to November 21, 1996. The number of shares available for granting additional options at the end of 1986 was 9,274,996 (12,111,642 at the end of 1985).

Requirements for shares of stock for incentive compensation plans as described in the Company's Proxy Statement may be met within certain restrictions either from unissued shares or from shares in treasury.

As of December 31, 1986, approximately 3,973 individuals were eligible to receive allotments under incentive compensation plan rules. Allotments were made for services rendered during 1986 to 3,628 employees.

23 Commitments and contingent liabilities

At December 31, 1986, the Company had minimum rental commitments under non-cancelable operating leases aggregating $2,333 million. Amounts payable over the next five years are: 1987 — $449 million; 1988 — $510 million; 1989 — $288 million; 1990 — $241 million; (102) and 1991 — $207 million.

Also at year-end 1986, NBC had approximately $1.19 billion of commitments to acquire broadcast material or the rights to broadcast television programs that require payments over the next five years.

Other commitments and contingent liabilities, consisting of guarantees, pending litigation, taxes and other claims, in the opinion of the management, are not considered to be material in relation to the Company's financial position.

(99) See our comment 28.

(100) *ARB No. 43* (1953) requires the disclosure of the details of stock option plans and of the currently outstanding options.

(101) At the end of 1986, the market price of a share of GE common stock was $86. The average price of the 10,759,000 options exercisable at the end of 1986 was $59.23. Thus, if all the options were exercised, the present owners' equity would be diluted approximately $288 million [= ($86.00 − $59.23) x 10,759,000 shares] in comparison to the issue of new shares at the current market price.

(102) Both the SEC and the FASB (*Statement No. 13*) require disclosure of material commitments under long-term noncancelable leases.

24 *Industry segment details* ⑩⑬

Revenues include income from all sources, i.e., both sales of products and services to customers and other income. Details of revenues for industry segment reporting are shown below. In general, it is GE policy to price sales ⑩④ from one component within the Company to another as

nearly as practical to equivalent commercial selling prices. Slightly less than one-fourth of external sales in 1986 were to agencies of the U.S. government, GE's largest single customer. Most of these sales were aerospace and aircraft engine products and services. ⑩⑤

Revenues
(In millions) For the years ended December 31

	Total revenues			Intersegment revenues			External revenues		
	1986	1985	1984	1986	1985	1984	1986	1985	1984
Aerospace	$ 4,318	$ 3,085	$ 2,622	$ 73	$ 33	$ 37	$ 4,245	$ 3,052	$ 2,585
Aircraft engines	5,977	4,712	3,835	57	87	104	5,920	4,625	3,731
Consumer products	4,654	3,220	3,466	180	131	129	4,474	3,089	3,337
Financial services	585	499	448	—	—	—	585	499	448
Industrial	4,711	4,762	4,495	596	561	322	4,115	4,201	4,173
Major appliances	4,107	3,617	3,650	—	—	—	4,107	3,617	3,650
Materials	2,331	2,119	2,280	35	37	51	2,296	2,082	2,229
National Broadcasting Company	1,817	—	—	2	—	—	1,815	—	—
Power systems	5,262	5,824	6,289	185	243	289	5,077	5,581	6,000
Technical products and services	3,266	2,317	2,402	160	113	112	3,106	2,204	2,290
All other	774	—	434	2	—	—	772	—	434
Corporate items & eliminations ⑩⑥	(1,077)	(903)	(990)	(1,290)	(1,205)	(1,044)	213	302	54
Total	$36,725	$29,252	$28,931	$ —	$ —	$ —	$36,725	$29,252	$28,931

Assets
(In millions) At December 31

Property, plant and equipment
For the years ended December 31

	1986	1985	1984	Additions			Depreciation, depletion and amortization		
				1986	1985	1984	1986	1985	1984
Aerospace	$ 2,175	$ 1,367	$ 1,182	$ 311	$ 157	$ 151	$ 111	$ 81	$ 61
Aircraft engines	4,665	4,034	3,328	332	333	356	194	161	136
Consumer products	3,530	2,199	2,178	429	171	236	155	107	121
Financial services	3,455	2,734	2,311	—	—	—	—	—	—
Industrial	3,141	2,896	2,927	258	213	271	196	179	164
Major appliances	1,448	1,509	1,437	101	146	111	95	78	75
Materials	3,602	3,276	2,928	608	551	696	262	244	194
National Broadcasting Company	3,385	—	—	385	—	—	28	—	—
Power systems	3,589	3,668	3,713	127	183	307	173	290	213
Technical products and services	3,251	1,706	1,795	859	107	158	185	60	95
All other	231	—	—	95	—	14	8	—	11
Corporate items & eliminations ⑩⑦	2,119	2,773	2,756	175	92	119	53	49	33
Total	$34,591	$26,162	$24,555	$3,680	$1,953	$2,419	$1,460	$1,249	$1,103

A reconciliation of total industry segment operating profit shown on page 35 with earnings before income taxes and minority interest is shown below.

Reconciliation of operating profit with earnings before income taxes and minority interest

(In millions)	1986	1985	1984
⑩⑦ Total industry segment operating profit	$4,310	$4,068	$3,779
Interest and other financial charges	(625)	(361)	(335)
Corporate items not traceable to segments, and intersegment eliminations	4	(275)	(164)
Earnings before taxes and minority interest	$3,689	$3,432	$3,280

Property, plant and equipment additions for 1986 included $1,638 million acquired with RCA.

The presentation of industry segments was modified in 1986 to reflect the acquisition of RCA during the year. Industry segments in which there are no changes because of the RCA acquisition are: aircraft engines, financial services, major appliances, materials and power systems. As discussed below, the other segments include portions of RCA operations commencing with June 1, 1986. Although the RCA acquisition directly affects only 1986 amounts, presentation of industry segments for prior years has been revised in certain instances to improve comparability. These revisions include: separate reporting of aerospace, formerly included in the technical products and

(103) *SFAS No. 14* requires disclosure of segment data. Segments are required to be defined both by kind of operation (consumer products, industrial power, etc.) and by location (United States, Far East, etc.).

(104) GE tells us that the *transfer prices* (see Glossary) are based on market prices, not on some other basis, such as cost, that other companies sometimes use.

(105) *SFAS No. 14* requires disclosure of this information about customers whose purchases represent 10 percent or more of a firm's revenues.

(106) The major difficulty in constructing meaningful and useful segment reports is the inability to allocate these "corporate items" to the major categories. They are truly common or joint costs of running the entire corporation but must be allocated to the various segments in order to present subtotals for segment earnings that would add up to the total earnings, $2,492 million for 1986. See *full costing* in the Glossary.

(107) Earnings of the individual segments sum to $4,310, an amount larger by $1,818 million than 1986 net income of $2,492. The details of the segment operating profit appear on page 35 of GE's annual report, which we have not reproduced. Excerpts from that page are given here:

For the years ended December 31 (In Millions)	1986	1985	1984
Operating Profit			
Aerospace..........................	$ 608	$ 437	$ 332
Aircraft engines	869	673	460
Consumer products...................	577	425	553
Financial services....................	488	420	355
Industrial...........................	182	252	79
Major appliances	462	399	381
Materials...........................	424	330	446
National Broadcasting Company..........	203	—	—
Power systems.......................	354	740	549
Technical products and services..........	112	22	(8)
All other............................	31	370	632
Total	$4,310	$4,068	$3,779

Note also, that assets of the individual segments sum to an amount smaller than total assets by $2,119 million. Hence rates of return computed for individual segments will overstate true rate of return. If a "true" rate of return for the company as a whole is defined to be net income over total assets, then GE's rate of return is 7.2 percent (= $2,492/$34,591). The incomes of the individual segments total $4,310 million and the sum of the segments assets is $32,472 (= $34,591 − $2,119) million. If one were computing rates of return for individual segments, then, the aggregate rate of return would average 13.3 percent (= $4,310/$32,472), an 85-percent increase. Some who criticize segment reporting have in mind the misleading inferences the unwary analyst (or politician or government regulator) might draw from computing rates of return for individual segments.

25 Geographic segment information

Revenues
(In millions) For the years ended December 31

	Total revenues			Intersegment revenues			External revenues		
	1986	1985	1984	1986	1985	1984	1986	1985	1984
United States	$33,543	$26,811	$25,963	$ 639	$ 671	$ 680	$32,904	$26,140	$25,283
Far East including Australia	—	—	1,017	—	—	440	—	—	577
Other areas of the world	4,384	3,650	3,330	563	538	259	3,821	3,112	3,071
Intracompany eliminations	(1,202)	(1,209)	(1,379)	(1,202)	(1,209)	(1,379)	—	—	—
Total	$36,725	$29,252	$28,931	$ —	$ —	$ —	$36,725	$29,252	$28,931

Operating profit
For the years ended December 31

	1986	1985	1984
United States	$3,563	$3,622	$3,270
Far East including Australia	—	—	159
Other areas of the world	740	435	331
Intracompany eliminations	7	11	19
Total	$4,310	$4,068	$3,779

Assets
At December 31

	1986	1985	1984
United States	$30,604	$22,495	$20,723
Far East including Australia	—	—	681
Other areas of the world	4,090	3,777	3,272
Intracompany eliminations	(103)	(110)	(121)
Total	$34,591	$26,162	$24,555

Geographic segment information is based on the location of the operation furnishing goods or services. U.S. revenues include exports to external customers, and royalty and licensing income from foreign sources. Commencing in 1985, data for Far East including Australia have been combined with other areas of the world. In prior years, operations of Utah International, GE's former affiliate, had been the most significant contributor to Far East including Australia.

Revenues, operating profit and assets associated with foreign operations are shown in the tables above. At December 31, 1986, foreign operation liabilities, minority interest in equity and GE interest in equity were $1,871 million, $112 million and $2,107 million, respectively. On a comparable basis, the amounts were

$2,158 million, $116 million and $1,503 million, respectively, at December 31, 1985; and $2,253 million, $118 million and $1,582 million, respectively, at December 31, 1984.

U.S. exports to external customers
(In millions)

	1986	1985	1984
Europe	$1,634	$1,215	$ 950
Pacific basin	985	965	1,125
Middle East and Africa	490	533	437
Americas	476	502	603
Other areas	124	134	140
Total	$3,709	$3,349	$3,255

26 Quarterly information (unaudited) ⓘ108

Operations ⓘ109

(Dollar amounts in millions; per-share amounts in dollars)	First quarter	Second quarter	Third quarter	Fourth quarter
1986:				
Sales of goods and services	$5,880	$7,785	$9,278	$12,268
Gross profit from sales	1,605	1,945	2,386	3,088
Net earnings	537	621	604	730
Net earnings per share	1.18	1.36	1.32	1.60
1985:				
Sales of goods and services	$6,197	$6,842	$6,521	$8,726
Gross profit from sales	1,732	1,952	1,700	2,059
Net earnings	500	576	563	638
Net earnings per share	1.10	1.26	1.24	1.40

Amounts for 1985 have been restated for the Company's change during 1986 from the "full cost" method to the

"successful efforts" method of accounting for oil and gas properties. Gross profit from sales is sales of goods and services less costs of goods and services sold.

Dividends and stock market

	Dividends declared		Common stock market price range	
	1986	1985	1986	1985
First quarter	58¢	55¢	$79⅜-66½	$65¼-55⅝
Second quarter	58	55	82⅝-71½	62¾-58
Third quarter	58	55	82½-71	64½-56¾
Fourth quarter	63	58	88¾-70⅝	73⅞-56¼

In the United States, GE common stock is listed on the New York Stock Exchange (its principal market) and on the Boston Stock Exchange. As of December 8, 1986, there were about 482,000 share owners of record.

(108) During 1976 the SEC defined a new class of footnotes with which the auditor is "associated" (to use the SEC's term), but which are not audited. The information here is in that class.

(109) During the year, GE (and other companies) are required to send quarterly (interim) financial statements to shareholders. The SEC requires companies to show in the annual statements the amounts of the interim earnings *after* all information for the year is available. If there is a difference, the company must explain why its interim reported numbers differ from the corresponding numbers shown in the annual report.

Balance Sheet for a Company Approaching Bankruptcy

On June 21, 1970, the Penn Central Company filed a bankruptcy petition for its major subsidiary, the Penn Central Transportation Company. On March 12, 1970, only three months before, the 1969 financial statements of the Penn Central Transportation Company had been issued. The balance sheet and income statement from those statements appear here. They reinforce one important point: analysis of the shareholders' equity section of a balance sheet need not give any indication of impending insolvency or bankruptcy.

At the end of 1969, Penn Central Transportation Company had retained earnings of almost half a billion dollars which was a part of shareholders' equity of over $1.8 billion. Much of this equity, however, was invested in track and roadbed, illiquid assets, for which there is no ready market. Penn Central could not dispose of these assets to raise funds. You can compute that at the end of 1968 and 1969, the Transportation Company had negative working capital; that is, current liabilities (as shown, plus debt due within one year) exceeded current assets. Working capital increased by about $18 million during 1969, but net quick assets—cash and receivables less current liabilities—decreased. The Company was in a less liquid position at the end of the year than at the start.

At the end of 1969, the Transportation Company had over $100 million of debt to repay in the following year. Although the Transportation Company had sufficient "net worth" to show almost half a billion dollars of retained earnings and almost two billion dollars of shareholders' equity, it did not have the funds to meet "only" a few hundred million dollars in current obligations. The company was approaching insolvency by the end of 1969, as can be discerned from these statements.

Like Penn Central Transportation Company, many bankrupt firms have positive net assets, or shareholders' equity, on the books at the time of bankruptcy.

Balance Sheet

Assets	December 31	1969	1968
Current Assets	Cash and temporary cash investments	$ 80,331,000	$ 46,915,000
	Accounts receivable and unbilled revenue ..	293,181,000	240,211,000
	Material and supplies, etc., at cost	104,303,000	88,692,000
	Total Current Assets	477,815,000	375,818,000
Noncurrent Assets	Investments and advances, at cost or less (notes 2 and 7).....................	1,139,038,000	1,217,796,000
	New Haven—net assets acquired, at cost (note 1)...........................	—	127,544,000
	Properties (notes 3, 6, 7 and 12)		
	Road, structures, etc.................	2,066,769,000	1,904,536,000
	Revenue equipment (rolling stock)......	1,662,759,000	1,745,448,000
	Other	96,051,000	90,541,000
		3,825,579,000	3,740,525,000
	Less accumulated depreciation and losses upon merger	902,731,000	992,036,000
	Total Properties—Net	2,922,848,000	2,748,489,000
	Deferred charges and sundry assets	56,939,000	43,703,000
	Total Assets	$4,596,640,000	$4,513,350,000

Liabilities and Shareholder's Equity

	December 31	1969	1968
Current Liabilities*	Notes payable (none to subsidiaries in 1969; $19,420,000 in 1968)	$ 102,048,000	$ 87,420,000
	Accounts payable and accrued expenses	396,407,000	356,519,000
	Total Current Liabilities* (excluding debt due within one year)	498,455,000	443,939,000
Long-Term Debt	Due within one year...................	106,058,000	76,716,000
	Due after one year	1,585,585,000	1,407,610,000
	Total Long-Term Debt (note 7)	1,691,643,000	1,484,326,000
Other	Estimated liabilities incurred upon merger (note 6)..........................	101,935,000	119,346,000
	Casualty and other claims..............	90,667,000	81,803,000
	Amounts payable to subsidiary companies ..	167,711,000	122,582,000
	Other	240,857,000	231,015,000
	Total Other	601,170,000	554,746,000
Shareholder's Equity	Capital stock—$10 par value. Authorized 27,000,000 shares; issued 24,113,703 shares (1968—24,085,329) (note 8)	241,137,000	240,853,000
	Additional paid-in capital (note 8)........	1,068,730,000	1,068,257,000
	Retained earnings (note 13)	495,505,000	721,229,000
	Total Shareholder's Equity	1,805,372,000	2,030,339,000
	Total Liabilities and Shareholder's Equity	$4,596,640,000	$4,513,350,000

Statement of Earnings and Retained Earnings

Current Earnings

	Year ended December 31	1969	1968
Income	Railway operating revenues	$1,651,978,000	$1,514,071,000
	Income from rental of properties, net	33,772,000	27,131,000
	Dividends and interest—consolidated subsidiaries	66,324,000	40,155,000
	Dividends and interest—other	2,661,000	15,451,000
	Net gain on sales of properties and investments........................	12,587,000	35,437,000
	Income under tax allocation agreements (note 5)...........................	21,543,000	19,038,000
	Total Income	1,788,865,000	1,651,283,000
Costs and Expenses	Railway operating expenses, excluding items listed below	1,296,397,000	1,173,761,000
	Depreciation, including depreciation on leased lines (note 3)	91,279,000	94,135,000
	Taxes, except Federal income	144,059,000	125,602,000
	Equipment and other rents, net (note 13)	183,802,000	169,292,000
	Interest on debt	96,764,000	68,787,000
	Guaranteed dividends and interest— leased lines	26,173,000	26,315,000
	Miscellaneous, net	6,719,000	(1,454,000)
	Total Costs and Expenses	1,845,193,000	1,656,438,0001
Earnings (Loss)	From ordinary operations (note 13)	(56,328,000)	(5,155,000)
	Extraordinary item (loss on investment in long-haul passenger service facilities) (note 12) ..	(126,000,000)	—
Net Earnings (Loss)	*For the year (notes 12 and 13)*..............	(182,328,000)	(5,155,000)

Retained Earnings

		1969	1968
	From prior years:		
	As previously reported	730,047,000	788,220,000
	Adjustment (note 13)..................	(8,818,000)	(6,436,000)
		538,901,000	776,629,000
	Cash dividends	43,396,000	55,400,000
	Balance at end of year	$ 495,505,000	$ 721,229,000

Accounting Magic

Generally accepted accounting principles permit alternative treatments for certain accounting events. The treatment a company chooses affects the financial statements that the company issues. In this section, we show how alternative accounting treatments of identical events can lead to reported income figures that are perhaps surprisingly different from each other.[1]

The Scenario

On January 1, two companies started in business. The two companies are alike except for their accounting treatment of several events. Conservative Company chooses the accounting alternatives that will minimize its reported income while High Flyer Company chooses the alternatives that will maximize its reported income. Both companies choose, where permitted, accounting methods that will minimize income taxes. The following events occur during the year.

1. Both companies issue common stock to raise funds necessary to commence a merchandising business.
2. Both companies purchase $6,000,000 of equipment that is assumed to have zero salvage value and estimated useful life of 8 years.
3. Both companies make the following purchases of merchandise inventory:

Date	Units Purchased		Unit Price		Cost of Purchase
January 1	85,000	@	$60	=	$ 5,100,000
May 1	95,000	@	$63	=	5,985,000
September 1	100,000	@	$68	=	6,800,000
Total	280,000				$17,885,000

4. During the year, both companies sell 210,000 units at an average price of $100 each so that each realizes sales revenues of $21,000,000.

---

[1]The idea and title for this example come from an article by Leonard Spacek, "Business Success Requires an Understanding of Unsolved Problems of Accounting and Financial Reporting," Arthur Andersen Pamphlet (September 25, 1959), pp. 19-28. Since the time Spacek prepared his illustration, there have been changes in generally accepted accounting principles, but several of the alternatives we illustrate were illustrated by him, too.

5. During the year, both companies have selling, general and administrative expenses, excluding officers' salaries, of $3,350,000.

6. At the end of the year, both companies "pay" bonuses of $150,000 to officers for jobs well done in addition to the $350,000 paid to them during the year in salaries. Conservative Company pays cash bonuses of $150,000 while High Flyer Company awards options for purchasing shares of common stock to its officers. Comparable options have market value of $150,000.

Accounting Alternatives

At the end of the year both companies prepare financial statements. Both must decide how to report the various events that occurred during the year. The following decisions made by each company are all generally acceptable.

Inventory Cost Flow Assumption.   Because not all goods purchased during the year were sold, each company must make an assumption about the cost of goods sold to be shown on the income statement and, simultaneously, about the cost of ending inventory to be shown on the balance sheet. Conservative Company makes a last-in, first-out (LIFO) cost flow assumption while High Flyer Company makes a first-in, first-out (FIFO) assumption. Because the beginning inventory is zero, the cost of goods available for sale by each company is equal to the purchases of $17,885,000 during the year. Both companies have 70,000 units in ending inventory. Conservative Company, using LIFO, reports a cost of goods sold of $13,685,000 (= $17,885,000 − 70,000 x $60) while High Flyer Company reports a cost of goods sold of $13,125,000 (= $17,885,000 − 70,000 x $68). Income tax regulations require a company to use LIFO in its financial statements if it uses LIFO for its tax return. High Flyer wants to report high income so does not use LIFO in its financial statements and, therefore, foregoes the savings in taxes from using LIFO on its tax returns.

Depreciation.   Conservative Company depreciates its equipment using the double-declining-balance method on its financial statements while High Flyer Company uses the straight-line method. Conservative Company takes a full year of depreciation in the year equipment is acquired, while High Flyer Company uses a half-year convention under which it takes only one-half year of depreciation in the first year. (The accelerated cost recovery system used by both companies for income tax reporting effectively requires that both take one-half year of depreciation on their tax returns.) Conservative Company therefore reports depreciation expense of $1,500,000 (= 2 x 1/8 x $6,000,000) while High Flyer Company reports depreciation expense of $375,000 (= 1/8 x $6,000,000 x 1/2).

Officers' Bonuses.   Conservative Company reports expense of $150,000 for the cash bonuses it pays while High Flyer Company reports no expense for the stock options granted. Under generally accepted accounting principles, the fair market value of qualified stock options granted to employees is not shown as an expense. (When the options are exercised, there will be an accounting transaction but the entry will record merely the cash received at the time of exercise.)

Published Income Statements

Income Tax Calculation.   We assume a combined federal and state income tax rate of 40 percent. Both companies show deductions for ACRS depreciation of equipment on the income tax return different from the amounts reported to shareholders. These are *timing differences*. That is, in subsequent years, the companies may report on their tax return amounts different in opposite directions from the amounts reported to shareholders. Consequently, each company reports deferred income taxes on its income statement and will show deferred taxes on its balance sheet. High Flyer Company reports smaller depreciation on the income statement than the amount of depreciation claimed on the tax return and will have deferred tax credits on its balance sheet. (This is the situation usually observed in most published annual reports.) Conservative Company reports larger depreciation on the income statement than the amount claimed on the tax return and will have deferred tax debits on its balance sheet. (This case is rarely observed. The phenomenon arises here because there is only one item of equipment being depreciated and the first-year conventions for tax reporting and financial reporting differ.) The following equation holds for both companies:

Income Tax Expense		Income Tax Payable		Deferred Tax Credits		Deferred Tax Debits
	=		+		−	

Conservative Company:

$ 786	=	$ 906	+	$ 0	−	$120

High Flyer Company:

$1,520	=	$1,190	+	$330	−	$ 0

The income statements for both companies appear below. As a result of its conservative treatment of accounting alternatives, Conservative Company reports net income and earnings per share about half of High Flyer Company's. Both companies used generally accepted accounting principles and each would receive a "clean" opinion from its auditor.

Accounting Magic Comparative Income Statements
For the Year Ending December 31
(Amounts in Thousands Except Per Share Amounts)

	Conservative Company		High Flyer Company	
	Financial Statement	Tax Return	Financial Statement	Tax Return
Sales Revenues	$21,000	$21,000	$21,000	$21,000
Expenses				
Cost of Goods Sold	$13,685	$13,685	$13,125	$13,125
Depreciation on Equipment	1,500	1,200[a]	375	1,200[a]
Officers' Compensation:				
Salaries	350	350	350	350
Cash Bonuses	150	150	—	—
Stock Options	—	—	0	0
Other Selling, General and Administrative Expenses	3,350	3,350	3,350	3,350
Expenses Before Income Taxes	$19,035	$18,735	$17,200	$18,025
Income Before Taxes.	$ 1,965	$ 2,265	$ 3,800	$ 2,975
Income Tax Expense[b]	786		1,520	
Net Income.	$ 1,179		$ 2,280	
Earnings Per Share in Dollars (500,000 Shares Outstanding)	$ 2.36		$ 4.56	

[a]Amounts based on ACRS, 5-year class; 20-percent of cost is deducted in first year: .20 × $6,000 = $1,200).
[b]Computation of Income Tax Expense:

Income Before Taxes.	$ 1,965	$ 2,265	$ 3,800	$ 2,975
Income Tax Expense on Current Income (at 40 percent)	$ 786		$ 1,520	
Income Tax Currently Payable		$ 906		$ 1,190
Income Taxes Deferred by Timing Difference for Depreciation:				
Dr. = .40 × ($1,200 − $1,500).	$ (120)			
Cr. = .40 × ($1,200 − $375)			$ 330	

Comparisons of Fund Flows

Until the time when the two companies paid their respective executive bonuses and income taxes, they were exactly alike in all economically significant respects. Because of the difference in executives' bonuses—Conservative Company paid in cash, while High Flyer granted stock options with the same value—Conservative Company paid out $150,000 more cash than did High Flyer for this item. High Flyer Company, in order to report higher net income, had to pay income taxes $284,000 (= $1,190,000 − $906,000) larger than did Conservative Company. Thus, after tax payments, Conservative Company, in a real sense, is considerably better off than is High Flyer. Overall, then, Conservative Company ends the year with $134,000 (= $284,000 − $150,000) more cash, or other liquid net assets, than does High Flyer.

You might find it instructive to construct statements of changes in financial position for each of the two companies. If you use cash as the definition of funds, you will find that Conservative Company generates $134,000 (= $284,000 tax savings − $150,000 higher bonus) more cash than does High Flyer.

If you use working capital (= current assets − current liabilities) as the definition of funds, you will find that High Flyer generates $426,000 more funds than does Conservative Company. The $560,000 (= $134,000 + $426,000) spread between these two amounts arises from the different cost flow assumptions for inventory. High Flyer uses FIFO; its ending inventory is valued at $68 per unit. Conservative Company uses LIFO; its ending inventory is valued at $60 per unit. The difference in inventory valuation is $8 per unit. Because there are 70,000 more units in ending inventory than in beginning inventory, the difference in the increase in working capital over the increase in cash is $560,000 (= $8 x 70,000). The choice of inventory flow assumption in times of changing prices has a major impact on published financial statements.

Managing Reported Earnings

The simple illustration for Conservative Company and High Flyer Company by no means exhausts the set of choices available to a firm to "manage" its earnings. Managing earnings refers to a process of taking deliberate steps within the constraints of generally accepted accounting principles to bring about a desired level of reported earnings. This section describes some of the techniques for managing earnings and offers arguments for and against an earnings management policy.

Techniques for managing earnings might be classified into three categories: (1) selection of accounting principles, (2) application of accounting principles, and (3) timing of asset acquisitions and dispositions. Some examples of actions in each of these categories are given next.

Selection of Accounting Principles

1. Revenue recognition—percentage of completion, completed contract, time of sale, installment.
2. Inventory cost-flow assumption—FIFO, LIFO, weighted average.
3. Depreciation method—straight-line, declining-balance, sum-of-the-years'-digits.
4. Leases—operating, capital.
5. Corporate acquisitions—purchase, pooling of interests.
6. Mineral resource activities—successful-efforts costing, full costing.

Application of Accounting Principles

1. Estimates of degree of completion of contracts on which the percentage-of-completion method is used
2. Estimates of service lives and salvage values of depreciable assets.
3. Estimates of uncollectible rate on accounts receivable.
4. Estimate of cost of warranty plans.
5. Treatment of indirect costs as product costs versus period expenses.
6. Classification of common stock investments as Marketable Securities, a current asset, or as Investment in Securities, a noncurrent asset.
7. Selection of actuarial cost basis for pension plan.
8. Selection of interest rates for capitalized leases and for pension accounting.

Timing of Asset Acquisitions and Dispositions

1. Timing of discretionary expenditures for research and development, advertising, and maintenance costs, which are recognized as expenses in the period when the costs are incurred.
2. Timing of the sale of property, plant, and equipment or of investments to accelerate or delay the recognition of a gain or loss.
3. Accelerating or delaying shipments of merchandise to customers at the end of a period.

These lists are not intended to be exhaustive. They do indicate the wide variety of avenues available to management to manage earnings.

Arguments For and Against Managing Earnings

The arguments for and against managing earnings vary both as to their underlying logic and to the evidence that is brought to bear in support of the position. We present the arguments here in as unbiased a manner as possible so that readers can make up their own minds.

Capital Market Efficiency. The major argument against managing earnings is that capital markets are efficient, in the sense that market prices adjust quickly and *in an unbiased manner* to publicly available information, and that earnings management is therefore a waste of valuable managerial time. An expanding number of theoretical and empirical studies have provided support for the efficiency of capital markets.[2] For example, several studies have examined the effects of changes in accounting methods on stock prices. Changes in accounting methods that have no real or economic effects (that is, those that do not affect cash flows) have been shown to have little effect on stock prices.[3] Using information from the financial statements and notes, the stock market at the aggregate level is able to distinguish changes with real effects from those that are merely "paper" changes and react accordingly.

Proponents of earnings management acknowledge this recent work but counter with three observations. First, all of the empirical work on market efficiency has looked at the aggregate market (for example, all stocks traded on the New York Stock Exchange). There are numerous examples of cases where the market has not been efficient at the individual-firm level (that is, in the pricing of securities for particular firms at a particular point in time). Proponents of this view point to examples where the market prices of particular firms' shares decreased dramatically after the effects of using specific accounting procedures were carefully analyzed and reported in the financial press.[4]

Second, the empirical work on market efficiency has focused for the most part on publicly-available information. There is little or no evidence to suggest that the market is able to access "inside" or non-public information. Information about the effects of changes in accounting methods is available in the financial statements and notes and has been studied empirically. However, information about management's efforts to manage earnings

---

[2]See Eugene F. Fama, "Efficient Capital Markets: A Review of Theory and Empirical Work," *Journal of Finance* (May 1970): 383-417.

Nicholas J. Gonedes and Nicholas Dopuch, "Capital Market Equilibrium, Information-Production and Selecting Accounting Techniques: Theoretical Framework and Review of Empirical Work," *Studies on Financial Accounting Objectives: 1974*, Supplement to Vol. 12, *Journal of Accounting Research*: 48-129; and Robert S. Kaplan, "Information Content of Financial Accounting Numbers: A Survey of Empirical Evidence," in: *Symposium of Impact of Accounting Research in Financial Accounting and Disclosure on Accounting Practice*, ed. by T. Keller and R. Abdel-Khalik (Durham: Duke University Press, 1978). See also Thomas R. Dyckman and Dale Morse, *Efficient Capital Markets and Accounting: A Critical Analysis*, 2nd ed. (Englewood Cliffs, N.J.: Prentice-Hall, 1986).

[3]See, for example, Ray Ball, "Changes in Accounting Techniques and Stock Prices," *Empirical Research in Accounting: Selected Studies, 1972*, Supplement to Vol. 10, *Journal of Accounting Research:* 1-38; Robert S. Kaplan and Richard Roll, "Investor Evaluation of Accounting Information: Some Empirical Evidence," *Journal of Business* (April 1972): 225-257; Shyam Sunder, "Relationship Between Accounting Changes and Stock Prices: Problems of Measurement and Some Empirical Evidence," *Empirical Research in Accounting: Selected Studies, 1973*, Supplement to Vol. 11, *Journal of Accounting Research*: 1-45.

[4]For several examples, see Abraham J. Briloff, *More Debits Than Credits* (New York: Harper & Row, 1976). For an analysis of these examples see George Foster, "Briloff and the Capital Market," *Journal of Accounting Research* (Spring 1979): 262-274.

by way of the judicious application of accounting principles or the timing of asset acquisitions or dispositions is usually not disclosed separately and consequently has not been adequately studied.

Third, proponents of earnings management note that most of the empirical work on capital market efficiency has focused on equity securities traded on the New York Stock Exchange. The efficiency of other capital markets (for example, the over-the-counter-market) as well as short-term credit and long-term debt markets has not been adequately tested.

Proponents of earnings management would conclude that capital markets are not necessarily efficient in all cases. If, by managing earnings, the firm is able to take advantage of these inefficiencies and obtain capital at a lower cost than if earnings management were not practiced, then the shareholders of the firm are better off.

Opponents of earnings management might be willing to accept the notion that some degree of inefficiency exists in capital markets. They would then argue that capital resources might get allocated in a less-than-socially-optimal way if, because of earnings management, certain firms are able to receive more resources than the otherwise would.

Management Incentives and Survival.   Because, over sufficiently long time periods, net income is equal to cash-in minus cash-out, some corporate managers acknowledge that earnings management is not particularly beneficial in the long run. They point out, however, that the long run is made up of a series of short-run periods in which shareholders' decisions to retain management are made. (See *agency theory* in the Glossary.) Shareholders, they would argue, do not want to see wide, unexpected fluctuations in earnings from year to year. Earnings management is necessary to smooth out these fluctuations and create the impression that management has operations "under control." Corporate managers also observe that all firms practice earnings management and that management's survival dictates that they do so as well to maintain the firm's position relative to other firms for management survival. They further point out that sufficient and convincing evidence for not managing earnings has not yet been provided. The other viewpoint has been explored principally by academic researchers who point to an expanding number of studies that call into question the perceived benefits of earnings management. Whether the two viewpoints can ultimately be reconciled depends on the results of continuing research on the relation between accounting numbers and stock prices.

Accounting Pronouncements

The following list of accounting pronouncements contains most of the generally accepted accounting principles.

Committee on Accounting Procedure (1939-1959)

Accounting Research Bulletins (ARBs)

ARB No.

Accounting Terminology Bulletins (ATBs)

ATB No.

Accounting Principles Board (APB), (1959-1973)

APB Opinions

Opinion No.

APB Statements

Statement No.

Financial Accounting Standards Board (FASB), (1973 to present)

Statements of Financial Accounting Standards

SFAS No.